W0009319

Supporting Users and Troubleshooting Desktop Applications on a Windows XP Operating System

Diana Huggins

Felicia Buckingham

CERTIFICATION

Supporting Users and Troubleshooting Desktop Applications on a Windows XP Operating System Exam Cram 2 (Exam 70-272)

Copyright © 2004 by Que Publishing

International Standard Book Number: 0-7897-3150-9

Library of Congress Catalog Card Number: 2003115741

Printed in the United States of America

First Printing: May 2004

08   07   06   7   6   5

Trademarks

All terms mentioned in this book that are known to be trademarks or service marks have been appropriately capitalized. Que Publishing cannot attest to the accuracy of this information. Use of a term in this book should not be regarded as affecting the validity of any trademark or service mark.

Warning and Disclaimer

Every effort has been made to make this book as complete and as accurate as possible, but no warranty or fitness is implied. The information provided is on an "as is" basis. The authors and the publisher shall have neither liability nor responsibility to any person or entity with respect to any loss or damages arising from the information contained in this book or from the use of the CD or programs accompanying it.

Bulk Sales

Que Publishing offers excellent discounts on this book when ordered in quantity for bulk purchases or special sales. For more information, please contact:

U.S. Corporate and Government Sales
1-800-382-3419
corpsales@pearsontechgroup.com

For sales outside the U.S., please contact:

International Sales
international@pearsoned.com

Publisher
Paul Boger

Executive Editor
Jeff Riley

Acquisitions Editor
Jeff Riley

Development Editor
Steve Rowe

Managing Editor
Charlotte Clapp

Project Editor
Sheila Schroeder

Copy Editor
Chuck Hutchinson

Indexer
Chris Barrick

Proofreader
Suzanne Thomas

Technical Editor
Marc Savage

Team Coordinator
Pamalee Nelson

Multimedia Developer
Dan Scherf

Interior Designer
Gary Adair

Cover Designer
Anne Jones

Page Layout
Kelly Maish

CERTIFICATION

Que Certification • 800 East 96th Street • Indianapolis, Indiana 46240

A Note from Series Editor Ed Tittel

You know better than to trust your certification preparation to just any-body. That's why you, and more than 2 million others, have purchased an Exam Cram book. As Series Editor for the new and improved Exam Cram 2 Series, I have worked with the staff at Que Certification to ensure you won't be disappointed. That's why we've taken the world's best-selling certification product—a two-time finalist for "Best Study Guide" in CertCities' reader polls—and made it even better.

As a two-time finalist for the "Favorite Study Guide Author" award as selected by CertCities readers, I know the value of good books. You'll be impressed with Que Certification's stringent review process, which ensures the books are high quality, relevant, and technically accurate. Rest assured that several industry experts have reviewed this material, helping us deliver an excellent solution to your exam preparation needs.

This book also features a preview edition of MeasureUp's powerful, full-featured test engine, which is trusted by certification students throughout the world.

As a 20-year-plus veteran of the computing industry and the original creator and editor of the Exam Cram Series, I've brought my IT experience to bear on these books. During my tenure at Novell from 1989 to 1994, I worked with and around its excellent education and certification department. At Novell, I witnessed the growth and development of the first really big, successful IT certification program—one that was to shape the industry forever afterward. This experience helped push my writing and teaching activities heavily in the cer-tification direction. Since then, I've worked on nearly 100 certification related books, and I write about certification topics for numerous Web sites and for *Certification* magazine.

In 1996, while studying for various MCP exams, I became frustrated with the huge, unwieldy study guides that were the only preparation tools available. As an experienced IT professional and former instructor, I wanted "nothing but the facts" necessary to prepare for the exams. From this impetus, Exam Cram emerged: short, focused books that explain exam topics, detail exam skills and activities, and get IT professionals ready to take and pass their exams.

In 1997 when Exam Cram debuted, it quickly became the best-selling computer book series since "...*For Dummies,*" and the best-selling certification book series ever. By maintaining an intense focus on subject matter, tracking errata and updates quickly, and following the certi-fication market closely, Exam Cram established the dominant position in cert prep books.

You will not be disappointed in your decision to purchase this book. If you are, please contact me at etittel@jump.net. All suggestions, ideas, input, or constructive criticism are welcome!

Ed Tittel

Expand Your Certification Arsenal!

Supporting Users and Troubleshooting a Windows XP Operating System Exam Cram 2 (Exam 70-271)

Dan Balter and Philip Wiest

ISBN 0-7897-3149-5

$29.99 US/$42.99 CAN/£21.99 Net UK

- Key terms and concepts highlighted at the start of each chapter
- Notes, Tips, and Exam Alerts advise what to watch out for
- End-of-chapter sample Exam Questions with detailed discussions of all answers
- Complete text-based practice test with answer key at the end of each book
- The tear-out Cram Sheet condenses the most important items and information into a two-page reminder
- A CD that includes MeasureUp Practice Tests for complete evaluation of your knowledge
- Our authors are recognized experts in the field. In most cases, they are current or former instructors, trainers, or consultants— they know exactly what you need to know!

To best friends.

—Felicia and Diana

About the Authors

Diana Huggins is currently an independent contractor providing both technical writing and consulting services. Prior to this, she worked as a senior systems consultant. Some of the projects she worked on include a security review of Microsoft's official curriculum, content development for private companies, as well as network infrastructure design and implementation projects.

Diana's main focus over the past few years has been on writing certification study guides. To complement her efforts, she also spends a portion of her time consulting for small- to medium-sized companies in a variety of areas and continues to work as an independent technical trainer.

Diana currently has her Microsoft Certified Systems Engineer (MCSE) and Microsoft Certified Trainer (MCT) Certification, along with several other certifications from different vendors. Although her focus is on the Information Technology industry, she also holds a bachelor's degree in education. Diana runs her own company, DKB Consulting Services. The main focus of the company is developing certification training courseware, online practice exams, as well as content delivery.

Felicia Buckingham is an independent contractor currently deploying Office XP for a provincial-wide electrical company. Prior to this, she spent several years in the technical training industry with a focus on Microsoft Office applications.

Felicia holds her Microsoft Certified Professional (MCP) and Microsoft Office Specialist (MOS) Master designations, along with several other certifications from various vendors. She specializes in Microsoft Office training and consulting.

Over the past few years, Felicia has contributed to several Microsoft Office study guides and has recently co-authored *Microsoft Excel 2003 Programming Inside Out*. During the past year, she has also established her own consulting company that specializes in Microsoft Office deployment, training services, and courseware development.

About the Technical Editor

Marc Savage is the Senior National Technical Advisor and Technical Trainer for Polar Bear Corporate Education Solutions. Combined with more than 7 years experience in microcomputer training and systems development in the private, public sector, and non-profit organisation sector his professional expertise is focussed particularly on providing companies with a clear vision and direction in regards to Microsoft products. Marc currently holds the following certifications: MCT, MCSE NT4, MCSE W2K, MCSA, CNE 4.11, A+, Network+. Marc lives in Ottawa, Canada with his lovely wife Lynne and two daughters Isabelle and Carolyne.

Acknowledgments

I'd like to first of all thank my son, Brandon, for always being so understanding and patient when I have deadlines to meet. He has just recently come to understand that, yes, you can buy Mom's books in the bookstore!

Thanks once again to Jeff Riley and Que Publishing for giving me the opportunity to work on yet another *Exam Cram 2* title and allowing me to continue with my passion for writing. It is always a pleasure working with you, Jeff!

I'd like to acknowledge my best friend and co-author Felicia Buckingham. You have been such a source of inspiration and support over the past few years. You truly are a wonderful mother, a talented author, and a great friend. Who would have thought five years ago that we would end up writing a book together? It has certainly been a pleasure working on this project with you.

Last, but certainly not least, thanks to Brady Buckingham for coming up with such a simple but fitting dedication!

—Diana

I would like to start by thanking Jeff Riley for the opportunity to work on this project. In addition, I would like to extend my gratitude to the whole Que Publishing team that worked on this project. Your hard work and dedication has made this project a success.

To my co-author and best friend, you are an inspiration to women everywhere. I am honored to have worked with you on this project and to be able to call you my friend.

To my family, I would like to thank you for your love and support. It is your understanding and encouragement that keeps me going as those deadlines approach. I also have a special thank you to my mother, a.k.a. Nana. You always helped me believe I could achieve anything if I set my mind to it. It is from this unwavering faith that I have been able to persevere. So Nana, this is for you.

—Felicia

We Want to Hear from You!

As the reader of this book, *you* are our most important critic and commentator. We value your opinion and want to know what we're doing right, what we could do better, what areas you'd like to see us publish in, and any other words of wisdom you're willing to pass our way.

As executive editor for Que, I welcome your comments. You can email or write me directly to let me know what you did or didn't like about this book—as well as what we can do to make our books better.

Please note that I cannot help you with technical problems related to the topic of this book. We do have a User Services group, however, where I will forward specific technical questions related to the book.

When you write, please be sure to include this book's title and authors as well as your name, email address, and phone number. I will carefully review your comments and share them with the authors and editors who worked on the book.

Email: feedback@quepublishing.com

Mail: Jeff Riley
         Executive Editor
         Que
         800 East 96th Street
         Indianapolis, IN 46240 USA

For more information about this book or another Que title, visit our Web site at www.examcram2.com. Type the ISBN (excluding hyphens) or the title of a book in the Search field to find the page you're looking for.

Contents at a Glance

Table of Contents

Introduction

Welcome to the *70-272 Exam Cram 2!* Whether this is your first or your fifteenth *Exam Cram 2* series book, you'll find information here that will help ensure your success as you pursue knowledge, experience, and certification. This introduction explains Microsoft's certification programs in general and describes how the *Exam Cram 2* series can help you prepare for the Microsoft Certified Desktop Support Technician, Microsoft Certified Systems Engineer, and Microsoft Certified Systems Administrator exams. Chapters 1–9 are designed to remind you of everything you'll need to know to take—and pass—the 70-272 exam. The two practice exams should give you a reasonably accurate assessment of your knowledge—and, yes, we've provided the answers and their explanations to the tests. Read the book and understand the material, and you'll stand a very good chance of passing the test.

Exam Cram 2 books help you understand and appreciate the subjects and materials you need to pass Microsoft certification exams. *Exam Cram 2* books are aimed strictly at test preparation and review. They do not teach you everything you need to know about a topic. Instead, we present and dissect the questions and problems we've found that you're likely to encounter on a test. We've worked to bring together as much information as possible about Microsoft certification exams.

Nevertheless, we recommend that you begin by taking the Self-Assessment that is included in this book, immediately following this introduction, to completely prepare yourself for any Microsoft test. The Self-Assessment tool will help you evaluate your knowledge base against the requirements for a Microsoft Certified Desktop Support Technician (MCDST) under both ideal and real circumstances.

Based on what you learn from the Self-Assessment, you might decide to begin your studies with some classroom training, some practice with Windows XP Professional and Office XP, or some background reading. On the other hand, you might decide to pick up and read one of the many study guides available from Microsoft or third-party vendors on certain topics, including the award-winning *Training Guide* series from Que Publishing. We also recommend that you supplement your study program with visits to www.examcram2.com to receive additional practice questions, get advice, and track the MCDST program.

We also strongly recommend that you install, configure, and work with Windows XP Professional, Office XP, and Windows 2000 Server or Windows Server 2003 because nothing beats hands-on experience and familiarity when it comes to understanding the questions you're likely to encounter on a certification test. Book learning is essential, but without a doubt, hands-on experience is the best teacher of all!

The accompanying CD contains MeasureUp exam-simulation software.

Taking a Certification Exam

After you've prepared for your exam, you need to register with a testing center. Each computer-based Microsoft Certified Professional (MCP) exam costs $125 (U.S.), and if you don't pass, you can retest for an additional $125 for each additional try. In the United States and Canada, tests are administered by Prometric and by VUE. Here's how you can contact them:

➤ **Prometric**—You can sign up for a test through the company's Web site, at www.2test.com. Within the United States and Canada, you can register by phone at 1-800-755-3926. If you live outside this region, you should check the Prometric Web site for the appropriate phone number.

➤ **VUE**—You can sign up for a test or locate the phone numbers for local testing centers through the Web at www.vue.com/ms.

To sign up for a test, you must possess a valid credit card or contact either Prometric or VUE for mailing instructions to send a check (in the United States). Only when payment is verified or your check has cleared can you actually register for the test.

To schedule an exam, you need to call the number or visit either of the Web pages at least one day in advance. To cancel or reschedule an exam, you must call before 7 p.m. Pacific Standard Time the day before the scheduled test time (or you might be charged, even if you don't show up to take the test). When you want to schedule a test, you should have the following information ready:

➤ Your name, organization, and mailing address.

➤ Your Microsoft test ID. (Inside the United States, this usually means your Social Security number; citizens of other nations should call ahead to find out what type of identification number is required to register for a test.)

➤ The name and number of the exam you want to take.

➤ A method of payment. (As mentioned previously, a credit card is the most convenient method, but alternate means can be arranged in advance, if necessary.)

After you sign up for a test, you are told when and where the test is scheduled. You should try to arrive at least 15 minutes early. You must supply two forms of identification—one of which must be a photo ID—and sign a nondisclosure agreement to be admitted into the testing room.

All Microsoft exams are completely closed-book. In fact, you are not permitted to take anything with you into the testing area, but you are given a blank sheet of paper and a pen (or, in some cases, an erasable plastic sheet and an erasable pen). We suggest that you immediately write down on that sheet of paper all the information you've memorized for the test. In *Exam Cram 2* books, this information appears on a tearout sheet inside the front cover of each book. You are given some time to compose yourself, record this information, and take a sample orientation exam before you begin the real thing. We suggest that you take the orientation test before taking your first exam, but because all the certification exams are more or less identical in layout, behavior, and controls, you probably don't need to do this more than once.

When you complete a Microsoft certification exam, the software tells you immediately whether you've passed or failed. If you need to retake an exam, you have to schedule a new test with Prometric or VUE and pay another $125.

 The first time you fail a test, you can retake the test as soon as the next day. However, if you fail a second time, you must wait 14 days before retaking that test. The 14-day waiting period remains in effect for all retakes after the second failure.

Tracking MCP Status

As soon as you pass any Microsoft exam, you attain MCP status. Microsoft generates transcripts that indicate which exams you have passed. You can view a copy of your transcript at any time by going to the MCP secure site and selecting Transcript Tool. This tool enables you to print a copy of your current transcript and confirm your certification status.

After you pass the necessary set of exams, you are certified. Official certification is normally granted after three to six weeks, so you should not expect to receive your credentials overnight. The package for official certification that arrives includes a welcome kit that contains a number of elements (see Microsoft's Web site for other benefits of specific certifications):

➤ A certificate that is suitable for framing, along with a wallet card and lapel pin.

➤ A license to use the applicable logo, which means you can use the logo in advertisements, promotions, and documents, and on letterhead, business cards, and so on. Along with the license comes a logo sheet, which includes camera-ready artwork. (Note that before you use any of the artwork, you must sign and return a licensing agreement that indicates you will abide by its terms and conditions.)

➤ A free subscription to *Microsoft Certified Professional Magazine*, which provides ongoing information about testing and certification activities, requirements, and changes to the MCP program.

Many people believe that the benefits of MCP certification go well beyond the perks that Microsoft provides to newly anointed members of this elite group. We're starting to see more job listings that request or require applicants to have MCP, MCSE, and other certifications, and many individuals who complete Microsoft certification programs can qualify for increases in pay or responsibility. As an official recognition of hard work and broad knowledge, one of the MCP credentials is a badge of honor in many IT organizations.

How to Prepare for an Exam

Preparing for any MCDST- or MCSE-related test (including Exam 70-272) requires that you obtain and study materials designed to provide comprehensive information about the product and its capabilities that will appear on the specific exam for which you are preparing. The following list of materials can help you study and prepare:

➤ The *Microsoft Office XP Resource Kit* (Microsoft Press, 2001).

➤ The *Microsoft Windows XP Professional Resource Kit, Second Edition* (Microsoft Press, 2003).

➤ The *Microsoft Windows Server 2003 Resource Kit* (Microsoft Press, 2003).

➤ The exam-preparation materials, practice tests, and self-assessment exams on the Microsoft Training and Services page, at `www.microsoft.com/traincert`. The Exam Resources link offers examples of the new question types found on the MCSE exams. You should find the materials, download them, and use them!

➤ The exam-preparation advice, practice tests, questions of the day, and discussion groups on the `www.examcram2.com` e-learning and certification destination Web site.

➤ Study guides. Several publishers, including Que Publishing, offer certification titles. Que Publishing offers the following:

  ➤ **The *Exam Cram 2* series**—These books give you information about the material you need to know to pass the tests.

  ➤ **The *Training Guide* series**—These books provide a greater level of detail than the *Exam Cram 2* books and are designed to teach you everything you need to know about the subject covered by an exam. Each book comes with a CD-ROM that contains interactive practice exams in a variety of testing formats.

  Together, these two series make a perfect pair.

➤ Classroom training. Certified Training and Education Centers (CTECs), online partners, and third-party training companies (such as New Horizons, ECPI, and Entré) all offer classroom training on Windows XP and Office XP. These companies aim to help you prepare to pass Exam 70-272 (or other exams). Although such training runs upward of $350 per day in class, most of the individuals lucky enough to partake usually find this training to be worthwhile.

➤ Other publications. There's no shortage of materials available about Windows XP and Office XP. The "Need to Know More?" resource sections at the end of each chapter in this book give you an idea of where we think you should look for further discussion.

This set of required and recommended materials represents a wide variety of sources and resources for Windows XP and Office XP and related topics. We hope you'll find that this book belongs in this company.

What This Book Will Not Do

This book will *not* teach you everything you need to know about computers or even about a given topic. Nor is this book an introduction to computer technology. If you're new to Windows administration and looking for an initial preparation guide, check out www.quepublishing.com, where you will find a whole section dedicated to the MCDST and other certifications. This book reviews what you need to know before you take the test, with the fundamental purpose dedicated to reviewing the information needed on the Microsoft 70-272 certification exam.

This book uses a variety of teaching and memorization techniques to analyze the exam-related topics and to provide you with ways to input, index, and retrieve everything you'll need to know to pass the test. Once again, it is *not* an introduction to Windows administration.

What This Book Is Designed to Do

This book is designed to be read as a pointer to the areas of knowledge you will be tested on. In other words, you might want to read the book one time, just to get an insight into how comprehensive your knowledge of computers is. The book is also designed to be read shortly before you go for the actual test and to give you a useful review in as few pages as possible. We think you can use this book to get a sense of the underlying context of any topic in the chapters—or to skim-read for Exam Alerts, bulleted points, summaries, and topic headings.

We've drawn on material from Microsoft's own listing of knowledge requirements, from other preparation guides, and from the exams themselves. We've also drawn from a battery of third-party test-preparation tools and technical Web sites, as well as from our own experience with Windows administration and the exam. Our aim is to walk you through the knowledge you will need—looking over your shoulder, so to speak—and point out those things that are important for the exam (Exam Alerts, practice questions, and so on).

Exam 70-272 makes a basic assumption that you already have a strong background of experience with the Windows XP Professional, Office XP, and Windows Server 2003 and/or Windows 2000 Server products and their applicable terminology. On the other hand, no one can be a complete expert. We've tried to demystify the jargon, acronyms, terms, and concepts. Also, wherever we think you're likely to blur past an important concept, we've defined the assumptions and premises behind that concept.

About This Book

If you're preparing for the 70-272 certification exam for the first time, we've structured the topics in this book to build upon one another. Therefore, the topics covered in later chapters might refer to previous discussions in earlier chapters.

We suggest that you read this book from front to back. You won't be wasting your time because nothing we've written is a guess about an unknown exam. We've had to explain certain underlying information on such a regular basis that we've included those explanations here.

After you've read the book, you can brush up on a certain area by using the index or the table of contents to go straight to the topics and questions you want to reexamine. We've tried to use the headings and subheadings to provide outline information about each given topic. We think, after you've been certified, you'll find this book useful as a tightly focused reference for supporting desktop users in a Windows XP and Office XP environment.

Chapter Formats

Each *Exam Cram* 2 chapter follows a regular structure and provides graphical cues about especially important or useful material. The structure of a typical chapter is as follows:

➤ **Opening hotlists**—Each chapter begins with lists of the terms you'll need to understand and the concepts you'll need to master before you can be fully conversant with the chapter's subject matter. A few introductory paragraphs follow the hotlists, setting the stage for the rest of the chapter.

➤ **Topical coverage**—After the opening hotlists, each chapter covers the topics related to the chapter's subject.

➤ **Alerts**—Throughout the topical coverage section, we highlight material most likely to appear on the exam by using a special Exam Alert layout that looks like this:

An Exam Alert stresses concepts, terms, software, or activities that will most likely appear in one or more certification exam questions. For that reason, we think any information found offset in Exam Alert format is worthy of unusual attentiveness on your part.

Even if material isn't flagged as an Exam Alert, *all* the content in this book is associated in some way with test-related material. What appears in the chapter content is critical knowledge.

➤ **Notes**—Where a body of knowledge is deeper than the scope of the book, we use notes to indicate areas of concern or specialty training.

 Cramming for an exam will help you through a test, but it won't make you a competent IT professional. Although you can memorize just the facts you need to become certified, your daily work in the field will rapidly put you in water over your head if you don't know the underlying principles of application development.

➤ **Tips**—We provide tips that will help you to build a better foundation of knowledge or to focus your attention on an important concept that will reappear later in the book. Tips provide a helpful way to remind you of the context surrounding a particular area of a topic under discussion.

➤ **"Exam Prep Questions"**—This section presents a short list of test questions related to the specific chapter topic. Each question is followed by an explanation of both correct and incorrect answers. The practice questions highlight the areas we've found to be most important on the exam.

➤ **"Need to Know More?"**—Every chapter ends with a section titled "Need to Know More?" This section provides pointers to resources that we've found to be helpful in offering further details on the chapter's subject matter. If you find a resource that you like in this collection, use it, but don't feel compelled to use all these resources. We use this section to recommend resources that we have used on a regular basis, so none of the recommendations will be a waste of your time or money. These resources might go out of print or be taken down (in the case of Web sites), so we've tried to reference widely accepted resources.

The bulk of the book follows this chapter structure, but there are a few other elements that we want to point out:

➤ **Practice exams**—The practice exams, which appear in Chapters 10 and 12 (with answer keys in Chapters 11 and 13), are very close approximations of the types of questions you are likely to see on the current Exam 70-272.

➤ **Answer keys**—These features provide the answers to the practice exams, complete with explanations of both the correct and incorrect responses.

➤ **Glossary**—The extensive glossary identifies important terms used in this book.

➤ **The Cram Sheet**—This valuable tool appears as a tear-away sheet inside the front cover of this *Exam Cram 2* book. It represents a collection of the most difficult-to-remember facts and numbers we think you should memorize before taking the test. Remember, you can dump this information out of your head onto a piece of paper as soon as you enter the testing room. This information usually includes facts that we've found require brute-force memorization. You need to remember this information only long enough to write it down when you walk into the test room. Be advised that you will be asked to surrender all personal belongings before you enter the exam room itself.

You might want to look at the Cram Sheet in your car or in the lobby just before you walk into the testing center. The Cram Sheet is divided into headings, so you can review the appropriate parts just before each test.

➤ **The CD**—The CD contains the MeasureUp exam-simulation software. For more information, visit www.measureup.com.

Self-Assessment

We included a self-assessment in this *Exam Cram 2* book to help you evaluate your readiness to tackle Microsoft certifications. It should also help you understand what you need to know to master the topic of this book—namely, Exam 70-272: "Supporting Users and Troubleshooting Desktop Applications on a Microsoft Windows XP Operating System." Before you tackle this self-assessment, though, let's address concerns you might have when pursuing certification as a Microsoft Certified Desktop Support Technician (MCDST) on Windows XP and what an ideal MCDST candidate might look like.

MCDSTs in the Real World

In the next section, we describe an ideal MCDST candidate, knowing full well that only a few real candidates will meet this ideal. In fact, our description of that ideal candidate might seem downright scary. But take heart: Although the requirements to obtain an MCDST may seem formidable, meeting them is by no means impossible. However, you should be keenly aware that getting through the process takes time, involves some expense, and requires real effort.

Increasing numbers of people are attaining Microsoft certifications, so the goal is within reach. You can get all the real-world motivation you need from knowing that many others have gone before you, so you can follow in their footsteps. If you're willing to tackle the process seriously and do what is required to obtain the necessary experience and knowledge, you can take—and pass—the certification tests involved in obtaining an MCDST.

In addition to MCDST, some of the other Microsoft certifications available include the following:

➤ **Microsoft Certified Systems Engineer (MCSE)**—By now, almost anyone who's been involved in the IT community for longer than a week has heard of the venerable MCSE certification. This premier-level certification is targeted at senior administrators who not only have responsibility to maintain and expand existing networks, but also to plan, design, and implement new networks using Microsoft technologies. This certification includes a total of seven exams.

➤ **Microsoft Certified Systems Administrator (MCSA)**— Microsoft has provided this newer certification for those Microsoft professionals who are not going to design networks but rather administer them. This certification includes three core exams and a single elective.

➤ **Microsoft Certified Solutions Developer (MCSD)**—This certification is aimed at software developers and requires one specific exam, two more exams on client and distributed topics, plus a fourth elective exam drawn from a different, but limited, pool of options.

➤ **Microsoft Certified Application Developer (MCAD)**—This certification is aimed at software developers functioning at a departmental level with one to two years of application-development experience. The MCAD certification requires two specific exams, plus a third elective exam drawn from a limited pool of options.

➤ **Microsoft Certified Database Administrator (MCDBA)**—This certification is aimed at database administrators and developers who work with Microsoft SQL Server. The MCDBA certification requires three core exams and one elective exam.

➤ **Other Microsoft certifications**—The requirements for these certifications range from one test (MCP) to several tests (MCSE).

The Ideal MCDST Candidate

This MCDST exam is aimed at experienced Windows XP and Office XP support technicians who need to demonstrate expertise in supporting desktop users in an Active Directory environment who are using Office XP on Windows XP Professional.

Microsoft specifies the following audience profile for this exam, which also summarizes the experience level that a typical MCDST candidate should possess:

➤ Candidates for this exam support end users who run Microsoft Windows XP Professional in a corporate environment or Microsoft Windows XP Home Edition in a home environment. They should have experience using applications that come with the operating system, such as Microsoft Internet Explorer and Microsoft Outlook Express, as well as the productivity applications used in a corporate environment, such as Microsoft Office applications.

➤ Candidates should be able to resolve operating system issues by telephone, by connecting to the end user's system remotely, or by visiting the end user's desktop. They should have a working knowledge of how to operate in a workgroup or Active Directory domain environment and how the end user is affected.

Even though you may not meet all these requirements, you can still become successfully MCDST certified with a little time and a little bit of practice, so stay with us!

Putting Yourself to the Test

The following series of questions and observations is designed to help you figure out how much work you must do to pursue Microsoft certification and what kinds of resources you should consult on your quest. Be absolutely honest in your answers; otherwise, you'll end up wasting money on exams you're not yet ready to take. There are no right or wrong answers—only steps along the path to certification. Only you can decide where you really belong in the broad spectrum of aspiring candidates.

Two things should be clear from the outset, however:

➤ Any technical background with operating systems and desktop applications is beneficial.

➤ Hands-on experience with Microsoft products and technologies is an essential ingredient to Microsoft certification success.

Educational Background

1. Have you ever taken any computer-related classes? [Yes or No]

   If Yes, proceed to question 2; if No, proceed to question 4.

2. Have you taken any classes on computer operating systems? [Yes or No]

   If Yes, you'll probably be able to handle Microsoft's architecture and system component discussions. If you're rusty, brush up on basic operating system concepts and general computer security topics.

   If No, consider some basic reading in this area. We strongly recommend a good general operating systems book, such as *Operating System Concepts, 6th Edition*, by Abraham Silberschatz and Peter Baer Galvin (John Wiley & Sons, 2001, ISBN 0-471-41743-2). If that title doesn't appeal to you, check out reviews for other, similar titles at your favorite online bookstore.

3. Have you taken any networking concepts or technologies classes? [Yes or No]

If Yes, you'll probably be able to handle Microsoft's networking terminology, concepts, and technologies (brace yourself for frequent departures from normal usage). If you're rusty, brush up on basic networking concepts and terminology, especially networking media, transmission types, the OSI Reference Model, and networking technologies such as Ethernet, token ring, and WAN links.

If No, you might want to read one or two books in this topic area. The two best books that we know of are *Computer Networks, 4th Edition*, by Andrew S. Tanenbaum (Prentice-Hall, 2002, ISBN 0-130-66102-3) and *Computer Networks and Internets with Internet Applications, 3rd Edition*, by Douglas E. Comer (Prentice-Hall, 2001, ISBN 0-130-91449-5).

Skip to the next section, "Hands-On Experience."

4. Have you done any reading on operating systems or networks? [Yes or No]

If Yes, review the requirements stated in the first paragraphs after questions 2 and 3. If you meet those requirements, move on to the next section.

If No, consult the recommended reading for both topics. A strong background will help you prepare for the Microsoft exams better than just about anything else.

Hands-on Experience

The most important key to success on all the Microsoft tests is hands-on experience. For this exam specifically, you will want to have experience with Windows XP Professional and Office XP Professional (including Outlook) in a Windows Server 2003 or Windows 2000 Server Active Directory network. If we leave you with only one realization after completing this self-assessment, it should be that there's no substitute for time spent installing, configuring, and using the various Microsoft products on which you'll be tested repeatedly and in depth.

5. Have you installed, configured, and worked with Windows XP Professional? [Yes or No]

If Yes, make sure you understand the basic concepts covered in the following exam:

> ➤ 70-270, "Installing, Configuring, and Administering Microsoft Windows XP Professional"

If you don't have a lot of experience with Windows XP Professional, you will want to spend several months working with it, including Internet Explorer and Outlook Express. You should pay particular attention to small details, especially within Internet Explorer.

6. Have you installed, configured, and worked with Office XP Professional? [Yes or No]

If No, you'll definitely want to spend some time getting to know Office XP Professional, both from a user's point of view and also from a support person's point of view. You'll need to be very familiar with some intricate configuration options.

 You can download objectives, practice exams, and other data about Microsoft exams from the Training and Certification page at **http://www.microsoft.com/traincert/**. Use the Microsoft Certifications link to obtain specific exam information.

Before you even think about taking a Microsoft exam, make sure that you've spent enough time with the related software to understand how it may be installed and configured, how to maintain such an installation, and how to troubleshoot that software when things go wrong. This experience will help you in the exam and in real life!

 If you have the funds, or your employer will pay your way, consider taking a class at a Certified Training and Education Center (CTEC). In addition to classroom exposure to the topic of your choice, you usually receive a copy of the software that is the focus of your course, along with a trial version of whatever operating system it needs, with the training materials for that class.

Testing Your Exam-Readiness

Whether you attend a formal class on a specific topic to get ready for an exam or use written materials to study on your own, some preparation for the Microsoft certification exams is essential. At $125 (U.S.) a try, pass or fail, you want to do everything you can to pass on your first try; that's where studying comes in.

We have included two practice exams in this book (Chapters 10 and 12), so if you don't score well on the first, you can study more and then tackle the second.

For any given subject, consider taking a class if you've tackled self-study materials, taken the test, and failed anyway. The opportunity to interact with an instructor and fellow students can make all the difference in the world, if you can afford that privilege. For information about Microsoft classes, visit the Training and Certification page at www.microsoft.com/education/partners/ctec.asp for Microsoft Certified Education Centers.

If you can't afford to take a class, visit the Training page at www.microsoft.com/traincert/training/find/default.asp anyway because it also includes pointers to free practice exams and to Microsoft Certified Professional Approved Study Guides and other self-study tools. Even if you can't afford to spend much at all, you should still invest in some low-cost practice exams from commercial vendors.

7. Have you taken a practice exam on your chosen test subject? [Yes or No]

If Yes and you scored 80% or better, you're probably ready to tackle the real thing. If your score isn't above that threshold, keep at it until you break that barrier.

If No, obtain all the free and low-budget practice tests you can find and start working. Keep at it until you can break the passing threshold comfortably.

When you want to assess your test-readiness, there's no better way than to take a good-quality practice exam and pass with a score of 80% or better. When we're preparing for an exam, we shoot for 90% or more, just to leave room for the "weirdness factor" that sometimes shows up on Microsoft exams.

What's Next?

After you've assessed your readiness, undertaken the right background studies, obtained the hands-on experience that will help you understand the products and technologies at work, and reviewed the many sources of information to help you prepare for a test, you're ready to take a round of practice tests.

When your scores come back positive enough to get you through the exam, you're ready to go after the real thing. If you follow our assessment regimen, you'll not only know what you need to study but also when you're ready to make a test date at Prometric (www.2test.com) or VUE (www.vue.com). Good luck!

Configuring, Customizing, and Troubleshooting the Operating System

Terms you'll need to understand:

✓ Program Compatibility Wizard
✓ Start menu
✓ Taskbar
✓ Multibooting
✓ NTFS
✓ Autoplay

Techniques you'll need to master:

✓ Customize the operating system to support applications
✓ Describe the methods for installing an application
✓ Troubleshoot applications on Windows XP
✓ Address file system and file permission problems on a multi-boot computer
✓ Configure Application Compatibility Settings

Configuring the Operating System to Support Applications

One of the major tasks of desktop support personnel is to troubleshoot problems with applications. This task may include troubleshooting installation problems or compatibility issues. To successfully troubleshoot such problems, you should have a general idea of how applications can be installed on Windows XP.

Installing Applications

Applications can be installed in a number of different ways. For example, an application can be installed from a Web site or from a CD-ROM that you purchased. Table 1.1 outlines several different methods for installing applications.

Table 1.1 Methods for Installing Applications	
Method	**Description**
Systems Management Server (SMS)	SMS is software designed to allow large organizations to easily and efficiently deploy critical business applications to users.
Group Policy Object (GPO)	Applications can be deployed using a GPO. Applications can be published to users or assigned to both users and computers.
Local (from CD)	Most applications that are purchased come with a CD that contains the executable used to install the application.
Network	Applications can be installed across the network. The required files must be placed in a shared folder.
MSI files	Some software vendors include MSI files that can be used to facilitate the installation of the application. An MSI file is also referred to as a Windows Installer Package.
MST files	MST files can be used to customize the installation of a Windows Installer Package. For example, an MST file may specify that only specific features of an application be installed.

Most applications purchased today are compatible with Windows XP. However, older applications may not be compatible. In these situations, you should run the *Program Compatibility Wizard*, discussed later in the chapter.

Most applications require very little interaction from the user other than clicking through a series of windows and accepting default installation settings. Many applications require you to provide only registration information. Most newer applications are installed automatically using a feature known as *autoplay*, or you are required to locate the application's installation executable (often Setup.exe).

Applications that support autoplay begin the installation as soon as the CD is inserted into the CD-ROM drive. If an application supports autoplay but the setup program does not automatically launch, verify that your CD-ROM has been enabled (through the Properties window for your CD-ROM drive). Another common method of installing an application is to locate the application's installation executable. After you've located the installation executable, simply double-click the icon to launch setup.

Configuring Application Compatibility Settings

Most programs run properly on Windows XP. The main exceptions are some older games and other programs that were written specifically for an earlier version of Windows. These programs may run poorly or not at all after you first upgrade to Windows XP. In most cases, though, you can use a compatibility mode in Windows XP to start these programs working again. Other programs that may not run properly on Windows XP include specialized drivers that are incompatible with Windows XP. Only an update from the manufacturer can resolve incompatible driver problems.

Most importantly, you make no trade-off. You do not give up any of the new features and excellent performance in Windows XP. Compatibility mode applies small pieces of code that support these older programs so they will work with Windows XP.

 NOTE

You can use a tool called QFixApp to determine any compatibility fixes that are required to resolve application compatibility issues. For more information, visit the following URL:

http://www.microsoft.com/technet/treeview/default.asp?url=/
technet/prodtechnol/winxppro/maintain/lgcyapps.asp

Changing Application Compatibility Settings

Often, you can identify compatibility issues by error messages such as that shown in Figure 1.1. In other cases, a program may not start, or it may perform erratically, with no error message to explain it. Then you should use the Program Compatibility Wizard to find the specific issue and available fixes.

Figure 1.1 The error window helps identify compatibility problems.

Using the Program Compatibility Wizard

You should run the Program Compatibility Wizard before you try other ways of updating your programs or drivers because it identifies compatibility fixes written specifically for Windows XP. If the wizard does not solve your problem, you can try other steps listed at the end of this chapter.

If a compatibility problem prevents you from installing a program on Windows XP, run the Program Compatibility Wizard on the Setup file for the program. The file may be called setup.exe or something similar, and is probably located on the Installation disc for the program.

To run the Program Compatibility Wizard, follow these steps:

1. Click Start, point to All Programs, point to Accessories, and then click Program Compatibility Wizard.

2. Follow the wizard's instructions to select the program's executable file, choose a compatibility mode, set the visual options, and then test the program.

The wizard prompts you to test your program in different modes and with various settings. For example, if the program was originally designed to run on Windows 95, set the compatibility mode to Windows 95, as shown in Figure 1.2, and try running your program again. The wizard also allows you to try different settings, such as switching the display to 256 colors and the screen resolution to 640×480 pixels. The wizard launches your program with the selected settings and allows you to test how the program works. The final page of the wizard enables you to select whether to permanently apply the compatibility settings, abandon the changes, or save them and run the wizard again to apply different settings. It is likely that you will need to repeat this process until you find the correct compatibility mode.

As an alternative to running the Program Compatibility Wizard, you can set the compatibility properties for a program manually by following these steps:

1. Right-click the program icon on your desktop or the shortcut on the Start menu for the program you want to run, and then click Properties.

2. Click the Compatibility tab and change the compatibility settings for your program.

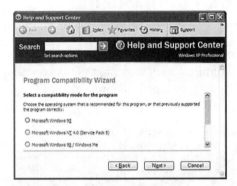

Figure 1.2   Use the Program Compatibility Wizard to set a program to run in a previous version of Windows compatibility mode.

The Compatibility tab, as shown in Figure 1.3, is available only for programs installed on your hard drive. Although you can run the Program Compatibility Wizard on programs or Setup files on a CD-ROM or floppy disk, your changes will not remain in effect after you close the program. For more information about an option on the Compatibility tab, right-click the option and then click What's This.

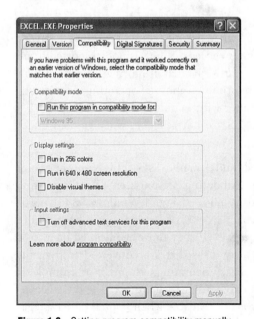

Figure 1.3   Setting program compatibility manually.

Configuring and Troubleshooting File System Access and File Permission Problems on Multiboot Computers

Multiple operating systems can be installed on a computer. This procedure is referred to as *multibooting*. You can configure a computer to multiboot with Windows XP and another operating system such as Windows 98.

 For multibooting to work, you should install the operating systems in a specific order. If you are multibooting Windows XP and Windows 2000, Windows XP should be installed after Windows 2000 has been installed. Generally, the rule of thumb is to install all non-Microsoft operating systems and earlier versions of Windows first. So, if you plan to multiboot Windows XP and Windows 98, Windows 98 should be installed first.

If you are multibooting a computer with Windows XP and an older operating system such as Windows 95, you must address compatibility issues in regards to the file system.

Normally, when you install Windows XP, it is recommended that you format partitions with the *NT File System (NTFS)* to take advantage of additional features not included with the *File Allocation Table (FAT)*, such as file-level security and encryption.

The main point to keep in mind when multibooting Windows XP with another operating system is file system access. NTFS is not supported by all operating systems. Therefore, any partitions that are formatted with NTFS will not be accessible when you boot under another operating system. For example, if you multiboot a computer with Windows XP and Windows 95, any partitions formatted with NTFS are not readable when booted under Windows 95.

Windows 2000 introduced the basic and dynamic disks. This is another point that must be considered when multibooting a computer. Older operating systems such as Windows NT 4.0, Windows 95, and Windows 98 use partitions as opposed to basic and dynamic disks. When you multiboot one of these operating systems with Windows XP, they must be installed on a basic disk that is formatted with FAT. Any disks that are converted to dynamic disks are not readable under the legacy operating systems. For example, if your computer is configured with two hard disks and one of the disks is converted to a dynamic disk, the disk is not readable when booted under a legacy operating system. This, however, is not an issue if you are multibooting with Windows 2000 because Windows 2000 supports dynamic disks.

If you plan to use applications under two different operating systems, you must install them on both partitions. For example, if you want to use Office under two operating systems, you must install the application twice.

Configuring Access to Applications on Multiuser Computers

Often a computer is shared among multiple users. However, you may not want all users to have access to every application that is installed on the computer. In such instances, you can use file permissions to control access to various applications. For example, certain applications may be used for specific job functions. One user performing one job function may not need access to applications required to perform another job function.

To take advantage of NTFS permissions to control access to applications, the applications must be installed on an NTFS partition. FAT and FAT32 do not support local permissions. Also, keep in mind that if you are multibooting and plan to use NTFS permissions to limit access to applications, the operating systems must support NTFS.

To control access to an application, locate the application's executable within Windows Explorer and use the Security tab from the application's properties window to configure which users can run the application.

If the Security tab is not available, you must turn off simple file sharing. See Table 1.4 for more information. To configure the permissions, you must also be the owner of the resource or have been granted the ability to do so by the owner.

Resolving Issues Related to Customizing the Operating System to Support Applications

Part of the responsibility of support personnel is to assist users in configuring and customizing their desktop to support applications. Windows XP allows users to configure various aspects of their computing environment including the Start menu, regional settings, and folder settings. For example, users can configure their Start menu to display certain programs that they use on a regular basis, making them more accessible and quicker to open.

The following sections address different ways Windows XP can be configured and customized to support applications.

Answering End-User Questions Related to the Customizing Operating System to Support an Application

As a desktop support technician, you need to be ready to answer questions from end users. This task may include answering questions for users who want to customize a certain aspect of their computing environment or troubleshooting problems that can arise due to misconfigurations.

Customizing the Start Menu and Taskbar

The *Start menu* and *taskbar* are two components located on the Windows desktop. By clicking the Start button on the desktop, you display the Start menu, which can be used to gain quick access to different areas or different programs installed on the computer. For example, you can launch a favorite program or open the Control Panel.

By default, the taskbar is located along the bottom of the desktop. The taskbar serves many purposes, one of which is fast switching between open programs. Each program that is currently running has a button on the taskbar, making it easy for a user to switch between programs. The taskbar also contains the Start button, the Quick Launch area, and the notification area.

Windows XP allows you to customize both the taskbar and Start menu to suit specific needs. In terms of troubleshooting, assisting end users with problems is easier if you have a general understanding of the different options for customizing both components.

Customizing the Taskbar

You can begin customizing the taskbar by right-clicking on the Start button and clicking the Properties option. Doing so opens the Taskbar and Start Menu Properties dialog box (see Figure 1.4). Using the settings available from the Taskbar tab, you can configure the appearance of the taskbar and notification area. Table 1.2 summarizes the different options available for customizing the taskbar appearance.

Figure 1.4　The Taskbar and Start Menu Properties dialog box.

Table 1.2　Options for Customizing the Appearance of the Taskbar	
Option	**Description**
Lock the Taskbar	The taskbar is locked in its current position on the desktop, so it cannot be moved.
Auto-hide the Taskbar	The taskbar is hidden on the desktop. The taskbar reappears when you point to the area of the desktop where the taskbar is located.
Keep the Taskbar on Top of Other Windows	This option ensures the taskbar is always visible.
Group Similar Taskbar Buttons	If the taskbar becomes too crowded with buttons, buttons for the same program are combined into a single button.
Show Quick Launch	The Quick Launch bar is displayed on the taskbar.

The remaining options are used to configure the notification area of the taskbar (the taskbar area that displays the clock). If you do not want the clock displayed, simply clear the Show the Clock option. You can also keep the notification area less cluttered by hiding inactive icons (those icons you have not recently clicked). After you select the Hide Inactive Icons option, you can use the Customize button to specify which items you want hidden when inactive.

Customizing the Start Menu

The Start menu in Windows XP is divided into distinct sections. The left side of the Start menu consists of pinned programs, recently used programs, and All Programs (see Figure 1.5).

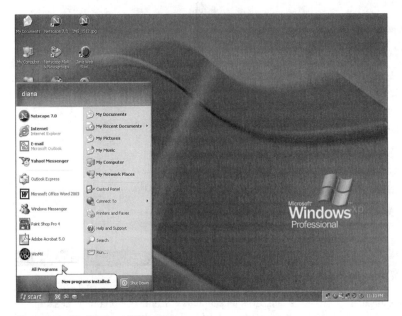

Figure 1.5 The Windows XP Start menu.

Pinned programs must be manually added to the Start menu. Your default email program and Web browser always appear, and additional programs can be added. Beneath the pinned programs are the recently used programs. The programs displayed here change as the most recently used programs replace those that have not been used. The All Programs option contains a submenu displaying all the programs currently installed on a computer.

You can pin a program to the Start menu by right-clicking the specific program and selecting Pin to Start menu. The program appears as a pinned program for the user who is currently logged on to the computer. You can also unpin a program by right-clicking the program on the Start menu and selecting Unpin.

Using the Start Menu tab from the Taskbar and Start Menu Properties dialog box, you can customize the appearance and behavior of the Start menu. After you click the Customize button, the Customize Start Menu dialog box appears (see Figure 1.6).

Figure 1.6   Customizing the appearance of the Start menu.

Using the General tab, you can change the size of the icons for programs displayed on the Start menu. You can also change the number of programs that appear on the frequently used list (the programs located below the separator line on the Start menu) and specify which programs are used to access the Internet and email. For example, if you use Internet Explorer for Web access, you will more than likely want this program displayed on the Start menu as opposed to a Web browser that you use less frequently.

Selecting the Advanced tab presents you with a number of other options you can use to customize the Start menu. Table 1.3 summarizes the various settings available.

Table 1.3 Advanced Options for Customizing the Appearance of the Start Menu	
Option	**Description**
Open Submenus When I Pause on Them with My Mouse	If the item contains a submenu, it is immediately displayed when pointed to.
Highlight Newly Installed Programs	New programs are highlighted in a different color on the All Programs list.
Start Menu Items	This option allows you to specify which items should be displayed on the Start menu.
List My Most Recently Opened Documents	If this option is selected, an item called My Recent Documents is displayed on the Start menu. Any documents recently opened are displayed on this list.

If you customize the Start menu using the Taskbar and Start Menu Properties dialog box, the changes are applied only to the user who is currently logged on to the computer.

Changing the Start Menu for Users

The Start menu can be customized for an individual user or for all users who log on to the computer. For example, if multiple users who require the same programs to perform their job functions share a computer, you can create a submenu off the Start menu containing shortcuts to all required programs. Conversely, you can perform the same procedure for an individual user.

To customize the Start menu for all users, follow these steps:

1. Right-click the Start button and click Open All Users.

2. Open the folder in which you want to create the submenu, such as the Programs folder.

3. Click File, point to New, and click Folder.

4. Type a name for the folder and press Enter.

5. Drag any programs that you want to appear on the submenu into the folder.

 To add a shortcut to the Start menu for all users, right-click the Start button and click Open All Users. From the File menu, point to New and click Shortcut. Browse to the location of the program and click OK. Click Next, type a name for the shortcut, and click OK.

To customize the Start menu for a specific user, follow these steps:

1. Right-click the Start button and click Explore All Users.

2. Locate the folder of the user for whom you want to customize the Start menu.

3. Click the Start menu.

4. Right-click the program or item for which you want to create a shortcut and select Create Shortcut. You can also drag or cut and paste the item into the user's Start menu or Programs folder.

Customizing Regional Settings

Regional settings affect how Windows XP and different programs display information such as numbers, currency, times, and dates. You can change regional settings by using the Regional and Languages Options applet within the Control Panel (see Figure 1.7).

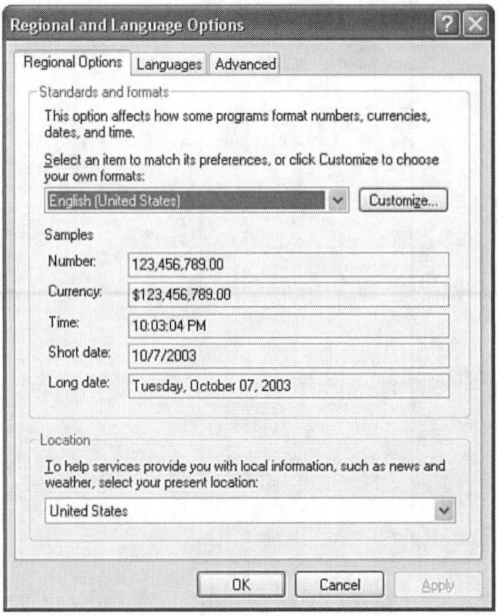

Figure 1.7   Customizing regional settings.

Using the Regional Options tab, you can select your specific locale, such as English (United States), to determine how certain items are formatted. Using the Customize button, you can manually configure how the different regional options are displayed.

Customizing Folder Settings

The Folder Options applet (see Figure 1.8) within the Control Panel can be used to change the behavior of folders and alter how information within folders is displayed. For example, you can change the program used to open files with a certain extension.

The General tab allows you to configure the behavior and appearance of folders within Windows XP. Under the Tasks section shown in Figure 1.8, you can configure whether common folder tasks are displayed in folders. By default, common tasks are displayed in folders. If you select the Use Windows Classic Folders option, the list of tasks are not displayed. Under the Browse Folders section, you can specify whether each folder is opened in a new window or in the same window. From the General tab, you can also configure how items are opened, using a single mouse click or a double mouse click.

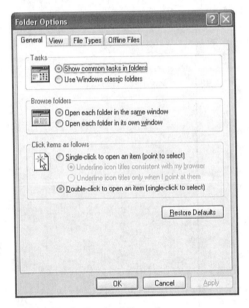

Figure 1.8 Configuring folder options.

The View tab contains a number of advanced settings used to control the behavior of folders and files. Some of the more common settings are summarized in Table 1.4.

Table 1.4 Advanced Options for Customizing the Behavior of Folders and Files	
Option	**Description**
Automatically Search for Network Folders and Printers	Windows periodically searches the network for shared folders and printers and displays them in My Network Places.
Display Simple Folder View in Explorer's Folders List	When a folder in the Folders List is selected, the contents and subfolders are displayed. All other folders are closed when another folder is selected.
Display the Contents of System Folders	The contents of system folders are displayed. By default, the contents are hidden.
Display the Full Path in the Address Bar	The complete path to an open folder or file is displayed on the address bar.

Table 1.4 Advanced Options for Customizing the Behavior of Folders and Files (continued)	
Option	**Description**
Display the Full Path in the Title Bar	The complete path to an open folder or file is displayed on the title bar.
Do Not Cache Thumbnails	Folder thumbnails are not cached. This can increase the amount of time required to open folders that contain thumbnails.
Do Not Show Hidden Files and Folders	Program and system files are not displayed in the file list for a folder.
Show Hidden Files and Folders	Program and system files are displayed in the file list for a folder.
Hide Extensions for Known File Types	File extensions are not displayed.
Hide Protected Operating System Files (Recommended)	Operating system files are not displayed in the list of files for a folder.
Launch Folder Windows in a Separate Process	Each folder is opened in a separate part of memory. This can increase stability but slow down performance.
Show Control Panel in My Computer	The Control Panel icon is displayed in My Computer.
Show Encrypted or Compressed NTFS Files in Color	Encrypted or compressed files and folders are displayed in different colors.
Use Simple File Sharing (recommended)	When simple file sharing is enabled, you can share folders with all users in your workgroup and make folders in your profile private. However, if you want to prevent specific users and groups from accessing your folders and files, simple file sharing must be disabled.

The Offline Files tab enables you to configure settings that apply to working with offline files (this way, you can work with files and programs stored on the network when a network connection is not present).

The File Types tab, shown in Figure 1.9, displays all the registered file types on the local computer. Each file extension listed is associated with a file type.

When you highlight a specific extension, such as DOC, detailed information is displayed, including the type of program used to open any files with that particular extension. For example, Microsoft Word is used to open any files with the .DOC extension. You can alter this by selecting the Change button. The Open With dialog box appears (see Figure 1.10). Here, you can select which program you want to use to open all files of that particular type.

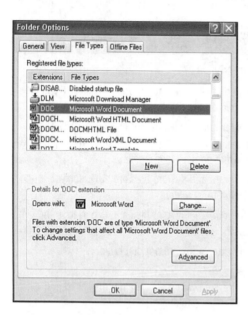

Figure 1.9 Configuring file types.

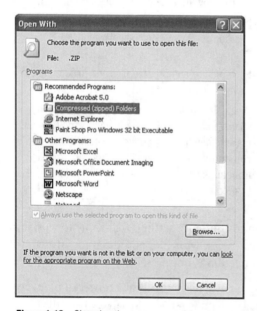

Figure 1.10 Changing the program used to open specific file types.

Customizing Fonts

Windows XP allows you to customize the way fonts are displayed on your desktop. For example, if you find a font is too small and difficult to read, you can increase the font size.

You can customize the way fonts are displayed by using the Display Properties dialog box. To do so, right-click the Windows XP desktop and click the Properties option. From the Display Properties dialog box, select the Appearance tab (see Figure 1.11).

Figure 1.11   Using the Appearance tab to customize Windows XP fonts.

As you can see in Figure 1.11, three options are available. The first two options enable you to change the look of windows and buttons as well as select a color scheme. The third option allows you to configure the size of the fonts.

 If you are working from a laptop or using a flat panel monitor, you may notice that text outlines can look blurry. You can fix this problem by selecting the Effects button available on the Appearance tab of the Display Properties window. Change the method used to smooth edges of screen fonts from Standard to ClearType.

Exam Prep Questions

Question 1

> A user has three partitions on her hard disk. Windows XP is installed on D. Windows 95 is installed on C. The user stores all her documents on partition E. When the user boots under Windows 95, she is unable to access the D partition. What is most likely causing the problem to occur?
>
> ○ A. The user does not have permission to access the drive.
> ○ B. The partition has been formatted with NTFS.
> ○ C. The partition is on a dynamic disk.
> ○ D. The hard disk has been converted to a basic disk.

Answer B is correct. A partition that has been formatted with NTFS is not accessible when booting under a legacy operating system such as Windows 95. Answer A is incorrect because permissions would not cause the drive to be inaccessible. Answer C is incorrect because Windows 95 cannot be installed on a dynamic disk. Answer D is incorrect because Windows 95 must be installed on a basic disk. Therefore, this would not cause a problem to occur.

Question 2

> You are trying to install an application on a desktop running Windows XP. You insert the CD into the CD-ROM drive, but nothing happens. The installation directions say that the application's installation executable should launch immediately. What should you do?
>
> ○ A. Run the application in compatibility mode.
> ○ B. Ensure you have the appropriate permissions to install the application.
> ○ C. Multiboot the computer with an older operating system. Reinstall the application under the new operating system.
> ○ D. Verify that autoplay has been enabled.

Answer D is correct. If the application's setup program does not launch automatically, verify that autoplay has been enabled. A compatibility problem would generate an error message. Before assuming this is the problem, verify the CD-ROM is enabled for autoplay. If it was a permissions problem, an error message would be generated. Therefore, answer A is incorrect. Answer B is incorrect because permissions are not causing the problem. Answer C is incorrect because multibooting would not solve the problem.

Question 3

A user reports that the Windows XP taskbar continually disappears from his desktop making it difficult for him to switch between open programs. What should you do?

○ A. Customize the Start menu to autohide the taskbar.

○ B. Select the Show Quick Launch option from the Taskbar and Start Menu Properties dialog box.

○ C. Select the Lock the Taskbar option from the Taskbar and Start Menu Properties dialog box.

○ D. Deselect the Autohide the Taskbar option from the Taskbar and Start Menu Properties dialog box.

Answer D is correct. If the Autohide the Taskbar option is selected, the taskbar is hidden on the desktop. The taskbar reappears when you point to the area of the desktop where the taskbar is located. Therefore, the problem can be solved by deselecting this option. Answer A is incorrect because the problem exists with the taskbar, not the Start menu. Answers B and C are incorrect because neither of these options would cause the taskbar to disappear and reappear.

Question 4

Multiple users share one of the computers on the network. All these users require access to the same group of programs. You want to allow logged-on users to access these programs more easily. What should you do?

○ A. Using the Taskbar tab from the Taskbar and Start Menu Properties dialog box, create a new submenu and add shortcuts to the appropriate programs.

○ B. Using the Start Menu tab from the Taskbar and Start Menu Properties dialog box, create a new submenu and add shortcuts to the appropriate programs.

○ C. Right-click the Start button and click Open All Users. Create a new folder and add shortcuts to the appropriate programs.

○ D. Right-click the Start button and click Explore All Users. Locate the Start Menu folder for the user currently logged on. Create a new folder and add shortcuts to the appropriate programs.

Answer C is correct. To customize the Start menu for all users who log on to the computer, you must right-click the Start button and click Open All Users. Answers B and D are incorrect because either of these options would customize the Start menu for the user who is currently logged on. The settings would not be applied to any other users. Answer A is incorrect because the Taskbar tab is not used to customize the Start menu.

Question 5

> You have installed Windows XP and Windows 95 on the same computer. Windows XP is installed on D, and Windows 95 is installed on C. You boot into Windows XP and install a new application. The application resided on partition D. When you boot into Windows 95, you cannot run the application. What should you do?
>
> ○ A. Reinstall the application under Windows 95.
>
> ○ B. Install the application on an NTFS partition.
>
> ○ C. Edit the permissions of the application's executable so you have the proper permissions.
>
> ○ D. Uninstall the application and install it on a shared partition.

Answer A is correct. If you are multibooting a computer, an application must be installed under each operating system. If not, the application is available only under the operating system on which the application was installed. Answer B is incorrect because Windows 95 cannot read NTFS partitions on a local computer. Answer C is incorrect because you can successfully run the application under Windows XP. Answer D is incorrect because the application must be installed under each operating system.

Question 6

> You are assisting a user with a configuration problem. When you open the contents of the Windows System folder, you notice that all the system files are visible. You want these files to be hidden from users. What should you do?
>
> ○ A. Deny the user access to each of the system files.
>
> ○ B. Use the Folder Options applet with the Control Panel to hide system files.
>
> ○ C. Configure the properties of each file so they are hidden.
>
> ○ D. Move the files you want hidden into an administrative share.

Answer B is correct. You can hide system files within Windows Explorer by using the Folder Options applet within the Control Panel. If you select the Do Not Show Hidden Files and Folders option, no program and system files are displayed. Answer A is incorrect because the files are still visible to users. Answer C is incorrect because this approach would require more administrative effort. Answer D is incorrect because program and system files cannot be moved.

Question 7

A user calls to report that each time she opens a Word document, Windows XP automatically launches WordPad. The user reports that the problem has been occurring for a week and now has to open Microsoft Word and browse for the documents. She wants Microsoft Word to launch when a document is opened. What is causing the problem?

○ A. The file association has been changed.

○ B. Microsoft Word has been uninstalled.

○ C. Microsoft Word must be run in compatibility mode.

○ D. Microsoft Word has been removed as a shortcut from the Start menu.

Answer A is correct. File extensions are associated with certain programs. When you open a file, a certain program launches automatically. More than likely, the file association has been changed so WordPad launches instead of Microsoft Word. Answers B and C are incorrect because the user can still open the program. Answer D is incorrect because a missing shortcut on the Start menu would not cause the problem.

Question 8

You multibooted a computer with three versions of Windows. The computer has four partitions. Windows XP resides on partition E, Windows 98 resides on partition D, and Windows 95 resides on partition C. Partition F is used for storing documents. The partitions are formatted as follows:

C	FAT16
D	FAT32
E	NTFS
F	FAT32

A user boots into Windows 95 and is unable to access files stored on partition E. What is causing the problem?

○ A. Windows 95 is not installed on an NTFS partition.

○ B. The user does not have permission to view the files.

○ C. Windows 95 cannot read from NTFS partitions.

○ D. The files have been hidden.

Answer C is correct. Windows 95 cannot read from any local partitions formatted with NTFS. Therefore, answers A, B, and D are all incorrect.

Question 9

> A user calls you for directions on how to change how his program's display values, such as the date, time, and currency. What should you tell him?
>
> ○ A. He must manually change the values in each program.
>
> ○ B. He must edit the settings using the Regional and Language Options within the Control Panel.
>
> ○ C. He must edit the settings using the Folder Options applet within the Control Panel.
>
> ○ D. He must edit the properties for each application executable.

Answer B is correct. You can change how programs display values such as time, date, and currency by using the Regional and Language Options applet within the Control Panel. Therefore, answers A, C, and D are incorrect.

Question 10

> A user needs to run a legacy application on her desktop. The desktop is currently running Windows XP. When you run the setup program for the application, you receive an error message that the program is not compatible with Windows XP. What should you do?
>
> ○ A. Nothing. Windows XP cannot run legacy applications.
>
> ○ B. Multiboot the computer with Windows 95. Install the application under this operating system.
>
> ○ C. Install the application using the Program Compatibility Wizard.
>
> ○ D. Contact the application's vendor for a newer version of the application.

Answer C is correct. If the application does not install under Windows XP, you should install the application using the Program Compatibility Wizard. Answer A is incorrect because Windows XP can run legacy applications. Answer B is incorrect because multibooting the computer is not necessary. Answer D is incorrect. Although this may be a possible solution, you should first try running the application in compatibility mode.

Configuring, Customizing, and Troubleshooting Internet Explorer

Terms you'll need to understand:

✓ Home page
✓ Internet Explorer
✓ Proxy server
✓ Toolbar

Techniques you'll need to master:

✓ Customize Internet Explorer
✓ Customize privacy settings
✓ Customize Internet Explorer connection settings
✓ Configure Internet Explorer security settings
✓ Troubleshoot Internet Explorer

Configuring and Troubleshooting Internet Explorer

Microsoft Internet Explorer 6.0 is included as part of Windows XP (earlier versions of Internet Explorer are included with earlier versions of Windows). As a result, *Internet Explorer* is one of the most popular Web browsers. Although the main function of Internet Explorer is to view Web content available from Internet- and intranet-based Web servers, it provides much more functionality than just this. For example, Internet Explorer can be used to access email and newsgroups.

Internet Explorer is customizable, meaning it provides you with a number of different options that can be configured to control how the Web browser functions. For example, you can control where and how temporary Internet files are stored, configure security settings, and modify a number of advanced settings.

You can begin customizing Internet Explorer by opening the Web browser, clicking Tools, and selecting Options. The Internet Options dialog box appears and presents you with a number of different tabs and settings.

In terms of troubleshooting, it is important that you are familiar with the various settings and what they are used for. This information will assist you in determining the cause of a problem when one does arise. The following sections describe the different settings available from the Internet Options dialog box.

Make sure you are familiar with the different settings available for customizing Internet Explorer.

General Settings

Using the General tab from the Internet Options dialog box (see Figure 2.1), you can configure the following settings:

➤ Home Page

➤ Fonts

➤ Temporary Internet Files

➤ Languages

➤ History

➤ Accessibility

➤ Colors

Figure 2.1   Using the General tab of the Internet Options dialog box.

Home Page

Each time you open Internet Explorer, an HTML page is displayed. It is referred to as the *home page*. By configuring the home page settings, you can specify which HTML page you want displayed when you open Internet Explorer. This is also the page you return to when you click the Home button on the *toolbar*.

You have three options when configuring the home page. When you select the Use Current button, the Web page that is currently open in your browser becomes the home page. When you select the Use Default button, the home page is set to the page configured when Internet Explorer was first installed. Selecting the Use Blank button displays a blank HTML page.

Temporary Internet Files

To improve performance and reduce the amount of time you spend waiting to view Web pages, Internet Explorer stores many of the Web pages and graphics you have viewed in a folder on your hard drive. The next time you revisit a Web site, Internet Explorer can use the content stored in the Temporary Internet Files folder to display the site content, instead of retrieving it from the Web.

Using the General tab, you can choose from three different buttons to configure temporary Internet files. The first button, Delete Cookies, deletes all cookies stored on your computer. The Delete Files button empties the contents of the Temporary Internet Files folder. This capability is useful if you are running low on disk space.

 When you visit an Internet site, cookies are created and stored on your computer. A *cookie* is a small text file that may store information including preferences for an Internet site or personal information, such as your email address.

Selecting the Settings button brings up a number of other options that you can configure for temporary Internet files (see Figure 2.2). You can configure when Internet Explorer checks for newer versions of Web pages that have been stored on your computer. You can choose any one of the following options to control how Internet Explorer updates stored Web pages:

➤ **Every Visit to the Page**—When you return to a Web page you have previously viewed, Internet Explorer checks for updates to the page. Keep in mind that with this option selected, browsing pages you have previously viewed can take longer.

➤ **Every Time You Start Internet Explorer**—When you return to a Web page viewed in a previous session, Internet Explorer checks for updates to the page. Selecting this option can improve performance when viewing Web pages you have viewed previously.

➤ **Automatically**—When you return to a Web page viewed in a previous session, Internet Explorer checks for updates to the page. However, if Internet Explorer determines that a Web page rarely changes, it checks for updates less frequently. This option provides the best performance when you are browsing Web pages.

➤ **Never**—Internet Explorer never checks for updates to Web pages you have viewed previously.

You can also allocate how much disk space is available for the Temporary Internet Files folder and change the default location where this folder is stored. For example, if you have limited disk space, you may want to decrease the amount allocated to your temporary Internet files. You can use the View Files button to open the Temporary Internet Files folder and the View Object button to view the ActiveX and Java controls that have been downloaded.

History

Internet Explorer keeps links to Web pages that you have recently viewed and stores them in the History folder. By default, links are kept in the

History folder for 20 days. If you have a limited amount of disk space, consider lowering this number. You can also clear the contents of the History folder by selecting the Clear History button.

Figure 2.2   Configuring additional Temporary Internet Files settings.

 You can use the remaining buttons on the General tab to further customize your browser, such as the colors and fonts. For example, you may want to increase the size of the font, making it easier to read.

Security and Privacy Settings

Many people who use the Internet are concerned about protecting their computer and personal information. Internet Explorer contains several security and privacy settings that you can take advantage of to secure your computer and maintain your privacy.

Using Security Zones

Internet Explorer allows you to group Web sites into different zones. Actions can be performed on the Web sites within a zone based on the zone's specific security settings. For example, you can configure Internet Explorer to automatically download any software from Web sites within the Trusted zone. Alternatively, you can configure your browser to prompt you before downloading any software from Web sites within other zones.

Security has also become a popular exam topic. Be sure you are familiar with the various security settings within Internet Explorer.

The Security tab (see Figure 2.3) available from the Internet Options dialog box displays four separate zones that are summarized in Table 2.1.

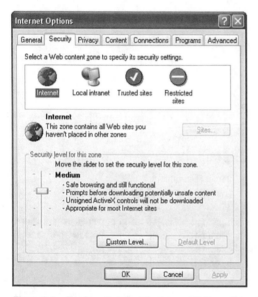

Figure 2.3 The Security tab of the Internet Options dialog box.

Table 2.1	Web Content Zones
Zone	**Description**
Internet	This zone contains the majority of sites that have not been placed in another zone.
Local Intranet	These sites exist within your organization's intranet.
Trusted Sites	These sites are those you trust not to damage your computer and/or data.
Restricted Sites	These sites are considered potentially harmful to your computer and/or data.

By default, Internet Explorer takes security precautions to protect your computer while you are browsing the Internet. All Web sites are placed within the Internet zone with a security level of *medium*. This setting allows you to safely browse the Internet but notifies you before downloading any content that may be unsafe.

You can add a Web site to a zone by selecting the specific zone, clicking the Sites button, and typing the address of the Web site (see Figure 2.4).

Figure 2.4   Adding a Web site to a security zone.

From the Security tab, you can also set the security level for a zone. For example, sites on your company's intranet are more than likely safe, so you can configure a low level of security for the Local Intranet zone.

Each zone is configured with a default security level. You can accept the default settings, or you can customize the security level to meet your specific needs. The security level for a zone can be changed by moving the slider to low, medium-low, medium, or high. Alternatively, more experienced users can define a custom level of security.

If a user is trying to access a Web site that requires some functionality that is disabled by the security level configured for the zone, add the Web site to the list of Trusted Sites.

Working with Privacy Settings

As mentioned previously, cookies are small text files stored on your computer as you visit different Web sites. A cookie contains information about your visit to the site including any personal information you provided, such as your email address.

Using the Privacy tab shown in Figure 2.5, you can configure which cookies are accepted and/or blocked. The default level of privacy for Internet Explorer is set to medium. You can change the privacy level by moving the slider.

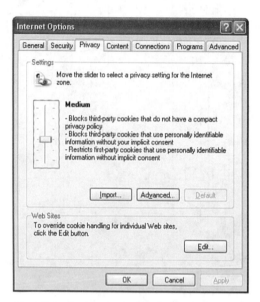

Figure 2.5 The Privacy tab of the Internet Options dialog box.

 You can change the privacy settings to block all cookies. Do so with caution because you may have difficulty using any sites that allow you to personalize information.

Content Settings

Using the Content tab shown in Figure 2.6, you can configure these three properties:

➤ Content Advisor

➤ Certificates

➤ Personal Information

Internet Explorer includes a feature known as the Content Advisor. This feature allows you to control the type of Web content that is acceptable for viewing. You can restrict certain content that you deem as inappropriate from being displayed by your browser. Although this is a great feature of Internet Explorer, it works only if the Web sites you are visiting have obtained security ratings.

Certificates verify the identity of an entity such as a user or computer. Internet Explorer uses personal certificates for Web sites that require you to verify your identity. Your browser uses Web certificates to verify the security of a Web site. For example, Web site certificates verify that you are downloading software from a reliable Web site.

Figure 2.6   The Content tab of the Internet Options dialog box.

Three buttons are available for certificates from the Content tab. The Clear SSL Slate button clears any client authentication certificates from the SSL cache (normally, these certificates remain in the cache until the computer is restarted). You can use the remaining two buttons, Certificates and Publishers, to view the certificate currently stored on the computer.

Two additional buttons are available under Personal Information: AutoComplete and My Profile. The AutoComplete feature displays possible Web site matches based on what is typed in the address bar. The AutoComplete Settings enable you to specify how you want to use AutoComplete. You also have the option of clearing the AutoComplete history (see Figure 2.7).

Internet Explorer allows you to create personal profiles that can include information such as your name, address, and phone number. Instead of your having to provide such information each time a Web site requests it, the Web site can access the information stored in your personal profile (with your permission). By selecting the My Profile button, you can create a new profile or select an existing profile from your address book to represent your profile.

Figure 2.7 Configuring AutoComplete Settings.

 By default, the Profile Assistant is enabled. This means you are prompted before your personal information is shared with a Web site. You can disable this feature altogether so your personal information is never shared with a Web site. To do so, use the Advanced tab of the Internet Options dialog box. Clear the Enable Profile Assistant option.

Connections Settings

You can use the different settings available on the Connections tab to specify how Internet Explorer will connect to the Internet (see Figure 2.8).

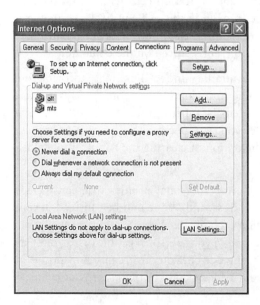

Figure 2.8 Using the Connections tab of the Internet Options dialog box.

If you need to create a connection to the Internet, you can select the Setup button. Doing so launches the New Connection Wizard, which walks you through the process of creating a new Internet connection.

Any dial-up and Virtual Private Network (VPN) Internet connections currently configured on the local computer are listed on the Connections tab. If you are connecting to the Internet through a *proxy server*, you can select the Settings button to configure the necessary proxy settings (see Figure 2.9). Table 2.2 summarizes the various settings in the Settings dialog box.

Figure 2.9   Configuring proxy settings for a dial-up and VPN Internet connection.

Table 2.2 **Dial-up and Virtual Private Network Settings**	
Setting	**Description**
Automatically Detect Settings	Proxy settings and configuration settings are automatically detected.
Use Automatic Configuration Script	Settings are retrieved from a file created by the network administrator. You must also specify the URL to the file or filename.

Table 2.2	Dial-up and Virtual Private Network Settings *(continued)*
Setting	**Description**
Use a Proxy Server for This Connection	Internet Explorer must connect to the Internet through a proxy server. You must provide the address and port number of the proxy server. By selecting the Advance button, you can configure which proxy server and port number to use for different protocols, such as HTTP and FTP. You can then create an exception list. When you try to access computers on the exception list, the proxy server is not used.
Bypass Proxy for Local Addresses	You select this option if you do not want to use a proxy server for local (intranet) addresses. Selecting this option can improve performance when accessing computers on your intranet.
Username	For dial-up connections, this account name is assigned to you by your Internet service provider.
Password	This password is assigned to you by your Internet service provider.
Domain	This domain name is assigned to you by your Internet service provider.

NOTE A proxy server stands between your computer or intranet and the Internet. The proxy server receives requests for Internet resources, such as a Web page, from clients on the intranet. The proxy server acts on behalf of the client and retrieves the requested resource from the Internet.

Using the settings available on the Connections tab, you can specify what Internet Explorer should do when a connection to the Internet is not available but one is required. You can select from one of the following options:

➤ **Never Dial a Connection**—Internet Explorer does not automatically establish a connection when one is not present but required. A connection must be established manually.

➤ **Dial Whenever a Network Connection Is Not Present**—Internet Explorer attempts to establish a connection using your default dial-up connections when a network connection is not available.

➤ **Always Dial My Default Connection**—Internet Explorer always attempts to connect using your default dial-up networking connection.

In some cases, Internet Explorer may access the Internet using the local area network (LAN) connection. For example, when you connect to the Internet using a high-speed connection such as a cable modem, the connection is

often established using your network connection, as opposed to a traditional Internet connection using a modem and analog line. Or if a computer is
on a company intranet, an Internet connection will more than likely be
established using the LAN connection. In any case, you may need to configure Internet Explorer to use a proxy server. You can do so by selecting the
LAN Settings button located near the bottom of the Connections tab. Refer
to Table 2.2 for a description of the available settings.

Programs Settings

Sometimes when you click a link on a Web site, Internet Explorer needs to
invoke another program such as an HTML Editor or an email program.
Using the Programs tab (see Figure 2.10), you can specify the default program
Internet Explorer should launch when a program of a specific type is required.
For example, you can configure Internet Explorer to launch Microsoft
Outlook when a link on a Web site needs to invoke an email program.

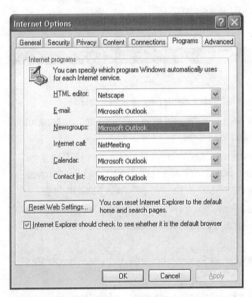

Figure 2.10   Configuring Internet programs.

Advanced Settings

Using the Advanced tab of the Internet Connections dialog box (see Figure
2.11), you can configure a number of different options such as specific
browser settings, the HTTP protocol Internet Explorer uses, and the way
your browser handles Java programs. Table 2.3 summarizes the different categories of settings you can configure.

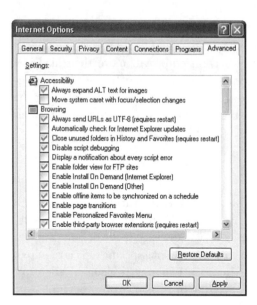

Figure 2.11 The Advanced tab of the Internet Options dialog box.

Table 2.3	Advanced Internet Options Settings
Setting	**Description**
Accessibility	These settings make Internet Explorer more accessible.
Browsing	These settings are used to configure how Internet Explorer behaves while you're browsing Web sites.
HTTP 1.1 Settings	These settings control whether Internet Explorer uses HTTP 1.1 for accessing Web sites. Some Web sites still use HTTP 1.0, so if problems occur displaying certain Web sites, uncheck these settings.
Microsoft VM	These settings tell Internet Explorer how to handle Java applets. For example, you can log all Java activity, which can be useful for troubleshooting.
Multimedia	These settings tell Internet Explorer how to handle multimedia files on Web sites.
Printing	The Print option available from the File menu within Internet Explorer enables you to print the contents of a Web page. Unless configured to do so, the background graphics and colors are not included with the printed image.
Search from the Address Bar	These settings customize the way Internet Explorer performs searches from the address bar when enabled to do so.
Security	These settings enable you to configure Advanced security settings to help protect your computer and data when accessing the Internet.

By default, some of the settings on the Advanced tab of the Internet Options dialog box are enabled and others disabled. If you make changes to any of the settings, you can easily return to the default settings by clicking the Restore Defaults button.

Resolving Issues Related to Customizing Internet Explorer

You customize Internet Explorer by using the Internet Options dialog box. This dialog box is your central location for the majority of customization in the Internet Explorer.

 Make sure you are familiar with the different ways to resolve issues related to Internet Explorer.

Home Page Error

The Home Page section on the General tab contains the default Web site you want loaded whenever you launch Internet Explorer. When a user's default home page has been changed, the user typically wants to know what happened. To modify the home page, type the new address in the Address text box. The next time Internet Explorer is opened, the requested home page is displayed.

Decreased Performance

A user may complain about decreased performance if the size of the Temporary Internet Files folder is set too high or too low. If the size is set unnecessarily high, the folder may fill the hard drive with outdated information. You can enter a lower number for the maximum Temporary Internet Files folder size. When the maximum size is reached, the older files are removed as needed. On the other hand, you do not want to set the maximum size too low because Internet Explorer can load Web sites from within this folder significantly faster than it would if it had to re-download the site by downloading it from the Internet. You can adjust this setting from the General tab of the Internet Options dialog box. Click the Settings button and type the new maximum size for the Temporary Internet files folder.

If the user's maximum folder size is reasonable but the folder is located on a drive that is becoming full, the solution is to move the folder to an alternate drive. To be able to maintain the folder size, you can use the Move Folder button on the Settings dialog box to change the location of the Temporary Internet Files folder to a different drive.

Privacy Requests

When users over-customize their privacy settings, you may receive requests to reduce the number of prompts to allow cookies. Some sites use cookies to keep track of details from one area to another, to let you view pages without re-entering a password.

Other sites might contain scripts that allow the site to greet you by name whenever you visit. Other sites use cookies for market research, to log what information you look at and what advertisements you click.

If a user has used configured Prompt setting to indicate when a Web site is trying to copy cookies to his system, the prompts that a user receives when browsing the Internet can easily become excessive. To access the Advanced Privacy settings, click the Advanced button on the Privacy tab of the Internet Options dialog box. You can then change the way cookies are handled. For example, you may want to accept First-party cookies but block Third-party cookies.

Another common problem that a user may report is not being able to utilize the customized features to frequently used Web sites. Some of the features are automatic logins, welcome screens, and local news and weather. To resolve this problem, you should lower the user's privacy setting.

Restricted Access to Web Sites

If a user complains about Web sites not appearing properly and messages popping up as the site is trying to load, the Security setting is probably set to high. If your company permits the adjustment of this setting, the user can eliminate the messages and view the site as it was originally designed. If the security settings are set too high, Java and ActiveX controls do not to load.

Connection Problems

Sometimes troubleshooting connectivity problems can be interesting during a help desk call. It is important to verify network connectivity first. A quick way to verify is to ensure that the user is not viewing a cached page or part of the company's intranet. Always verify that the user is not working offline.

When users have portable computers, they may also have two hardware profiles. In this case, ensure the user has logged in using her office profile versus her roaming or home profile. After you have verified that the user has her network card enabled, you can check to see whether she has access to other network resources, such as mapped drives and email. When you are confident that the user has access to other company resources, check to see that the LAN settings are configured appropriately. You can verify the LAN settings from the Connections tab of the Internet Options dialog box. Have the user click the LAN Settings button.

Exam Prep Questions

Question 1

> John is the desktop support technician for a small insurance company. A user calls to report that a blank HTML page appears each time he opens Internet Explorer. John verifies that the user can still access Web sites by typing in a URL. What should John do?
>
> ○ A. Verify that the correct proxy settings have been configured using the Connections tab of the Internet Options dialog box.
>
> ○ B. Verify that the site has been added to the list of Trusted Sites using the Security tab of the Internet Options dialog box.
>
> ○ C. Verify that the computer has been assigned an IP address.
>
> ○ D. Verify that the default home page is correctly configured using the General tab of the Internet Options dialog box.

Answer D is correct. Each time Internet Explorer is launched, a home page is displayed. If Internet Explorer is configured to use a blank home page, a blank HTML page is always displayed. This page can be changed using the General tab of the Internet Options dialog box. Answer A is incorrect because other Web pages are accessible from the user's computer. Answer B is incorrect because Trusted Sites are those Internet sites considered safe. Answer C is incorrect because the user can successfully gain access to the Internet, eliminating IP addressing as the problem.

Question 2

> Which of the following settings will have the best performance when browsing Web pages you have previously viewed?
>
> ○ A. Every Visit to the Page
>
> ○ B. Every Time You Start Internet Explorer
>
> ○ C. Automatically
>
> ○ D. Never

Answer C is correct. When you select Automatically, Internet Explorer checks for updates to any Web pages you viewed during a previous session. However, if a Web page's content rarely changes, Internet Explorer checks for updates less frequently. Answers A and B are incorrect because either of these two options would decrease performance. Answer D is incorrect because Internet Explorer would never check for updates to pages you have previously viewed.

Question 3

Your browser is configured with the settings shown below. Which of these statements is correct?

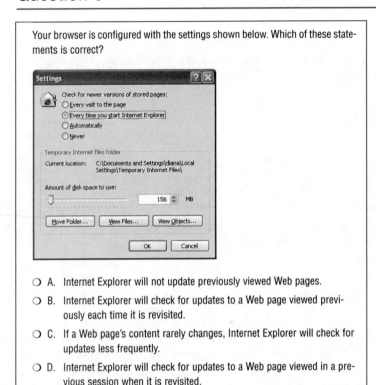

- ○ A. Internet Explorer will not update previously viewed Web pages.
- ○ B. Internet Explorer will check for updates to a Web page viewed previously each time it is revisited.
- ○ C. If a Web page's content rarely changes, Internet Explorer will check for updates less frequently.
- ○ D. Internet Explorer will check for updates to a Web page viewed in a previous session when it is revisited.

Answer D is correct. If you select the Every Time You Start Internet Explorer option to check for updates, Internet Explorer checks for updates to a Web page that has been viewed in a previous session. Therefore, answers A, B, and C are incorrect.

Question 4

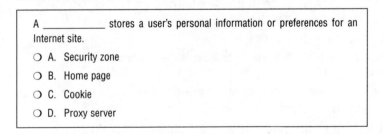

A _____ stores a user's personal information or preferences for an Internet site.
- ○ A. Security zone
- ○ B. Home page
- ○ C. Cookie
- ○ D. Proxy server

Answer C is correct. A cookie is a small text file that may store information such as your preferences for an Internet site or personal information, such as your email address. Answer A is incorrect because security zones are used to group Web sites for the purpose of applying security settings. Answer B is incorrect because a home page is the Web page displayed each time the Web browser is opened. Answer D is incorrect because a proxy server retrieves Web content on behalf of computers on the private network and blocks unwanted Internet traffic from reaching the intranet.

Question 5

A user reports that he is running out of disk space on his C drive. Internet Explorer is configured with the default settings. You want to free up disk space as well as limit the amount of space that stored Web pages and graphics consume. What should you do? Choose two correct answers.

❑ A. Change the location of the Temporary Internet Files folder.

❑ B. Change the amount of disk space allocated to the Temporary Internet Files folder.

❑ C. Delete all cookies on the computer.

❑ D. Clear the contents of the Temporary Internet Files folder.

Answers B and D are correct. Using the Internet Options dialog box, you can delete the file within the Temporary Internet Files folder. If the user has a limited amount of disk space, you can change the amount of disk space for the Temporary Internet Files folder. Answer A is incorrect because the question does not indicate that the computer is configured with a second drive. Answer C is incorrect because cookies take up a small amount of disk space.

Question 6

A user indicates that the C drive on her computer is almost full after extensive research for her current project. The user's main source of information was the Internet. What are the possible problems? (Choose all that apply.)

❑ A. The Temporary Internet Files folder is too large.

❑ B. The Temporary Internet Files folder is too small.

❑ C. The Temporary Internet Files folder is an appropriate size but located on a small drive.

❑ D. The Temporary Internet Files folder needs to be purged.

Answers A, C, and D are correct. The Temporary Internet Files folder may be too large and therefore filling the C drive. However, if the folder is an appropriate size, it should be moved to a drive that has enough free space to accommodate the temporary Internet files. It is also possible that the temporary files are not required and should be deleted from the system. Answer B is incorrect because the problem is that the C drive has reported that it is reaching its capacity.

Question 7

All client computers on your network access the Internet through a proxy server. Your company hosts a Web server on the private network that all users require access to. You want to improve performance for users when they access any Web pages hosted on the internal Web server. What can you do?

- O A. Increase the amount of disk space for the Temporary Internet Files folder.
- O B. Configure the properties of Internet Explorer on each computer not to use a proxy server.
- O C. Configure Internet Explorer to bypass the proxy server for local addresses.
- O D. Add the company Web site to the list of Trusted Sites.

Answer C is correct. Performance can be improved by configuring Internet Explorer to bypass the proxy server for local addresses. Because the Web server is on the intranet, the proxy server is not required. Answer A is incorrect because this approach would only increase the amount of information that can be stored in the Temporary Internet Files folder. Answer B is incorrect because this approach would result in client computers having no Internet connectivity. Answer D is incorrect because security zones are used to group Web sites for the purpose of applying security settings.

Question 8

Your company hosts a Web server on the internal network. To which security zone should the site be added?

- O A. Internet
- O B. Local Intranet
- O C. Trusted Sites
- O D. Restricted Sites

Answer B is correct. The Local Intranet security zone is used to group the sites that exist within your organization's intranet. Therefore, answers A, C, and D are incorrect.

Question 9

A user reports that he had difficulty logging in to his laptop, so he used a local logon. The user now indicates that his default home page is reverting to an unavailable Web page. What is the problem?

- ○ A.   The Web server is down.
- ○ B.   The exchange server is down.
- ○ C.   The user does not have access to network resources.
- ○ D.   The user's home page is not a valid address.

Answer C is correct. The user indicated that he logged on to the system using a local logon and does not have access to network resources, including the Internet. Answers A and B are incorrect; the user does not have access to these servers because he has logged on to the system locally. Answer D is incorrect because the user does not have access to an Internet connection to test whether the address is valid.

Question 10

A user indicates that she receives error messages indicating Java and ActiveX controls will not load when certain Web sites are loaded. What is the problem?

- ○ A.   The security level is set to medium.
- ○ B.   The privacy level is set to medium.
- ○ C.   The security level is set to high.
- ○ D.   The privacy level is set to high.

Answer C is correct. When set to high, the security level does not allow Java or ActiveX controls to load. Answers A, B, and D are incorrect because they do not restrict Java or ActiveX controls.

Configuring, Customizing, and Troubleshooting Outlook Express

Terms you'll need to understand:

✓ Outlook Express
✓ Newsgroups
✓ Address book
✓ Email
✓ Preview pane
✓ Import
✓ Export

Techniques you'll need to master:

✓ Create and configure email and newsgroup accounts
✓ Troubleshoot email and newsgroup accounts
✓ Manage data in Outlook Express
✓ Customize Outlook Express
✓ Resolve issues related to customizing Outlook Express

Configuring and Troubleshooting Email and Newsgroup Accounts

Outlook Express is an email and newsgroup client that is installed along with Internet Explorer. Although Outlook Express is not actually a part of the Web browser, it integrates with the browser to extend Internet Explorer's functionality.

To effectively troubleshoot problems that can arise with Outlook Express, you should be familiar with performing some of the basic tasks that include setting up an email account and newsgroups. These topics are discussed in the following sections.

Configuring Email Accounts in Outlook Express

Outlook Express is a fully functional email client that seamlessly integrates with Internet Explorer. It provides many capabilities you would find with other email clients such as address book and data management. Outlook Express even integrates with Hotmail, so you can retrieve *email* from an ISP and Hotmail (if you have a Hotmail account).

Creating an Email Account

To send and receive email using Outlook Express, you must set up a new email account. To do so, follow these steps:

1. Click Start, point to All Programs, and select Outlook Express.

2. From the Tools menu, click Accounts. The Internet Accounts dialog box appears.

3. Select the Mail tab, click the Add button, and click the Mail option. This action launches the Internet Connection Wizard.

4. Type a display name. This name will appear on any outgoing messages. Click Next.

5. Type your email address. The network administrator or your ISP provides this information when you sign up for an account. Click Next.

6. Use the drop-down arrow to select the type of incoming mail server: POP3, IMAP, or HTTP. Then provide the names of the incoming and outgoing mail servers (see Figure 3.1). Click Next.

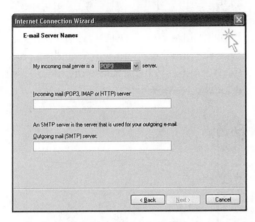

Figure 3.1 Configuring the names of email servers.

7. Type the username and password for the account. Again, your ISP or network administrator provides this information. Click Next.

8. Click Finish to close the Internet Connection Wizard.

Configuring Email Account Properties

After you have created an email account, you can edit the properties at any time through Outlook Express. For example, you can change the display name that will appear in the From box on all your outgoing messages.

To edit the properties of an existing email account, follow these steps:

1. Within Outlook Express, click Tools and select the Account option.

2. From the Internet Accounts window, select the Mail tab.

3. Highlight the email account you want to configure and click the Properties button.

4. The properties window for the email account appears (see Figure 3.2).

 Be sure you are familiar with different tabs and settings available for configuring an email account. When troubleshooting email problems, you first should verify that these settings are correctly configured. Be prepared to encounter exam questions pertaining to this topic.

From the General tab shown in Figure 3.2, you can change some basic account information. Under Mail Account, you can type a descriptive name for the account. You can also configure your name and organization. The name will appear in the From box on all your outgoing messages. You can also edit the email address and reply address. If you want users to reply to an email address other than the one from which you send, you can type the appropriate email address in the Reply Address box. If you want Outlook Express to check for new messages for the email account when sending and receiving, click the Include This Account When Receiving Mail or Synchronizing option at the bottom of the window.

Figure 3.2   Open the properties window for an email account.

Using the Servers tab, shown in Figure 3.3, you can configure the name of the mail servers and authentication information. Under Server Information, specify the protocol used for your incoming mail server as well as the names of your incoming and outgoing mail servers.

To receive mail, you must be authenticated. Under Incoming Mail Server, type the user account name and password for the email account. Select the Remember Password option to have Outlook Express remember the password. If this option is not selected, you are prompted to provide the password when Outlook Express checks for new email. If your outgoing mail server requires authentication, select the My Server Requires Authentication option and click the Settings button. In the resulting dialog box, shown in Figure 3.4, you have the option of using the same credentials used for the incoming mail server, or you can specify unique credentials.

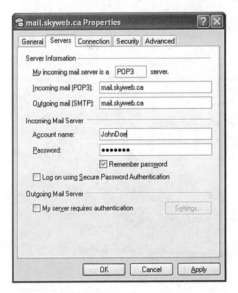

Figure 3.3   Using the Servers tab from an email account's properties window.

Figure 3.4   Configuring credentials for an outgoing mail server.

Using the Connections tab, shown in Figure 3.5, you can configure how Outlook Express connects to the Internet. If you do not select the Always Connect to This Account Using option, Outlook Express connects to the Internet using the settings configured in Internet Explorer. Conversely, you can override the settings in Internet Explorer and specify the dial-up or LAN connection Outlook Express should use to connect to the Internet.

Digital certificates verify that you are who you say you are. If you have been assigned a digital certificate, you can use it to digitally sign all your outgoing messages. You can configure the signing certificate and encrypting preferences for an email account using the Security tab, as shown in Figure 3.6.

Figure 3.5 Configuring how Outlook Express connects to the Internet.

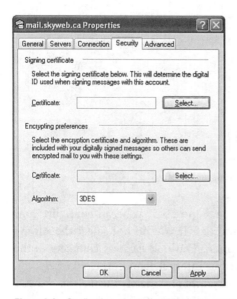

Figure 3.6 Configuring security settings for an email account.

The Advanced tab provides a number of other settings that you can configure for an email account. These settings are outlined in Table 3.1.

Table 3.1 Advanced Email Account Settings	
Setting	Description
Outgoing Mail (SMTP)	Specifies the port to connect to for the outgoing mail server. The default value is port 25.
This Server Requires a Secure SSL Connection	Specifies whether to use the Secure Sockets Layer protocol. This option can be enabled for outgoing and/or incoming mail servers.
Incoming Mail (POP3)	Specifies the port to connect to for incoming mail. The default value is port 110.
Server Timeouts	Specifies how long to wait for a response from a mail server before stopping an attempt to send or receive mail.
Break Apart Messages Larger Than	Specifies that messages larger than the value identified here are broken into smaller messages. This option is available because some older mail servers are unable to handle messages larger than 64KB.
Leave Copy Messages on Server	Specifies that a copy of all received messages are left on the mail servers.
Remove from Server After	Specifies when messages stored on the incoming mail server should be deleted.
Remove from Server When Deleted from "Deleted Items"	Specifies that messages deleted from the Deleted Items folder are also deleted from the mail server.

Troubleshooting Email Accounts

One of the most common problems users encounter when using Outlook Express is the inability to send or receive email messages. Often this is related to problems with Internet connectivity (refer to Chapter 7, "Configuring and Troubleshooting Network Connectivity," for tips on verifying Internet connectivity). If Internet connectivity is not the root of the problem, a good starting point for troubleshooting the problem is to identify the error message. This message usually gives you a good indication as to what the problem is.

If a user is able to connect to her Internet service provider (ISP) or has a LAN connection but is unable to send or receive email, verify that all the information is correct within the email account properties window. The settings configured here should match those of the ISP or local mail servers.

If a user reports that a timeout message appears when downloading email messages, try increasing the server timeout value using the Advanced tab from the account properties window (refer to Table 3.1).

If a user is unable to send and receive email, there is a good chance that a setting for the email account does not match those of the ISP. This is one of the first issues you should verify when troubleshooting such a problem.

Accessing Newsgroups Using Outlook Express

Another feature of Outlook Express is its capability to function as a newsreader. A newsreader is required to access newsgroups.

Newsgroups provide a means for people to exchange news, share information, and voice opinions. Individual newsgroups are normally dedicated to a specific topic and used by people with common interests. They serve as a type of message board where someone can post a comment or opinion (depending on the purpose of the newsgroup) that can be read by anyone else who accesses the newsgroup.

Accessing Newsgroups Through Outlook Express

Newsgroups are hosted on a server, so the first step in setting up Outlook Express is to add a newsgroup server. Your network administrator or ISP provides the name of the newsgroup server.

Follow the steps outlined here to add a newsgroup server in Outlook Express:

1. Select Tools and click the Accounts option.

2. From the Internet Accounts dialog box, click the News tab.

3. Click the Add button and select News.

4. Type your name and click Next. This name will appear when you post messages to a newsgroup.

5. Type your email address and click Next.

6. Enter the name of the news server supplied by your ISP or network administrator. If the news server requires credentials, select the My News Server Requires Me to Log On option. Click Next.

7. Type the user account name and password that will be used to access the news server. Click Next.

8. Click Finish.

A news server provides various newsgroups that you can subscribe to. After you have completed the preceding steps, you can view a list of newsgroups available on your news server and subscribe to the ones that interest you by following these steps:

1. Within Outlook Express, select the news server you have added under the folder list. A window appears informing you that you have not subscribed to any newsgroups. Click Yes to subscribe now.

2. The Newsgroups Subscriptions dialog box appears and displays all the newsgroups available on the news server. Select a newsgroup of interest and click the Subscribe button.

3. Repeat step 2 for any additional newsgroups you want to subscribe to. The newsgroups you subscribed to are displayed in Outlook Express.

4. To read the messages posted to a newsgroup, click the name of the newsgroup. The messages are displayed in the right pane.

Troubleshooting Newsgroups

Most problems with newsgroups are related to users not being able to connect to a news server or not being able to view any newsgroups. You can use the following points to assist in troubleshooting newsgroup-related issues:

➤ Verify that the user can connect to his ISP.

➤ If a user can connect to her ISP but cannot view any newsgroups, verify the settings for the news account. The settings configured should match those of the ISP.

➤ Using the Server tab from the news account properties window, verify that the correct news server name has been specified. If the user must log on to the news server, ensure that the correct username and password are being used.

➤ Verify that the correct port number has been specified. Most news servers use port 119.

➤ If the connection times out, increase the server timeout value on the Advanced tab for the news account.

Resolve Issues Related to Customizing Outlook Express

Like most other programs, Outlook Express can be customized to meet a user's specific needs. Support personnel should be familiar with the different options available for customizing Outlook Express. Knowing what the different settings are used for helps in determining the cause and solution to a problem related to customization.

Customizing the View of Outlook Express

If you do not like the layout of Outlook Express, you can alter it to meet your preferences. For example, if you do not want your list of contacts to appear on the bottom-left side in Outlook Express, you can configure it not to do so.

To customize the view of Outlook Express, click View and select the Layout option. You receive the Window Layout Properties dialog box (see Figure 3.7). Here, you can select the different components you want to have visible within the Outlook Express interface.

Figure 3.7 Customizing the view within Outlook Express.

If you want to be able to view the contents of email messages without having to open them in a separate window, you can enable the *preview pane*.

Customizing Outlook Express Options

Outlook Express offers numerous options that you can use to customize the email program. From a troubleshooting perspective, you need to be familiar with the various options to be able to solve Outlook Express–related issues.

Be sure you are familiar with the different settings available for customizing Outlook Express. One of the best ways to do this is to open Outlook Express and click through the various tabs.

Sending and Receiving Messages

To access the Outlook Express options, click the Tools menu and select Options. You receive the Options dialog box, as shown in Figure 3.8. From the General tab, you can configure how Outlook Express will send and receive messages. Following are some of the options:

➤ **Play Sound When New Messages Arrive**—Outlook Express plays a sound when a new message is received.

➤ **Send and Receive Messages at Startup**—Outlook automatically checks for new messages and sends any messages in your Outbox each time it is started.

➤ **Check for New Messages Every**—Outlook Express checks for new messages at the interval you specify. If you are not connected to the Internet when Outlook Express attempts to check for new messages, you can remain offline or have Outlook Express establish an Internet connection.

Maintaining Outlook Express

By default, Outlook Express stores a user's personal message store on the local computer within his profile. Outlook Express allows you to change this location. For example, if you want users' personal message stores to be stored on a server where they can be backed up regularly, you can change the location. To do so, click the Tools menu and select Option. Select the Maintenance tab and click the Store Folder button (see Figure 3.9). In the window that appears, you can type the new path indicating where the email should be stored.

Figure 3.8   Configuring Outlook Express options.

Figure 3.9   Changing the location of the message store.

As you can see in Figure 3.9, several other options are available for maintaining Outlook Express. Table 3.2 outlines the various settings.

Table 3.2 Outlook Express Maintenance Settings	
Setting	**Description**
Empty Messages from Deleted Items Folder on Exit	If this option is selected, Outlook Express automatically deletes all messages in the Deleted Items folder when the program is closed. Otherwise, messages in the Deleted Items folder must be manually deleted.
Purge Deleted Messages When Leaving IMAP Folders	Outlook Express deletes IMAP messages marked for deletion when you leave an IMAP folder.
Compact Messages in the Background	Messages are compacted in the background, but you can still work within Outlook Express.
Delete Read Message Bodies in Newsgroups	Outlook Express deletes newsgroup messages that have been read upon exit.
Delete News Messages X Days After Being Downloaded	All newsgroup messages are deleted after they have been on your computer for the specified number of days.
Compact Messages When There Is X Percent Wasted Space	Storage files are compacted when the percentage of wasted space reaches the value specified.
Clean Up Now	Messages stored on your computer are cleaned up.

 You can use the Maintenance tab from the Outlook Express Options dialog box to enable logging. Outlook Express saves all commands to and from a mail server into a log file that can be used for troubleshooting.

Configuring File Attachment Security

Most viruses these days are spread through email attachments. Because it is difficult for users to know attachments may contain a virus, they often open them mistakenly. Outlook Express 6 allows you to control the file attachments that users are allowed to open.

 Although Outlook Express 6 provides a way of blocking certain attachments from being opened, this feature is not a substitute for running antivirus software.

To configure file attachment security in Outlook Express, click the Tools menu and select Options. From the Security tab, shown in Figure 3.10, select the Do Not Allow Attachments to Be Saved or Opened That Could Potentially Be a Virus option.

Figure 3.10 Configuring file attachment security.

Although selecting this option does increase security, it may restrict more file types than you want. Using the Folder Options applet (discussed in Chapter 1, "Configuring, Customizing, and Troubleshooting the Operating System"), you can select which individual file types can be opened. To turn off this restriction for specific file types, follow these steps:

1. Click Start and select Control Panel.

2. Within the Control Panel, open the Folder Options applet.

3. Select the File Types tab. Highlight the file type for which you want to remove the restriction and click the Advanced button.

4. Uncheck the Confirm After Download option. Click OK.

As you can see in Figure 3.10, several other security settings can be configured. For increased security, consider setting the security zone to Restricted. Also, select the Warn Me When Other Applications Try to Send Mail as Me option. This setting can help prevent programs, mainly viruses, from accessing your address book and sending email to your contacts.

Using Signatures

Outlook Express can be configured to add a signature to all outgoing messages. You can do so using the Signatures tab, shown in Figure 3.11.

Figure 3.11 Adding signatures to outgoing messages.

To create a new signature, click the New button and rename the title of the signature to something more descriptive, making the signature more identifiable. Edit the text to display the information you want added to all outgoing messages. Select the Add Signatures to Outgoing Messages option. If you do not want your signature added to reply or forwarded messages, clear the box beside the option Don't Add Signatures to Replies and Forwards. Click OK.

Working with Identities

Often in a workplace or a home office, more than one user shares a single computer. Chances are each user will want to customize various programs, such as Outlook Express, to meet her own personal needs and preferences.

Using the Identities feature in Outlook Express, multiple users can share a single computer while maintaining their own email separately.

To create a new identity within Outlook Express, follow these steps:

1. Select the File menu, point to Identities, and click Add New Identity.

2. Type the name of the user.

3. Select the Require a Password option and create a password. This step is optional; however, it increases security.

4. Click OK. A window appears asking whether you want to switch to the new identity. If you click Yes, you are prompted to set up Outlook Express for the new user. If you answer No, you are returned to the Outlook Express interface.

 You can quickly switch between identities in Outlook Express by selecting the Switch Identities option from the File menu.

Managing Data in Outlook Express

As a desktop support technician, you need to know not only how to set up Outlook Express, but also how to perform various tasks within the program. At some point, you will more than likely receive calls from end users requesting your assistance on performing a task.

Importing and Exporting Mail

Outlook Express allows you to *import* and *export* mail messages to and from other email programs such as Microsoft Outlook.

To export mail messages, click File, point to Export, and select Messages. In the Choose Profile dialog box, select the program you want to export your mail messages to (for example, Microsoft Outlook). From the Export Messages dialog box, select the folders you want to export and click OK.

To import mail messages, click File, point to Import, and select Messages. Select the email program you want to import your messages from and click Next. Select the folders you want to import into Outlook Express and click Next. Then click Finish.

Managing Email Messages

If you receive a high volume of email messages, you may want to change the way Outlook Express processes them. For example, you may want messages from a specific person to be sorted and placed into a specific folder or highlighted in a different color.

By creating rules in Outlook Express, as shown in the following steps, you can change how incoming mail messages are processed:

1. Within Outlook Express, click the Tools menu option, point to Message Rules, and click Mail.

2. Select one or more conditions for the rule. For example, if you select Where the From Line Contains People, the mail message must be from a specific person before any processing actions are performed (see Figure 3.12).

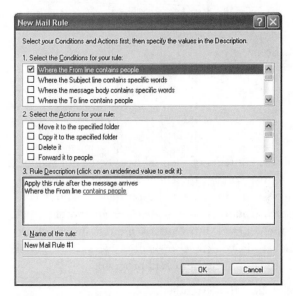

Figure 3.12 Configuring rule conditions.

3. After you have specified the conditions, you must edit the value for each condition by selecting the hyperlink under Rule Description.

4. Specify the actions for the rule. Outlook Express will take these actions if a mail message meets all the conditions.

5. Edit the values for the actions by selecting the hyperlink under Rule Description. For example, if you select the rule Move It to the Specified Folder, you then have to edit the value of the rule and tell Outlook Express which particular folder mail should be placed in.

6. Type a descriptive name for the rule.

7. Click OK.

Managing Address Books

Most email programs allow you to configure and maintain an *address book*. This feature is similar to a traditional paper-based address book where you store the names, addresses, and phone numbers of your contacts. Using the address book included with Outlook Express, you can store the following information about a person or contact:

➤ Name of the contact

➤ Email address

➤ Physical address

➤ Business-related information

➤ Personal-related information

➤ NetMeeting details

➤ Digital ID information

Users often rely heavily on the contents of their address books for sending email because the address books contain the email addresses of their contacts. Outlook Express allows you to import and export address book contacts. For example, if a user has address book contacts from another email program, you can import the contacts into Outlook Express instead of re-creating all the entries. Conversely, you can also export a user's address book from Outlook Express for use within another email program.

To import an address book, follow these steps:

1. From within Outlook Express, click the File menu, point to Import, and click Address book.

2. Browse to the location of the address book (.wab) and then click Open.

 If you are importing an address book that is stored in another format, such as **.csv**, click the File menu, point to Import, and select Other Address Book.

As already mentioned, Outlook Express also allows you to export an address book—for example, if you want to use your existing contacts and information within another email program. You can export an address book by clicking the File menu within Outlook Express, pointing to Export, and clicking the Address Book option. Select an export format for the address book and click Export.

Compacting Folders in Outlook Express

Outlook Express stores messages as entries within a database. Over time, these databases can grow in size and, as a result, degrade performance and consume a large amount of disk space. The reason is that when a message is deleted within Outlook Express, even if it is removed from your Deleted Items folder and out of your view, it still consumes disk space. So, over time, all the hidden records, which you thought were deleted, slow down performance and take up disk space.

Outlook Express allows you to compact your folders, which essentially removes all the records that have been marked for deletion from your computer. Compacting should improve performance and free up disk space.

By default, Outlook Express is configured to compact folders automatically during periods of inactivity. You can turn off this feature using the Maintenance tab from the Options dialog box. However, should you choose to disable this feature, you should manually compact your folders once a month. You can do so by selecting the Clean Up Now button located on the Maintenance tab and clicking Compact from the Local File Clean Up dialog box.

If you receive the **Cannot compact, folder is in use** error message, close down Outlook Express. Then reopen the application and try running the Compact feature again.

Blocking Senders

Many users receive unwanted email in their Inboxes. Outlook Express allows you to control the senders from whom you receive email. For example, if you continually receive spam email from a specific email address, you can block the sender. After a sender is blocked, you will no longer receive email from that sender in your Inbox.

To block a sender, highlight an unwanted message within your Inbox, click the Message menu, and select the Block Sender option. A message appears informing you that the sender is blocked. Click Yes to confirm this action.

Exam Prep Questions

Question 1

You are working as a help desk support technician for a small insurance company. A new user reports to you that Outlook Express continually prompts her
for a password when checking for new messages. She does not want to continually have to type in her password. What should you do?

○ A. Change the security zone using the Security tab from the Outlook
Express Options dialog box.

○ B. Open the properties window for the email account and select the
Remember Password option on the Servers tab.

○ C. Open the properties window for the email account and select the
Servers tab. Click the My Server Requires Authentication option.

○ D. Open the Options dialog box for Outlook Express. From the General
tab, select the Automatically Log On to Windows Messenger option.

Answer B is correct. Outlook Express can be configured to remember the
password for an email account so you are not prompted to type it in when
Outlook Express checks for email. You can configure this setting by opening
the properties window for the email account, selecting the Servers tab, and
clicking the Remember Password option. Answer A is incorrect because a
security zone is used to apply security settings. Answer C is incorrect because
this option is selected if your outgoing mail server requires authentication.
Answer D is incorrect because this option is used to configure Outlook
Express to automatically log you on to Windows Messenger.

Question 2

You are currently using Outlook Express as your email client. You want all messages from your boss to be placed in a specific folder when they are received.
What should you do?

○ A. Import all email messages from your boss into the specific folder.

○ B. Create a rule that moves all email messages from your boss into a
specific folder.

○ C. Manually move each message into a specific folder after you read
them.

○ D. Outlook Express does not support this functionality.

Answer B is correct. To change how Outlook Express processes received mail messages, you must create a rule. A rule can be created to move all messages received from a specific person or email address into a specific folder. Answer A is incorrect because the Import function is used to import mail messages from another program into Outlook Express. Outlook Express does allow you to manually move individual messages into a different folder. However, doing so would require more effort than creating a rule that will do it automatically. Therefore, answer C is incorrect. Answer D is incorrect because rules in Outlook Express allow you to configure how received mail messages are processed.

Question 3

A user reports that Outlook Express is performing slowly. Upon investigation, you also discover that the user has limited disk space. You want to improve application performance while, at the same time, reclaim some of the wasted disk space. What should you do?

- ○ A. Empty the Deleted Items folder.
- ○ B. Compact the messages using the Maintenance tab from the Options dialog box.
- ○ C. Clear the Temporary Internet Files folder using the General tab from the Internet Options dialog box.
- ○ D. Export all the user's messages from Outlook Express.

Answer B is correct. By using the compact feature in Outlook Express, you can reclaim wasted disk space and improve application performance. When folders are compacted, messages marked for deletion are removed from the computer. Answer A is incorrect because this will not purge all unwanted information from the computer. Deleted messages are removed only from the user's view. Answer C is incorrect because the information stored within the Temporary Internet Files folder is used for browsing the Internet. Clearing the contents of this folder will free disk space but not improve performance of Outlook Express. Answer D is incorrect. The export function is used to move messages from Outlook Express into another email program such as Outlook.

Question 4

> You are the help desk technician for a small consulting firm. One of the users recently received an email message with an executable attachment. You want to prevent users from opening attachments that could be potentially harmful. What should you do?
>
> ○ A. Have users forward all email messages with attachments to you before opening them.
>
> ○ B. Change the program used to open executables to Outlook Express.
>
> ○ C. Using the Options dialog box, configure Outlook Express to block attachments that could be potentially harmful.
>
> ○ D. Using the Options dialog box, configure Outlook Express to notify you when another program attempts to send an email.

Answer C is correct. Outlook Express can be configured to block attachments that can be potentially harmful to a computer. You can enable this option by using the Security tab within the Options dialog box. Therefore, answers A and B are incorrect. Answer D is incorrect because this option is used to prevent viruses from sending email to contacts in your address book.

Question 5

> You are working as a support technician for an Internet service provider. A home user calls to report that she is unable to send and receive email. However, she can successfully browse the Internet. You verify that the user is logging in with the correct username and password. What else should you do?
>
> ○ A. Verify that the user's modem is working correctly.
>
> ○ B. Verify that the settings for the dial-up connection are properly configured.
>
> ○ C. Check the email account properties to verify that they match those of the ISP.
>
> ○ D. Verify that Outlook Express is configured to check for new messages.

Answer C is correct. When you are troubleshooting email problems, one of the first things you should do is verify that the settings configured for the email account match those of the ISP. For example, make sure the user has specified the correct name of the POP3 server. Answers A and B are incorrect because it has already been established that the user can browse the Internet. Answer D is incorrect because Outlook Express is unable to connect to the mail servers.

Question 6

A user calls to indicate that he has been recently receiving a large amount of spam email in his Inbox. This unwanted email is received several times throughout the day and must be manually deleted. The user is concerned that some of the emails may contain viruses and does not want to receive them anymore. What should you do?

- ○ A. Create a rule that places all email from the sender into another folder.

- ○ B. Configure Outlook Express to automatically empty the contents of the Deleted Items folder when it is closed.

- ○ C. Block the email address of the sender.

- ○ D. Create a rule that places all incoming email from the sender into the Deleted Items folder.

Answer C is correct. If the user does not want to receive any email from the sender, the sender's email address should be blocked. Any email from a blocked sender will not be received. Therefore, answers A, B, and D are incorrect.

Question 7

You are troubleshooting an email problem for a user. When the user attempts to receive email, the error message shown in the figure below. What should you do?

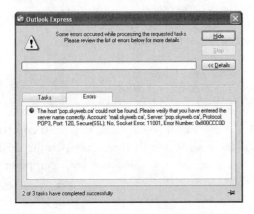

○ A. Verify that the user is typing the correct password from the email account properties window.

○ B. Check that the username is correct from the email account properties window.

○ C. Check that the name of the incoming mail server is correct from the email account properties window.

○ D. Verify that the user is connecting to the default POP3 port of 120 on the mail server.

Answer C is correct. The error indicates that the incoming mail server cannot be found. One of the first things you should check is that the name of the incoming mail server is correctly configured. Answers A and B are incorrect because the error message does not indicate a problem with authentication. Answer D is incorrect because the default POP3 port is 110. You can see by the error message that the user is connecting to the correct port.

Question 8

One of the users in your organization has a home office. He is able to receive email from his home or office computer. However, he reports that any email he receives on one computer is not available on the other computer. What should you do?

○ A. Instruct the user to forward a copy of all received emails to himself.

○ B. Have the user work offline when in his home office.

○ C. Using the General tab from the Outlook Express Options dialog box, configure Outlook Express not to connect to the Internet when checking for new messages.

○ D. Using the Advanced tab from the email account properties window, configure Outlook Express to leave a copy of all messages on the server.

Answer D is correct. Outlook Express can be configured to store a copy of all received email messages on the mail server (if the server permits this). The received email messages can then be available from both computers. Therefore, answers A, B, and C are incorrect.

Question 9

You have set up Outlook Express for a new user. She can successfully send and receive email. The user calls you in regards to the Outlook Express interface. She wants to be able to view the content of received messages without having to open each one in a new window. What should she do?

- ○ A. Open the Windows Layout Properties dialog box and enable the preview pane.
- ○ B. Open the Options dialog box for Outlook Express and enable Outlook Express to go directly to the Inbox when started.
- ○ C. Open the Options dialog box for Outlook Express and enable Outlook Express to display folders with unread messages.
- ○ D. Create a new rule that displays the preview pane for all received messages.

Answer A is correct. To display the preview pane, you must open the Windows Layout Properties dialog box and enable the preview pane. Therefore, answers B and C are incorrect. Answer D is incorrect because rules are used to configure how Outlook Express handles incoming email.

Question 10

Users in your company currently use Outlook Express. However, all users are being migrated to Microsoft Outlook. You want to move email messages from Outlook Express into Microsoft Outlook. What should you do?

- ○ A. Use the Export function of Outlook Express.
- ○ B. Use the Save As function within Outlook Express and save all messages into a **.pst** file.
- ○ C. Import the messages into a **.pst** file. Import the messages into Microsoft Outlook.
- ○ D. Back up the mail messages and restore them in Microsoft Outlook.

Answer A is correct. You can use the Export function within Outlook Express to copy all mail messages (as well as the address book) into Microsoft Outlook. Therefore, answers B, C, and D are incorrect.

4

Configuring, Customizing, and Troubleshooting Office Applications

Terms you'll need to understand:

✓ Administrative installation point

✓ Transform (**.mst**) file

✓ Windows Installer package

✓ Proofing Tools

✓ Template file

Techniques you'll need to master:

✓ Install Office XP

✓ Troubleshoot Office XP installations

✓ Configure Office XP default settings

✓ Customize toolbars in Microsoft Office

✓ Troubleshoot customization issues with Office XP

✓ Configure Office Proofing Tools

Installing Office

You will encounter two different types of Office installations: a *fresh installation* and an *upgrade*. A fresh installation is performed on a system that has not had a version of Microsoft Office installed previously. An upgrade installation is performed on a system that has had a previous version of Microsoft Office installed.

 You should be comfortable installing, configuring, and customizing Office XP software.

Determining the Type of Installation Required

If a previous version of Microsoft Office is not currently installed on your computer, you need to determine which option is appropriate for your scenario. The following options are available in the Choose the Type of Installation dialog box:

➤ To quickly install the most commonly used Office XP applications, tools, and features, select the preconfigured installation. Choose the Install Now Option.

➤ To install everything, including all optional tools and features, select the Complete option.

➤ To control exactly which applications, tools, and features are installed, select the Custom option.

With any of these choices, you can change the default installation location by typing or browsing to a new folder path in the Install To text box.

If a previous version of Office was installed on your computer, you see an additional option in the Choose the Type of Installation dialog box during the setup. The Upgrade Now option is available only when a previous version of Office is installed on your computer. During the installation, the previous Office version is removed, replacing each application with the new version.

Performing a CD-Based Installation

Before you begin the installation, you need the Office XP CD, a valid product key, and access to a CD-ROM drive. This drive can be local or a shared CD-ROM drive on the network.

The following steps guide you through the Installation Wizard process:

1. Insert the first Office XP CD into the CD-ROM drive. If the autoplay feature is disabled, open the Explorer window and view the contents of the CD. Run the Setup.exe program in the root folder of the Office CD.

2. Enter the appropriate details in the User Information dialog box, including name, initials, organization, and product key (see Figure 4.1). Click Next.

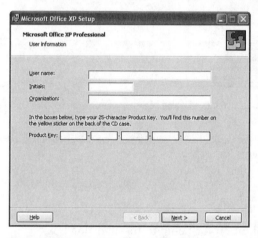

Figure 4.1   The User Information dialog box.

The product key is located on a label on the Office CD container. You cannot install Office XP without a valid product key.

3. You must accept the End-User License Agreement (EULA) in the End-User License Agreement dialog box to proceed with the installation. Click Next.

4. In the Choose the Type of Installation You Need dialog box, shown in Figure 4.2, select the type of installation you want to perform. You can choose either Complete, which installs all options available, or Custom, which enables you to choose the components you want to install. Also, select the location where the Office XP program files will be stored. Then click Next.

Figure 4.2 The Choose the Type of Installation You Need dialog box.

The remaining steps apply only if you have selected the Custom option, regardless of whether this is an upgrade or fresh installation.

5. In the Choose Which Application for Setup to Install dialog box, choose the applications to install. The available options are

➤ To quickly install the common features for the applications you selected, as well as the typical Office tools, select Install Applications with the Typical Options.

➤ To choose the specific application features and Office tools that will be installed, select Choose Detailed Installation Options for Each Application.

After you have made your selection, click Next.

6. If you selected the Detailed Installation Options for Each Application, Setup displays the Choose Installation Options dialog box, shown in Figure 4.3. Select the specific application features and Office tools that you want to install. Then click Next.

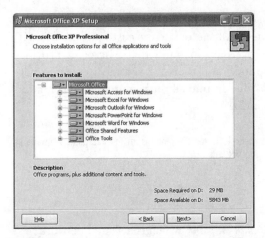

Figure 4.3   The Choose Installation Options dialog box.

To control the installation of a particular application, tool, or feature, expand the hierarchy in the Choose Installation Options dialog box if necessary to reveal the component; then click the down arrow to open the menu of choices. Choose Run From My Computer to install the component, choose Run All From My Computer to install the component plus all components beneath it in the hierarchy, choose Installed On First Use to have Office automatically install the component the first time you attempt to use it, or choose Not Available to omit installing the component.

7. If you had a previous version of Office installed on your computer when you ran Setup, the Remove Previous Versions dialog box is displayed. Choose whether to have Setup remove your previous Office version, preserve your complete previous Office installation, or remove one or more specific applications from your previous installations. Then click Next.

8. Setup displays the Begin installation dialog box, which shows a list of the applications that will be installed. Click Install to complete the installation.

Performing a Network-Based Installation

In a networked environment, provided that you have obtained the required licenses from Microsoft, you can copy all the Office XP files to a single shared network folder and then allow all users to install Office XP directly from that folder over the network rather than from the product CD. Not only does this method eliminate the need to distribute CDs to all users, but it also allows you to fully customize and automate the Office XP installation. With a customized installation, users are not required to enter the details into the Setup dialog boxes but can run a standard Setup file.

You can use the following procedure to set up and install Office XP on a network. This procedure allows you to fully automate the customized Office XP installations on users' computers. Keep in mind that Microsoft provides many additional techniques, options, and tools for setting up custom network installations of Office XP. You can find all the required documentation and tools in the Office Resource Kit.

NOTE   The Office Resource Kit is available for download from the Microsoft Web site at **http://www.microsoft.com/office/ork**.

1. Create an *administrative installation point*, which is a shared network folder that contains all the Office files required to install Office on a user's computer. To convert a shared network folder to an administrative installation point, run Office Setup using the /a flag. For instance, if the Office CD is on drive D, you execute the following command using the Run option from the Start menu: d:\Setup.exe /a. Figure 4.4 displays the Run dialog box with the required command.

Figure 4.4   The Run dialog box displays the Setup program with the required switch to begin a network installation.

Next, in the Administrative Installation Setup dialog box, enter your organization name, the path of the shared folder you want to use as the administrative installation point, and the product key. In the End-User License Agreement dialog box, accept the license agreement and click Install.

NOTE   If the product key is omitted, each user will have to enter a valid product key when installing Office XP.

2. Use the Custom Installation Wizard to create a transform (.mst) file to automate the customization of the Office XP installation on a user's computer. The Custom Installation Wizard is included in the Office Resource Kit. When you run it, it begins by displaying an informational dialog box.

On the second wizard dialog box, enter the path of the Windows Installer package file that will be used to install Office XP. You can find this file in the administrative installation point folder that you set up in step 1.

The Windows Installer package file has a name such as **msoffice.msi**. This file contains default settings that Setup uses to install Office XP. These settings are modified by the *transform file* that you create in step 2.

3. In the third dialog box, enter a name and location for the transform file that you're creating. The best place to save this file is in the administrative installation point folder you set up in step 1.

In the next series of wizard dialog boxes, approximately 20, select all the options that you want to apply when users install Office XP on their individual computers. You can click Finish in any of these wizard dialog boxes to use the defaults for all installation options you haven't yet set.

4. Have each user install Office XP by running the setup.exe program in the administrative installation point folder you created in step 1. When running setup.exe, the user must pass the Transforms command-line parameter specifying the location of the transform file you created in step 2. For instance, if you created the administrative installation point in the \\admin\c\admininstallpoint\ network folder and named the transform file New Custom Setup file.mst, a user could install Office XP by choosing Run from the Start menu in Windows and entering the following into the Run dialog box:

```
\\admin\c\AdminInstallPoint\setup
transforms="\\admin\c\AdminInstallPoint\
New Custom Setup file.mst" /qb
```

The entire command line should be entered on a single line in the Run dialog box.

Deploying Office through Group Policy

Another method of deploying Microsoft Office XP (as well as other software applications) is using Group Policy. Group Policy includes software installation features that you can use to perform mass installations of and to maintain Microsoft Office.

Group Policy settings are contained within a Group Policy Object (GPO). The GPO can be linked to any level of the Active Directory hierarchy, which essentially determines the scope of the GPO settings. For example, applying a GPO to a specific OU means that only those accounts within the OU are affected by the GPO settings.

Microsoft Office XP is designed to function within an environment that uses group policies for software installation and maintenance. By using features of Microsoft Office XP and Active Directory, you can deploy a custom configuration of the software to a specific group of users and computers.

Microsoft Office XP can be deployed using a GPO in three different ways:

➤ **Assigned to computers**—With this method, Microsoft Office XP is installed the next time the computer is restarted. The software is then available to all users.

➤ **Assigned to users**—With this method, a shortcut is placed on the users' desktop. When a shortcut for one of the Office applications is opened, the software is automatically installed. Applications that are assigned to users are resilient.

➤ **Published to users**—With this method, Microsoft Office XP can be installed using the Add/Remove Programs applet.

 When deploying software using a GPO, remember that applications can be assigned to users and/or computers. However, applications can be published only to users, not computers.

Activating Office XP

After you install Office XP on your computer, you are required to activate the software. If you do not activate Office, you can start Office applications only 50 times; then you will be required to activate the software to avoid running the software in Reduced Functionality Mode. Reduced Functionality Mode prevents you from saving or creating new documents and from using certain features within the applications. Activation involves connecting with

Microsoft on the Internet or by telephone. Figure 4.5 displays a sample warning message when activation is required.

Figure 4.5 The Activation Wizard dialog box.

The first time you open an Office application, the Office Application Wizard is displayed. The wizard allows you to activate Office XP using the following options:

➤ To activate Office XP via the Internet, select the Activate By Using the Internet option and then click Next. Follow the wizard's instructions to connect to Microsoft's Office XP activation site and complete the activation. You can manually connect to the Internet before clicking Next, or you can have the wizard use your default Internet connection. You need to provide only your country of residence; supplying additional personal information is optional. The wizard automatically activates your Office XP installation.

➤ To activate the product by calling a Microsoft customer service agent, select the Activate by Using the Telephone option and then click Next to see complete instructions for calling the agent and completing the activation process.

The next dialog box provides the telephone number for calling the agent from your country and displays your unique Installation ID. You need to provide that ID to the agent, who will then give you a Confirmation ID. When you enter the Confirmation ID into the wizard dialog box and continue, the wizard activates your Office XP installation.

➤ To skip the activation and immediately run the application, click Activate Later. Keep in mind that you can run the product a total of 50 times before activating. The Office Activation Wizard continues to pop up every time an Office XP application is opened until the activation has been completed.

Using the Volume Licensing Product Key

A *Volume License Product Key (VLK)* is a product key issued to a corporate customer under a specific license agreement. Each VLK is associated with a particular customer and type of product for which the customer is licensed. For each type of license agreement, one VLK is issued per enrollment agreement per product family. For Microsoft Open License customers, the VLK is provided on the Open License order confirmation. These VLKs are to be used when the product prompts for it at installation or when you create a custom image. A VLK must be used with volume licensing media; therefore, it cannot be used with retail full-packaged product or OEM CD media.

 Volume License Product Key (VLK) is available for both Windows XP and Office XP. You also can purchase VLKs for individual applications within Office XP, such as Word, Excel, Access, PowerPoint, and Outlook.

When you use a VLK during the deployment of Office XP, you must enter it when building your network image. After you have set up your image using the VLK, the end user will not be prompted for a product key when installing from that network image. However, you must still work within the Microsoft license agreement that you have signed. In simple terms, you must acquire a separate license for the software you install for each computer or user. Use varies according to the terms of your agreement and the terms of each product license.

The majority of volume licensing customers deploy products over their network. When setting up the network share, the system administrator can preapply the VLK so that end users installing the software from that point will not be prompted for a product key. The same can be done when creating customized CDs.

Troubleshooting an Office Installation

You can rerun Office Setup in maintenance mode at any time to add or remove specific features, reinstall Office XP, or remove Office XP from your computer. You can also use maintenance mode if you have been having serious problems with one or more programs or features and you suspect that the program files or Registry settings may have become corrupted. To use Setup in maintenance mode, complete the following steps:

1. Open the Add or Remove Programs applet from the Windows Control Panel, select the Microsoft Office XP item from the list, and click the Change or Remove button (see Figure 4.6).

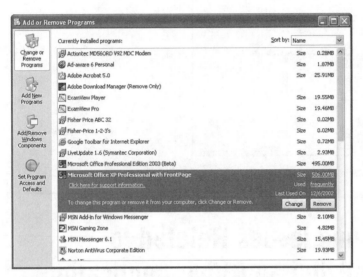

Figure 4.6   The Add or Remove Programs applet displays the Change and Remove buttons for the Office XP installation.

2. In the opening Setup dialog box named Maintenance Mode Options, shown in Figure 4.7, select one of the following options:

   ➤ To add or remove one or more Office applications or features, select Add or Remove Features. Setup displays the same installation options you selected when you most recently ran Setup. You need to change only the installation options for features you want to add or remove; the rest of the installation is not disturbed.

   ➤ To force Setup to reinstall all Office XP files and redo all Registry settings and necessary repairs, select Detect and Repair Errors in My Office Installation. If in doubt about which option to select, choose this simpler option first and select the more radical Reinstall Office option only if your problem persists.

   ➤ To remove Office XP from your computer, select Uninstall Office.

 Another way to have Office XP detect and repair errors in your Office XP installation is to choose the Detect and Repair command from the Help menu of any Office application. This command provides an additional option that discards your customized settings and restores all defaults.

Figure 4.7   The Maintenance Mode Options dialog box.

Resolving Issues Related to Customizing an Office Application

The working environment in Microsoft Office applications can easily be changed to a user's preference. Some custom settings apply only to the open application; however, other settings modify all applications within the Microsoft Office suite. For example, the Default File Locations setting applies to all Microsoft Office applications. You set the file locations in the Options dialog box in Microsoft Word. In contrast, the default font used in the blank document template named Normal.dot affects only new Word documents.

A common problem occurs when a user unintentionally modifies blank templates for Word, Excel, or PowerPoint. There is a simple solution to this problem. Office provides a fail-safe feature that re-creates the blank template if it cannot find the blank template while creating a new file. To remove all customizations to the blank template, including custom toolbars and menus, simply delete the old, blank template and allow the program to re-create the blank template when the program is opened.

Re-creating a blank template removes all customized settings. For users who have not customized their application settings, this method solves their problem. However, power users who rely heavily on their customizations will not approve of the loss of their macros, custom toolbars, or menu modifications. Always back up the *template file* before you delete. This way, you have something to fall back on if the user was unaware a customization had been applied.

Follow these steps to re-create the `Normal.dot` template for Microsoft Word:

1. Click Start and then select Search.

2. In the left pane, select All Files and Folders.

3. In the All or Part of a File Name box, type `normal.dot`.

4. In the Look In drop-down list, choose the drive where Microsoft Office XP is currently installed.

5. Click Search to begin your search.

 If your search does not locate a **Normal.dot** template file, verify that your search includes system folders. To include system folders, click the More advanced options link in the Search Results window and check the Search System Folders option. After you have verified that the system folders are being searched and your search does not locate a **Normal.dot** template file, the search result then indicates that no modifications have been made to the blank template file in Microsoft Word. The **Normal.dot** file is stored in a file format only after customizations have been applied to the blank document or application window.

6. When the search is complete, right-click `Normal.dot` and then select Rename. If multiple `Normal.dot` files are located, you need to rename all files that have been found.

 If multiple people use the system that requires a new **Normal.dot** template file, you must verify the location of the **Normal.dot** template file for each individual user and rename that particular file **Normal.old**.

7. In the Name box, type `Normal.old` and press Enter. Rename any additional files that were located during the search.

8. Open Microsoft Word. Word automatically creates the new `Normal.dot` template file.

Customizing Toolbars

The method to customize toolbars is the same for all applications in the Microsoft Office suite. To access the Customize dialog box, shown in Figure 4.8, select View, point to Toolbars, click Customize, and then select the Toolbars tab.

Figure 4.8 The Customize dialog box.

 An alternative method to open the Customize dialog box is to right-click an open toolbar and select Customize from the shortcut menu.

Each Microsoft Office suite application has its own specific toolbars. You will notice similarities between the applications—for example, the Standard toolbar. The Standard toolbar always contains the New, Open, Save, Cut, Copy, and Paste icons. However, the specific applications have additional icons that pertain to the program. Figure 4.9 shows the Standard toolbar for Microsoft Word, and Figure 4.10 shows the Standard toolbar for Microsoft Excel. Compare the two toolbars and notice that each toolbar has additional buttons specific to the particular program.

Figure 4.9 The Standard toolbar for Microsoft Word.

Figure 4.10 The Standard toolbar for Microsoft Excel.

If a user is having a problem with a toolbar, be sure to open the troublesome application before troubleshooting the toolbar in question.

Using the Toolbar tab of the Customize dialog box (refer to Figure 4.8), you can configure various settings that include

➤ Activating or deactivating toolbars

➤ Creating a new toolbar

➤ Renaming a toolbar

➤ Deleting custom toolbars

➤ Resetting a toolbar

➤ Assigning a keyboard combination to a command

Follow these steps to add a button to an existing toolbar:

1. Click the View menu, point to Toolbars, and click Customize.

2. In the Customize dialog box, click the Commands tab. Under Categories, select the category from which you want to add the button.

To change which features are displayed in the Commands list, click a new category from the Category list on the left pane of the dialog box.

3. To add a button to a toolbar, drag a button from the Commands list to the desired toolbar.

When you use Full Screen view, all toolbars and menu bars are hidden. The Full Screen toolbar should appear floating within the application window unless the user has turned it off. To exit Full Screen view, press Escape to return to the previous program view.

Make sure you are able to configure and customize built-in toolbars in all Office XP applications.

Configuring Proofing Tools

Microsoft Office *Proofing Tools* is an add-in that supplies a collection of tools, such as spelling and grammar checkers, thesauri, and AutoCorrect lists, for more than 45 languages. Microsoft Office comes with built-in proofing tools for commonly used languages. For example, the English version of Office includes proofing tools for French and Spanish, as well as English. By installing Office Proofing Tools, you add those same capabilities for many more languages. This makes it even easier to quickly and accurately enter and edit text in the languages you want, creating powerful, professional, and error-free documents.

When you install Office Proofing Tools, the following tools are added to most Office programs:

➤ Spelling checkers and their accompanying dictionaries

➤ Grammar and writing style checkers

➤ Thesauri for checking synonyms

➤ Hyphenators

➤ AutoCorrect lists

➤ AutoSummarize

➤ Input Method Editors (IMEs)

➤ Word breakers

➤ Simplified/traditional Chinese translator

➤ Tools for working with Korean text, such as Hangul Hanja converter and Hanja dictionary

➤ Additional bilingual dictionaries

Microsoft Office XP Proofing Tools is available for purchase at shop.microsoft.com or a licensed reseller.

You should be comfortable configuring Office XP Proofing Tools.

Personalizing Office Features

Office includes many features that you can customize to users' particular needs. Some of the features were mentioned earlier in this chapter; however, another feature in particular is worth mentioning. You can customize the My Places bar of the Open dialog box to specific network drives, local drives, or folders by following these steps:

1. Within any Office application, select the File menu and then select Open.

2. Navigate to the folder or drive that you want to add to the My Places bar. Click the folder or drive to select the item.

3. Click the Tools button on the toolbar and select Add to My Places (see Figure 4.11). The new button is displayed at the bottom of the My Places bar list.

Figure 4.11   The Add to My Places menu option from the Tools button in the Open dialog box.

The Open dialog box default size is set up to show five default icons; however, you can resize the dialog box to display the additional icons. An alternative solution to enlarging the dialog box is to change the My Places bar view to small icons to display more icons.

Saving Your Settings Wizard

You can easily modify menus and toolbars to include additional options and buttons. However, a common end-user request is to locate a missing toolbar button. If you have verified that the option is not hidden because of the personalized toolbars, you need to add the button manually or reset the toolbar. You can reset the menus and toolbars to their original design by using the Customize dialog box.

For power users who have customized the Office suite applications, these settings are an integral part of their working environment. Resetting the menus and toolbars will cause the loss of their efforts and create unhappy end users.

To prevent the loss of customized settings, Office XP includes a new feature called the Save My Settings Wizard. You now can create a file of customized settings, including menu, toolbar, and template modifications. Store the file either locally or on the company network, and any time you need to re-apply a user's customizations to an Office XP-equipped computer, you can use that profile to re-create the work environment.

To prepare the profile, click the Windows Start menu, choose All Programs, select Microsoft Office Tools, and then click Save My Settings Wizard.

Save these settings locally, either to a company's network or to your own backup disk. The settings file is small enough to save on a floppy. If your hard drive melts down, and you need to reinstall Office, you can easily restore your settings from this file.

As a backup and for those times when you want to personalize another edition of Office but don't want to haul around a disk, we also recommend saving your profile to Microsoft's secure online server. There's no charge (all you need is a Passport account), and Microsoft swears that it cannot access this information. You can retrieve this file using any Internet-connected computer and then use it to restore that PC's Office XP to your personal settings.

Follow these instructions to save your current settings using the wizard:

1. Close all applications from the Microsoft Office suite.

2. Click the Start Menu, choose All Programs, select Microsoft Office Tools, and click the Save My Settings Wizard (refer to Figure 4.12).

3. When the Welcome to the Save My Settings Wizard dialog box opens, click Next to begin the wizard.

4. In the Save or Restore Settings dialog box, select the Save the Settings from This Machine option to back up your current customizations (refer to Figure 4.13). Then click Next.

5. In the Choose to Save to the Web or a File dialog box, select the Save the Settings to a File option (refer to Figure 4.14).

6. Click the Browse button to navigate to the location where you want to store your file.

7. Type the name of the file and click Save.

8. Click the Finish button to complete the wizard.

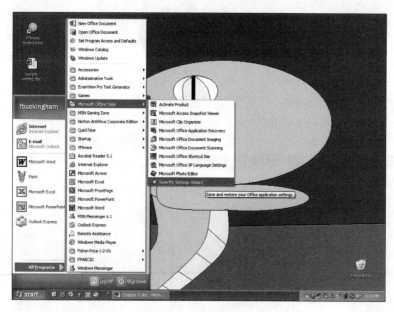

Figure 4.12 The Save My Settings Wizard menu option.

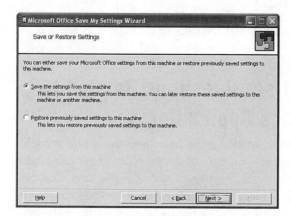

Figure 4.13 The Save or Restore Settings dialog box.

When you need to restore the settings stored in the backup file, you use the same wizard to complete this task. The following instructions explain how to restore the user's customizations:

1. Close all applications from the Microsoft Office Suite.

2. Click the Start Menu, choose All Programs, select Microsoft Office Tools, and click the Save My Settings Wizard (see Figure 4.12).

3. When the Welcome to the Save My Settings Wizard dialog box opens, click Next to begin the wizard.

4. In the Save or Restore Settings dialog box, select the Restore Previously Saved Settings to This Machine option to restore the customizations (see Figure 4.13). Then click Next.

5. In the Choose to Restore from the Web or from a File dialog box, choose the location of the backup file was stored (see Figure 4.14).

6. Click Finish to restore the Office XP customizations.

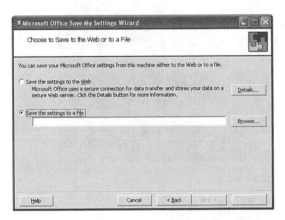

Figure 4.14   The Choose to Save to the Web or a File dialog box.

Answering End-User Questions Related to Customizing Office Applications

When an end user calls with a question regarding customizing Office applications, you need to listen to the symptoms of the problem. Don't get caught up in the end user's ideas as to what is causing the problem. These ideas can send you off in the wrong direction. The symptoms always tell the whole story. Allow the end user to inform you of the problem and then start verifying the details after the explanation of the problem is complete.

The number-one cause of a difficult call is to assume the end user has solved the problem. Listen to the symptoms, determine when the problem was first noticed, and then do not make any assumptions. Verify each fact.

Exam Prep Questions

Question 1

A user has received a new laptop and requests that his Office customizations be applied to his new system. What can be done to apply the user's customizations to his new system?

○ A. Run the Save My Settings Wizard on the user's current system and then run it on the new laptop.

○ B. Copy the **Normal.dot**, **presentation.pot**, and **xluser.xlt** files from the user's existing system and replace the existing copies on the new laptop.

○ C. Re-create the customized settings on the new laptop.

○ D. Copy the user's profile from the existing system onto the new laptop.

Answer A is correct. To prevent the loss of customized settings, you can create a file of customized settings, including menu, toolbar, and template modifications. Store the file either locally or on the company network, and any time you need to re-apply the user's customizations to an Office XP–equipped computer, you can use that profile to re-create the work environment. Answers B and D are incorrect because these options do not offer viable solutions. Answer C is also incorrect. Although this answer does provide a solution, it does not present the most efficient one.

Question 2

A power user indicates that some features are missing from her current installation of Microsoft Word. You have verified that you cannot access the thesaurus. What is the problem with the user's computer?

○ A. The Office XP installation needs to be repaired.

○ B. The user does not have Word installed.

○ C. The user has customized the Format menu.

○ D. The user has a Typical Office XP installation.

Answer D is correct. The Typical Office XP installation does not contain the thesaurus. Answer A is incorrect because the user has not reported an error with the installation. Answer B is incorrect because Word is installed. Answer C is incorrect because the thesaurus is located on the Tools menu, not the Format menu.

Question 3

A user reports that the Paste button is missing from the Standard toolbar. What should you do?

- ○ A. After verifying that the user has not customized the toolbar, reset the toolbar in the Customize dialog box.
- ○ B. Reset the Standard toolbar.
- ○ C. Open the Customize dialog box and drag the Paste button onto the Formatting toolbar.
- ○ D. Inform the user to press Ctrl+V because the Paste button is gone.

Answer A is correct. You can reset the toolbar using the Customize dialog box. Answers B and C are incorrect because these options do not solve the problem. Answer D is incorrect. Although the user can press Ctrl+V, pressing this key combination does not solve the problem of the missing Paste button.

Question 4

A user calls and reports that Excel hangs whenever he accesses the Import Data feature. After further investigation, the user indicates that Excel has had other performance problems. What should be done?

- ○ A. Remove the Excel application.
- ○ B. Install the Import Data feature.
- ○ C. Repair the Office installation.
- ○ D. Remove the Office installation and perform a Custom installation.

Answer C is correct. You should repair the Office installation using the Detect and Repair option from the Help menu. You can also repair the installation from the Add or Remove Programs applet. Answer A is incorrect because removing the Excel application does not solve the problem with the current Excel installation. Answer B is incorrect because the Import Data feature is currently installed. Answer D is incorrect because you do not need to remove the entire Office installation and reinstall.

Question 5

A user reports that she had her system rebuilt approximately a month ago. She has not had any problems with her Windows XP system. However, today she opened Microsoft Word, and several menu options are unavailable. What is the problem?

- ○ A. The Office XP product key has expired.
- ○ B. The user has a virus.
- ○ C. The user's permissions have been customized with a domain policy to restrict access to some Office features.
- ○ D. The Office XP installation has not been activated.

Answer D is correct. The Office XP installation allows a user to open the Office applications 50 times before activation is required. When the user exceeds this number, the programs allow her to view files but not create new files or modify the existing files. Answer A is incorrect because the product key does not expire. Answer B is incorrect because no known virus disables Office features. Answer C is incorrect because there is no mention that a domain policy has been applied. It is also not possible for a domain policy to disable features within Office.

Question 6

A user indicates that the blank template in Word contains part of a file he was working on the previous day. Each time he creates a new file, the text appears. What should be done?

- ○ A. The **Normal.doc** template should be re-created.
- ○ B. The **Normal.dot** template should be edited to remove the unwanted text.
- ○ C. The **Normal.dot** template should be re-created.
- ○ D. The **Blank.dot** template should be edited to remove the unwanted text.

Answer B is correct. The Normal.dot template file stores several customized settings as well as the text. To ensure that customizations are not lost, the Normal.dot file should be edited to remove the text. Answers A and D are incorrect because the blank template is named Normal.dot. Answer C is also incorrect; when the Normal.dot template is re-created, it loses all configuration settings the user has modified.

Question 7

A user reports that the Office XP installation window periodically appears on her screen while she is using the Office programs. She already has installed the suite and thinks her system is broken. What is occurring?

○ A. The applications are set to Install on First Use.

○ B. The most commonly used features are installed; however, the remaining features are set to Install on First Use.

○ C. The Office installation needs to be repaired.

○ D. A domain policy is applying software patches.

Answer B is correct. The Office XP window appears as features set to Install on First Use are used. Answer A is incorrect because the user indicates that the Office XP installation windows appear as she is using the applications. Answer C is incorrect because the Office installation is intact. Answer D is incorrect because there is no indication that a domain policy has been applied.

Question 8

A user's computer has recently been upgraded to Office XP. He reports that the menus are shorter than those in the previous version. He wants to know where the missing menu options are located. What is the problem?

○ A. The Personalized menus are turned on.

○ B. The Customized menus are turned on.

○ C. The Personalized toolbars are turned on and cause the menus to show only the buttons displayed on the toolbars.

○ D. The Customized toolbars are turned on and cause the menus to show only the buttons displayed on the toolbars.

Answer A is correct. Personalized menus automatically customize menus and toolbars based on how often the user uses the commands. When the user first starts an Office program, only the basic commands appear. Then as he uses the program, the menus and toolbars adjust so that only the commands and toolbar buttons he uses most often appear. Answer B is incorrect because the feature is called *Personalized menus*. Answers C and D are incorrect because the buttons used on the toolbar do not affect the menu commands in view in the program menus.

Question 9

A new user indicates that she has lost all toolbars and menu options. What do you need to do to solve this problem?

○ A. Reset all toolbars and menus.

○ B. Re-create all toolbars and menus.

○ C. Repair Office XP to return all options to their default settings.

○ D. Exit Full Screen view by pressing Escape.

Answer D is correct. When in Full Screen view, you can either press Escape or click the Close Full Screen View button. Answers A and B are incorrect because the toolbars and menus are hidden from view. Answer C is also incorrect; when you repair an Office XP installation, customizations remain intact.

Question 10

A user indicates that the Tables toolbar is not in view. How does he activate the Tables toolbar?

○ A. Click the Table menu and select Toolbar.

○ B. Click the View menu and select Toolbars and the Tables toolbar.

○ C. Click the View menu and select Toolbars and then Tables and Borders.

○ D. Right-click any active toolbar and select Tables from the pop-up menu.

Answer C is correct. To activate the Tables and Borders toolbar, the user can either right-click on an active toolbar and select Tables and Borders, or click the View menu and select the Toolbars submenu and the Tables and Borders option. Answers A, B, and D are incorrect because they do not open the Tables and Borders toolbar.

Configuring, Customizing, and Managing Outlook

Terms you'll need to understand:

✓ Outlook
✓ Newsgroup
✓ Inbox Repair Tool
✓ Import
✓ Export
✓ AutoArchive
✓ Personal folder

Techniques you'll need to master:

✓ Configure Mail Accounts in Outlook
✓ Configure Outlook Newsgroup Reader
✓ Configure Outlook Advanced options
✓ Manage Outlook data

Configuring Email Accounts in Outlook

Email account configuration is the fundamental reason for setting up *Outlook* on a user's system. It is that user's communication tool to fellow employees and the outside world. You are required to support users when configuring and customizing Outlook.

Make sure you are familiar with how to configure email accounts in Outlook.

Adding a New Email Account

Follow these steps to create a new email account using the Email Accounts Wizard:

1. From the Tools menu, select the Email Accounts option.

2. Choose the View or Change Existing Email Accounts option, as shown in Figure 5.1. Click Next.

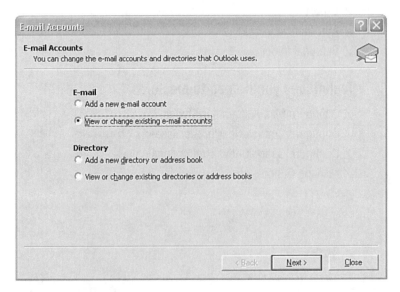

Figure 5.1   The Email Accounts dialog box.

3. Click Add and choose the type of mail server for the new account. The options available are Microsoft Exchange Server, POP3, IMAP, HTTP, and Additional Server Types. The server descriptions are included below the options, as shown in Figure 5.2. Click Next.

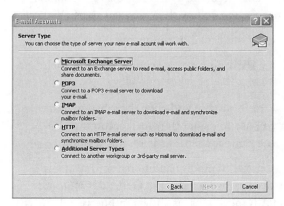

Figure 5.2   The Server Type dialog box.

4. Enter the User Information, Server Information, and Logon Information in the Internet Email Settings dialog box. Figure 5.3 displays sample settings for a new POP3 mail account. Click Next.

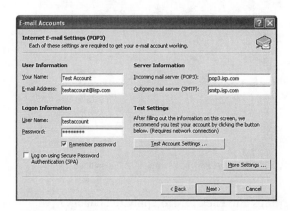

Figure 5.3   The Internet Email Settings page of the Accounts dialog box.

To increase security on a shared system, you may want to deselect the Remember Password option. It requires users to enter their passwords each time the server checks for new messages or tries to send messages.

5. In the Email Accounts dialog box, examine all the email accounts configured with Outlook. Click Finish to close the dialog box.

Modifying an Existing Email Account

Some properties can be changed after an account has been created. To make the changes, you must access the properties of the email account. The properties window includes these tabs: General, Outgoing Server, Connection, and Advanced. To modify the settings, follow these general steps:

1. From the Tools menu, select the Email Accounts option.

2. Select the View or Change Existing Email Accounts option. Click Next.

3. Select the account you want to modify and click the Change button. The same window that you use to create the email account is displayed. You can modify the standard settings from this window.

4. Click the More Settings button to modify additional settings. The Internet Email Settings dialog box includes the General, Outgoing Server, Connection, and Advanced tabs, as shown in Figure 5.4.

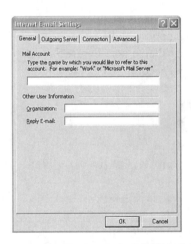

Figure 5.4   The Internet Email Settings dialog box where you can modify more settings.

5. Modify the required settings and click OK to apply the changes.

6. Click Next to return to the Email Accounts dialog box and then click Finish.

  You should know where to find each of the email account property settings.

The Internet Email Settings dialog box (accessed in step 4 of the preceding steps) includes several advanced features that you can access only from this dialog box. Tables 5.1 through 5.4 summarize the options available on each tab.

Table 5.1	The General Tab Options
Option	**Description**
Mail Account	The descriptive name that you want to refer to the account
Organization	The company name that uses the account
Reply Email	The email address used to reply to incoming messages

Table 5.2	The Outgoing Server Tab Options
Option	**Description**
My Outgoing Server (SMTP) Requires Authentication	This check box should be selected when the SMTP server requires authentication.
Use Same Settings as the Incoming Mail Server	This is the default setting when you check the My Outgoing Server (SMTP) Requires Authentication option. You use this option when the SMTP server uses the same settings as the incoming mail server. This option is available only when authentication is required.
Log On Using	This option enables you to enter an alternative username and password to receive incoming messages. Select the Remember Password option if you do not want to enter the password when sending and receiving messages. This option is available only when authentication is required.
Log On to Incoming Mail Server Before Sending Mail	This feature should be selected if you usually work with Outlook offline and need to connect to the mail server to send and receive messages. This option is available only when authentication is required.

Table 5.3	The Connection Tab Options
Option	**Description**
Connect Using My Local Area Network (LAN)	This option allows you to set Outlook to receive messages using the LAN connection. You can also check the Connect Via Modem When Outlook Is Offline option when the LAN connection is unavailable.
Connect Using My Phone Line	This option allows you to send and receive email using your dial-up connection if you do not have access to a LAN.

Table 5.3 The Connection Tab Options *(continued)*

Option	Description
Connect Using Internet Explorer's or 3rd Party Dialer	This option enables you to specify the Internet Explorer connection settings.
Use the Following Dial-Up Networking Connection	This option enables you to specify the dial-up connection to use if multiple dial-up connections are configured on your system. This option is available if the Connect Via Modem When Outlook Is Offline or the Connect Using My Phone Line option is selected.
Properties	This option displays the dial-up connection properties window. This option is available if the Connect Via Modem When Outlook Is Offline or the Connect Using My Phone Line option is selected.
Add	This option starts the New Connection Wizard if the appropriate dial-up connection is not available. This option is available if the Connect Via Modem When Outlook Is Offline or the Connect Using My Phone Line option is selected.

Table 5.4 The Advanced Tab Options

Option	Description
Server Port Numbers	This option enables you to configure the port numbers for the incoming and outgoing servers.
Server Timeouts	This option enables you to configure the length of time before the server will time out when sending or receiving messages.
Delivery	This option enables you to determine whether messages are stored on the server after their delivery, as well as the length of time they are stored on the server.

Removing an Email Account

When an email account is no longer necessary, you can remove the account from your list of email accounts by using the following guidelines:

1. From the Tools menu, select the Email Accounts option.

2. Select the View or Change Existing Email Accounts option. Click Next.

3. Select the account you want to delete and click the Remove button.

4. Click Yes in the Account Manager dialog box, as shown in Figure 5.5, to verify that you want to remove the account.

Figure 5.5 The Account Manager dialog box.

5. Click Finish to close the Email Accounts dialog box.

Configuring and Troubleshooting Newsgroup Account Configurations

Outlook has its own newsreader that enables you to gain access to various types of *newsgroups*, download and read news messages, and post replies to them. You can find newsgroups on practically any subject, such as an Internet Usenet group or an internal company newsgroup.

If you have not previously set up a newsreader, Microsoft Outlook automatically sets up the Microsoft Outlook Newsreader. If you have set up a different newsreader, you can start it from within Outlook. To open the Outlook Newsreader, point to the View menu, select Go To, and then click News. If you have configured newsgroups previously, you can view these groups immediately.

Make sure you are familiar with how to configure newsgroups from Outlook.

Setting Up a Newsgroup Account

To set up a new newsgroup account, you need to verify the newsgroup server with your Internet service provider before you begin the following steps:

1. From Outlook, point to the View menu, select Go To, and click News.

2. After the Microsoft Outlook Newsreader window opens, click the Set Up a Newsgroups Account link, as shown in Figure 5.6.

3. In the Your Name dialog box, enter your display name. Click Next.

4. In the Internet News Email Account dialog box, enter the email address where other members can respond to your messages. Click Next.

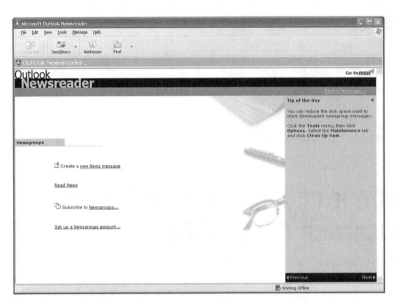

Figure 5.6 The Microsoft Outlook Newsreader window.

5. In the Internet News Server Name dialog box, enter the news server name that your ISP has supplied you. Click Next.

6. Click Finish to complete the wizard.

7. When the wizard is complete, you are prompted to download newsgroups from the news server you selected, as shown in Figure 5.7. Click Yes.

Figure 5.7 The request to download newsgroups window.

8. The download process may take several minutes, depending on your connection speed and the number of newsgroups the news server hosts. Figure 5.8 displays the progress of the download.

9. When the download is complete, you can search and then subscribe to the desired newsgroups.

Figure 5.8   The downloading newsgroups from the news server window.

Subscribing to a Newsgroup

After you have configured a newsgroup account, you can search and then subscribe to newsgroups by following these steps:

1. From the Microsoft Outlook Newsreader window, click the Subscribe to Newsgroups link.

2. Use the Newsgroup Subscriptions window to search for newsgroups based on keywords. Type Microsoft in the Display Newsgroups Which Contain text box.

3. Select a newsgroup from the list and click the Subscribe button.

4. Click the Subscribed tab to view all newsgroups you are currently subscribed to.

Using Outlook with Multiple Email Accounts

When you are using multiple email accounts within Outlook, establishing some organization is important. You may have multiple accounts that could include your personal work email address, a general inquiry email address, or your supervisor's email address. Receiving all messages within the same Inbox could be confusing, and managing the information would be difficult. To assist in organization, you may want to set up multiple Inboxes to receive messages for each account. You can add shortcuts to the Outlook Shortcuts bar to allow you to view whether new messages have been received. After the folders are created, you must create rules to move the messages into the appropriate folders.

Adding Multiple Inbox Folders

To create new Inbox folders, follow these general guidelines:

1. Select the Folder List option from the View menu.

2. Right-click the Inbox folder and select New Folder. The Create New Folder dialog box opens.

3. Enter the new folder name in the Name text box.

4. Select the type of folder you are creating from the Folder Contains drop-down list.

5. Select the place where the folder will be located. If you are creating a mail folder, select the Inbox folder. Figure 5.9 displays the completed dialog box.

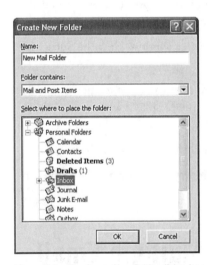

Figure 5.9 The Create New Folder dialog box.

6. Click OK. The Add Shortcut to Outlook Bar dialog box appears, as shown in Figure 5.10.

Figure 5.10 The Add Shortcut to Outlook Bar dialog box.

7. Click Yes to add a button to the My Shortcuts bar.

Creating Mail Rules to Organize Incoming Messages

To set up new rules that automatically move messages into specific folders, follow these instructions:

1. Click the Inbox shortcut to view the contents of your Inbox.

2. Select the Organize button on the Standard toolbar. The Organize feature is displayed.

3. Select New Mail Folder from the Move Message drop-down list.

4. In the Create a Rule area, enter the email address of the messages you want to move into the new mail folder. Figure 5.11 displays sample information to create a new rule that will move all new messages for pop3.isp.com to the new mail folder.

Figure 5.11   The Organize feature in the Outlook window.

5. Click Create. The apply rule to new messages dialog box appears, as shown in Figure 5.12.

Figure 5.12   The apply rule to new messages dialog box.

6. Click Yes.

Sending Mail When Multiple Mail Accounts Are Configured

When multiple email accounts are configured within Outlook, you must select which account any outgoing message is to be sent from. Notice the Accounts button has been added beside the Send button on the Standard toolbar. The Accounts button drop-down list includes all email accounts that have been configured within Outlook. Select the account you want to send the message with and click Send. Figure 5.13 displays the Accounts drop-down list with a list of email accounts available.

Figure 5.13   The Accounts drop-down list.

Customizing Outlook Settings

Outlook can be customized to suit the users' needs. You can find the main area for configuration in the Options dialog box opened through the Tools menu. The Options dialog box is organized into six tabs: Preferences, Mail Setup, Mail Format, Spelling, Security, and Other. Several options contained within the Options dialog box can be accessed through individual menu items; however, this dialog box is organized to allow for centralized configuration.

 Make sure you are familiar with the various configuration options available in Outlook.

Modifying Settings on the Preferences Tab

The Preferences tab is displayed by default when you open the Options dialog box. This tab gives you access to all the major Outlook components, as shown in Figure 5.14. Table 5.5 describes the available options from the Preferences tab.

Table 5.5	The Preferences Tab Options
Option	**Description**
Email	This option enables you to configure the appearance of messages and the way they are handled when new messages are sent and received.
Calendar	This option enables you to customize the appearance of the calendar.
Tasks	This option enables you to customize the appearance of tasks.
Contacts	This option enables you to configure the default settings for contacts and the journal feature.
Notes	This option enables you to customize the appearance of notes.

Figure 5.14   The Preferences tab.

Each section of the Preferences tab contains buttons that open their own dialog boxes for further configuration.

Modifying Settings on the Mail Setup Tab

The Mail Setup tab focuses on configuring mail accounts, send/receive options, data files, and dial-up options. Figure 5.15 displays the Mail Setup tab, and Table 5.6 summarizes the options available.

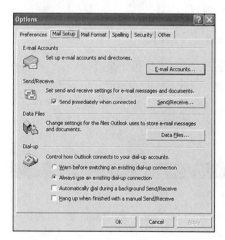

Figure 5.15   The Mail Setup tab.

Table 5.6 The Mail Setup Tab Options	
Option	**Description**
Email Accounts	This section contains an Email Accounts button that opens the Email Accounts Wizard. This is the same wizard you see when using the Tools menu and selecting Email Accounts.
Send/Receive	This option sets whether messages are sent immediately when connected. The Send/Receive button is also available to send and receive messages if currently connected. This button is also on the Standard toolbar in the main Outlook window.
Data Files	The Data Files button opens the management tool for the PST files used within Outlook. The PST files store all information within Outlook: email messages, contacts, appointments, tasks, notes, and journal entries.
Dial-up	These options determine how Outlook connects to the dial-up accounts configured within the application.

Modifying Settings on the Mail Format Tab

The Mail Format tab allows you to configure outgoing messages. You can set the default message format, such as HTML, rich text, or plain text. You can also set Word to be the default editor so you can take advantage of Word features to edit the messages.

You can also configure the outgoing messages with background colors or images using the stationery feature. These defaults can be changed within individual messages if necessary.

In a business environment, it is important to include details about the sender, position, contact information, and company the sender works for. To save time, you can create a signature for all outgoing messages. You can customize it according to messages being created versus messages responded to. Figure 5.16 displays the Mail Format tab, and Table 5.7 explains the available options.

Table 5.7 The Mail Format Tab Options	
Option	**Description**
Message Format	These options enable you to configure the default mail format for outgoing messages.
Stationery and Fonts	These options enable you to customize the default stationery used in outgoing messages.
Signature	These options enable you to configure the default signatures for outgoing messages.

Figure 5.16   The Mail Format tab.

Modifying Settings on the Spelling Tab

On the Spelling tab, you can configure how Outlook deals with spelling errors within outgoing messages. Figure 5.17 displays the Spelling tab, and Table 5.8 outlines the options available.

Figure 5.17   The Spelling tab.

Table 5.8	The Spelling Tab Options
Option	**Description**
General Options	These options are similar to the Spelling options available in Word.
Edit Custom Dictionary	This option enables you to modify the **custom.dic** file, which contains the manual entries into the dictionary.
International Dictionaries	This option enables you to configure the default dictionary used to check the spelling within outgoing messages.

Modifying Settings on the Security Tab

The Security tab determines what level of security is applied to outgoing messages. You can set these options to determine the level of security on outgoing messages, as well as verify that, when using Outlook to search the Internet, you are viewing only secure content.

Figure 5.18 displays the Security tab, and Table 5.9 explains the options available.

Figure 5.18 The Security tab.

Table 5.9	The Security Tab Options
Option	**Description**
Secure Email	These options enable you to configure encryption and digital signatures to verify that messages sent and received are secure.
Secure Content	The Zone Settings are similar to the configuration options found on the Security tab in the Internet Explorer Options dialog box.
Digital IDs (Certificates)	This option enables you to set the digital certificates on outgoing messages to verify your identity.

Modifying the Other Tab

The Other tab is a collection of misfit configuration settings. You can view the Advanced Options, AutoArchive settings, Preview Pane configuration, and Instant Messaging settings. Figure 5.19 displays the Other tab, and Table 5.10 describes the options available.

Figure 5.19   The Other tab.

Table 5.10 The Other Tab Options	
Option	**Description**
General	This section contains the Advanced Options button that sets the Startup and Appearance options.
AutoArchive	This option enables you to configure the AutoArchive settings to determine the frequency and way items are treated during the archive process.
Preview Pane	This option enables you to configure the way messages are treated when the preview pane is in use.
Instant Messaging	This option enables instant messaging within Outlook. The Options button opens the Options dialog box, which is similar to the MSN Messenger Options dialog box.

Managing Outlook Data

Outlook has become an integral part of users' daily job responsibilities. It is the leading source of communication in the workforce. Many users rely on the information contained within Outlook to be able to complete their daily responsibilities at work.

You will find that users who rely heavily on Outlook will require their problems be resolved quickly.

 Make sure you are familiar with the different ways to manage Outlook data.

Using Data File Management

You use the Data File Management dialog box to determine where your PST files are located. You can open this dialog box from the File menu. The data files currently configured in your Outlook application are listed here. Select a data file in the list; then click Settings for more details or click Open Folder to display the folder that contains the data file.

 To move or copy PST files, you must shut down Outlook first.

As good as Outlook is, it lacks any viable system for backing up your valuable Outlook information. Here's what you need to know about backup for Outlook: Outlook stores information in a data file called a *personal folder* file with a .pst extension.

The easiest way to back up all your Outlook information is to copy your PST file—in most cases, Outlook.pst—to a network drive or to your local hard drive.

Outlook enables you to archive your data to a file called Archive.pst; when you do, your oldest data is placed into that file. From Outlook, point to Tools, select Options, click the Other tab, and then click the AutoArchive button. Now you can set your Outlook program to automate the archive process so that the process runs every few days.

If your PST files are not stored on a network drive that has a good backup strategy, you should implement your own backup plan. Copy all PST files to a CD or network drive on a daily, weekly, or monthly basis. You need to determine which scenario is a good fit for your environment.

Follow these steps to archive all items that are older than a specified date:

1. Open Outlook.

2. Select the Archive option from the File menu to open the Archive dialog box, as shown in Figure 5.20.

Figure 5.20   The Archive dialog box.

3. Select the Archive This Folder and All Subfolders option. Expand the Personal Folders item if necessary.

4. Enter an appropriate date in the Archive Items Older Than text box.

5. Check the Include Items with "Do Not AutoArchive" Checked option. This option backs up all items to your Archive.pst file.

6. Click the Browse button and navigate to the location where you want to store the Archive.pst file.

7. Click OK. The status bar displays the items being moved to the Archive.pst file. This process may take a few minutes, depending on the number of items being archived.

Importing and Exporting Data

You can use Outlook's *Import/Export* feature to back up your data, as well as add new data to your existing Outlook PST file.

The Export feature copies the specified data intact to a file, whereas the Archive feature (described in the preceding section) copies only old data to the archive file.

To export, open Outlook, click File, and then select Import and Export. The Import and Export Wizard starts. Select Export to a File and click Next. Then select Personal Folder File (.pst) and click Next. Select Personal Folders at the top of the dialog box to back up all your Outlook data. Make sure that the Include Subfolders check box is checked and click Next. Select a destination for the folder. Outlook labels the backup file backup.pst, and you can set the destination by placing the drive letter before the destination filename. For example, if your Zip drive is drive E:, you just type E:\ backup.pst. It's a good idea to select Do Not Export Duplicate Items in the Options box. Finally, click Finish, and your Outlook data is exported.

The advantage of using the Export feature is that you can choose to export any of the individual Outlook folders. This way, you can effectively back up individual items such as your Calendar folder or your entire contents within the Outlook.pst file.

To restore a PST file into your current Outlook data, you can use the same utility that exported the data. Open the Import and Export Wizard and use the same option to import the data into Outlook. Select the File menu and choose the Import and Export option. To import the contents of an existing Personal Folder File (.pst), select Personal Folder File (.pst) and click Next. Enter the location of the PST file in the File to Import text box and click Next. At this stage, you can select to import all folders such as Inbox, Contacts, Deleted Items, or Sent Items. If you want to import all data, be sure to place a check mark by the Include Subfolders option. To complete the Import and Export Wizard, click Finish.

Repairing Corrupted Data

To fix corrupted PST files, you can use the *Inbox Repair Tool*. However, the tool isn't always able to repair every PST file. It works by repairing the PST file's header and then deleting anything in the file that it doesn't understand. So if a PST file's header is damaged, as may be the case for corruption that occurs during a version upgrade, the tool should have no trouble making the repair. But if the data within the file is corrupt, the Inbox Repair Tool will likely destroy what's left of the file. That's why it's always a good idea to make a backup of the PST file before running the Inbox Repair Tool.

The Inbox Repair Tool, named scanpst.exe, is located in the *drive*:\Program Files\Common Files\System\MSMapi\1033\ directory of any system that is running Windows XP. Other versions of Windows also include the Inbox Repair Tool, but the tool's location varies among earlier versions.

Exam Prep Questions

Question 1

> A user indicates that he continually receives messages that his Inbox is full. He is required to delete his messages before he can receive or send mail. What do you suggest to prevent loss of information?
>
> ○ A. Archive historical messages on a weekly basis.
>
> ○ B. Clear the deleted items on exit.
>
> ○ C. Move important messages to the C drive.
>
> ○ D. Set up a rule that organizes messages into Custom Mail folders.

Answer A is correct. Outlook enables you to archive your data to the Archive.pst file, which places your oldest data into that file. Therefore, answers B, C, and D are incorrect.

Question 2

> When Outlook is open, a user receives an error message when trying to close MSN Messenger, as shown in the following figure. How can you prevent this message from appearing?

> ○ A. Uninstall MSN Messenger.
>
> ○ B. Repair Outlook.
>
> ○ C. Disable instant messaging in Outlook.
>
> ○ D. Disable instant messaging in MSN Messenger.

Answer C is correct. To prevent the error message from appearing, you must disable instant messaging from Outlook. Answer A would prevent the message from appearing but would remove the instant messaging capability permanently from the user's system. This is not the best answer. Answer B is incorrect because Outlook is functioning properly. Answer D is incorrect because you cannot disable instant messaging in MSN Messenger.

Question 3

A user indicates that when she is at home, she can search the Internet but cannot retrieve email on her laptop. What is the problem?

- A. In the Internet Settings dialog box, both the Connect Using My Local Area Network Connection (LAN) option and the Connect Via Modem When Outlook Is Offline option are not selected.
- B. In the Email Account Settings dialog box, both the Connection Using My Local Area Network option and the Connect Via Modem When Outlook Is Offline option are selected.
- C. In the Customize dialog box, the Connection Using My Local Area Network option and the Connect Via Modem When Outlook Is Offline option are selected.
- D. The user does not have a valid Internet connection.

Answer A is correct. The user must use a dial-up connection to check for new messages when the LAN connection is not available. Answer B is incorrect because the Connection option is not available from the Email Account Settings dialog box. Answer C is incorrect because the Connection option is not available from the Customize dialog box. Answer D is incorrect because the user indicated that she is able to search the Internet.

Question 4

A user indicates that he is responsible for responding to general inquiries received from the generic company email address, but he would like to respond to these messages with his personal company address. The user mentions that he can select the account from the accounts list when he sends messages, but he finds it cumbersome. What can you do to help this user?

- A. The user is already accomplishing the task, and no other options are available.
- B. Configure the default email address to the generic company account.
- C. Configure the Reply Email address to the user's company account.
- D. Configure the Forward Email address to the user's company account.

Answer C is correct. To help the user set up his email account to automatically reply using his personal company address, you can set the Reply Email address on the General tab in the Internet Email Settings dialog box. Answer A is incorrect because the Reply Email address can be set to the user's personal company address. Answer B is incorrect because the user wants to use his personal company address to respond to the messages. Answer D is incorrect because the option does not exist.

Question 5

A user reports that she receives hundreds of messages daily. She is having difficulty organizing her incoming mail. What do you suggest to assist the user?

○ A. Set up custom mail folders and rules to organize the messages by priority or sender.

○ B. Set up rules to prioritize incoming messages.

○ C. Use an auto-reply message.

○ D. Use the Out of Office assistant.

Answer A is correct. The user should set up custom mail folders and rules to organize the messages into new folders. Answer B is incorrect because rules cannot prioritize incoming messages. Answer C is incorrect because the user is trying to organize incoming messages. Answer D is incorrect because the user is not trying to configure an Out of Office message.

Question 6

A user returns from maternity leave and reports that her Outlook information is gone. What is the problem?

○ A. The information was deleted.

○ B. The information was lost due to corruption.

○ C. The items were AutoArchived.

○ D. The Outlook information was exported to a backup file.

Answer C is correct. The information was AutoArchived. Answer A is incorrect because the user did not report the loss of other resources. Answer B is incorrect because the user did not indicate she received error messages. Answer D is incorrect because the user would have exported the backup file and then would not have reported it lost.

Question 7

A user is reading through his archived messages in Outlook and has indicated that some messages do not contain the message text. What should you do?

- ○ A. Restore the **Archive.pst** file to its original location.
- ○ B. Run the Inbox Repair Tool.
- ○ C. Reboot the system.
- ○ D. Apply the latest patches to the Office XP software.

Answer B is correct. The Inbox Repair Tool tries to repair the header of the PST file. Answer A is incorrect because the user did not indicate that he moved the Archive.pst file. Answer C is incorrect because rebooting does not affect the data in Outlook. Answer D is incorrect because the latest patches to the Office XP software do not affect the data.

Question 8

A user reports that when a new appointment is created the reminder appears 24 hours before the appointment. She wants the reminder to appear 30 minutes before the appointment. How do you resolve this problem?

- ○ A. From the Options dialog box, select the Other tab and adjust the default reminder to 30 minutes.
- ○ B. From the Options dialog box, select the Calendar tab and adjust the default reminder to 30 minutes.
- ○ C. From the Options dialog box, select the Preferences tab, click the Calendar Options button, and change the default reminder to 30 minutes.
- ○ D. From the Options dialog box, select the Preferences tab and modify the default reminder to 30 minutes.

Answer D is correct. The default reminder is located on the Preferences tab in the Options dialog box. Therefore, answers A, B, and C are incorrect because they do not contain the default reminder setting.

Question 9

A user wants to adjust the Archive settings in Outlook to automatically archive messages older than 30 days. Where can he set these options?

- ○ A. Archive dialog box
- ○ B. AutoArchive dialog box
- ○ C. Data File Management dialog box
- ○ D. Backup dialog box

Answer B is correct. The AutoArchive dialog box is available from the Other tab in the Options dialog box. The AutoArchive button displays the configuration options available with the AutoArchive feature. Answer A is incorrect because the Archive dialog box is used to initiate the archive feature manually. Answer C is incorrect because the Data File Management dialog box is used to manage the PST files configured in Outlook. Answer D is incorrect because the Backup dialog box is not a valid feature.

Question 10

When a user receives messages from her home office, they do not appear in her Inbox when she returns to her office computer. The user indicates that mail received on one computer is not available on the other computer. What should you do?

- ○ A. Configure the delivery of messages to be retained on the mail server.
- ○ B. Modify the server timeouts to allow the messages to be downloaded.
- ○ C. Verify the user's Internet connection in her home office.
- ○ D. Modify the user's account to use a mandatory profile.

Answer A is correct. To allow the user to view all her mail regardless of location, you must configure the delivery of the messages so that the mail server stores the mail after delivery. Answer B is incorrect because the mail server has not timed out. Answer C is incorrect because the user reports that she has received messages at her home office, but they do not appear in her Inbox when she returns to her office computer. Answer D is incorrect because a mandatory profile does not affect how mail messages are affected after delivery.

Configuring and Troubleshooting Hardware

Terms you'll need to understand:

✓ Drivers
✓ Device Manager
✓ CDR-ROM
✓ CDRW-ROM
✓ Hard drive
✓ Network drive
✓ System Restore
✓ Printer

Techniques you'll need to master:

✓ Manage drivers
✓ Troubleshoot storage devices
✓ Install local and network printers
✓ Troubleshoot issues with printer drivers
✓ Troubleshoot issues with printers and print jobs

Resolving Hardware Issues

The *Device Manager* enables you to check the status of computer hardware and update device *drivers* on the computer. It contains diagnostic features to resolve device conflicts and change resource settings. To access the Device Manager, you must open the System applet from the Control Panel. The Device Manager button is located on the Hardware tab, as shown in Figure 6.1.

Figure 6.1 The Hardware tab of the System applet.

Make sure you can install, update, and configure device drivers.

Managing Drivers

The Device Manager provides a graphical view of the hardware that is currently installed on the computer. The device drivers and resources associated with that hardware are listed in the properties of each device. Figure 6.2 demonstrates how the Device Manager provides a central point to change the way the hardware is configured.

The Device Manager enables you to maintain, configure, and troubleshoot the devices physically connected to the computer system. The following items outline some of the available functionality:

➤ Determine whether the hardware is working properly on the computer.

➤ Change hardware configuration settings.

➤ Identify the device drivers loaded for each device and obtain information about each device driver.

➤ Change advanced settings and properties for devices.

➤ Install updated device drivers.

➤ Disable, enable, and uninstall devices.

➤ Reinstall the previous version of a driver with the Roll Back feature.

➤ Identify device conflicts and manually configure resource settings.

➤ Print a summary of the devices configured on your computer.

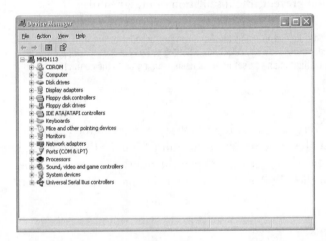

Figure 6.2 The Device Manager window.

Viewing Driver Properties

When viewing Driver properties, you can determine the file version of the device driver. In the Device Manager window, an icon appears next to device drivers to indicate they are digitally signed by Microsoft.

Windows device drivers and operating system files have been digitally signed by Microsoft to ensure their quality. A Microsoft digital signature is an assurance that a particular file is from that manufacturer and has been verified by Microsoft to function properly with Windows XP.

Depending on how your computer is configured, Windows either ignores device drivers that are not digitally signed, displays a warning when it detects device drivers that are not digitally signed, or prevents you from installing device drivers without digital signatures. Figure 6.3 displays the Driver tab of the properties window of a network interface card.

You can configure how the system responds to unsigned files by opening the System applet in the Control Panel and clicking the Hardware tab. In the Device Manager box on the Hardware tab, click the Driver Signing button to display the Driver Signing Options dialog box. There, you can set your system to the following options:

➤ **Ignore**—This option allows files to be installed regardless of the digital signature.

➤ **Warn**—This option displays a message before allowing the installation of an unsigned file. It is the default option.

➤ **Block**—This option prevents the installation of unsigned files.

 When you are logged in using the Administrator account or are a member of the Administrator group, you can select Apply Setting as System Default to apply the driver signing configuration you set up to all users who log on to the computer.

The File Signature Verification Utility enables you to monitor and troubleshoot digital signatures. You can access the utility from the Run command on the Start menu. Type `sigverif.exe` to open the utility window. After the utility opens, you can click the Advanced button to configure the verification options.

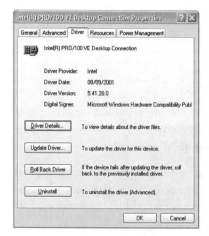

Figure 6.3 A Device Driver properties window.

Configuring Device Manager Views

You can configure the Device Manager to display device information in various views. The following views are available:

> **Devices by Type**—Displays devices by the type of device installed. The connection name is listed below the type.

> **Devices by Connection**—Displays devices by how they are connected to your computer. Each device is listed under the hardware to which it is connected.

> **Resources by Type**—Displays the status of all allocated resources by the type of device using these resources. The resources are direct memory access (DMA), channels, input/output ports (I/O ports), interrupt request (IRQ), and memory addresses.

> **Resources by Connection**—Displays the status of all allocated resources by connection type. The resources are DMA channels, I/O ports, IRQ, and memory addresses.

> **Show Hidden Devices**—Includes non–Plug-and-Play devices (devices with earlier Windows device drivers).

 NOTE Two types of devices are hidden by default in Device Manager. Non–Plug-and-Play devices, printers, and other classes of devices that are not typically useful in configuring or troubleshooting hardware issues are hidden. Also hidden are devices that were previously attached but are not connected to the computer at the present time, also known as *nonpresent devices*. Typically, you do not need to view hidden devices unless you need to configure or troubleshoot hardware.

Updating or Changing a Device Driver

You need to ensure that the latest device driver for each device is loaded in Windows XP. Manufacturers frequently update their drivers to fix problems and take advantage of operating system features. These drivers are usually available from the manufacturers' Web sites; Microsoft also maintains driver files for many devices on its Web sites.

When downloading drivers, read the manufacturer's instructions before attempting to use the files to update the device. Downloaded driver files are typically compressed into a self-executing file that needs to be extracted to use the driver. In the Hardware Update Wizard, click to select the Have Disk option; then click the Browse button to locate the driver files.

Because using the Device Manager is the most convenient method to update existing drivers, follow these steps to install updated drivers:

1. From the Device Manager, expand the type of device you want to update or change.

2. Right-click the specific device you want to update or change and select the Properties option.

3. Select the Driver tab and click the Update Driver button to open the Hardware Update Wizard, as shown in Figure 6.4.

Figure 6.4 The Hardware Update Wizard.

4. Accept the default option, Install the Software Automatically. Choose the Install from a List or Specific Location option if you have the updated driver so you can indicate the file location. Click Next.

5. Windows searches for an updated driver and instructs you if an updated driver has been found. Install the updated driver and click Finish.

Rolling Back to a Previous Version of a Driver

You use the *Roll Back* feature when you encounter problems after installing a driver. Such problems include error messages when you access the device, faulty device behavior, and even the inability to start Windows.

To use the Roll Back feature with Windows XP, open the Device Manager and follow these steps:

1. Right-click the device for which you want to reinstall the previous version of the driver and click Properties.

2. Click the Drivers tab.

3. Click the Roll Back Driver button.

 The Roll Back feature certainly sounds like a blessing; however, for it feature to be effective, the original driver must still be stored on the system. If the driver has been removed or deleted, the Roll Back feature cannot install the previous driver. The Roll Back feature can also install the previous driver, but if it was not functioning properly, you simply install a nonfunctional driver.

Troubleshooting Device Drivers

Each device has its own device driver, but you can take some standard steps to troubleshoot driver problems. If a problem occurs with a device, a status box is displayed on the device in the device list. If the Device Status box displays a problem, click Troubleshoot to launch the Windows XP troubleshooter for this device type. The troubleshooter asks you to supply information and answer questions as prompted.

If you cannot resolve the problem using the troubleshooter, visit the manufacturer's Web site. You are probably not the first person to encounter this problem, and the solution may be posted on the Web site. Table 6.1 summarizes the various symbols that may appear with a device that is not functioning properly.

Table 6.1 Symbols Indicating Problems with Hardware Devices	
Symbol	**Explanation**
A black exclamation point (!) on a yellow field	The device is not functioning properly.
A red *X*	The device as been disabled.
A blue *i* on a white field	The device was manually configured.
A green question mark (?)	A compatible driver is installed, but the device may not have all the functionality available.

 If a device's status is Disabled, that is usually the result of user action and does not necessarily mean the device has a problem. However, sometimes users disable a device because it was causing a problem, so you should try enabling it to see whether it affects another device negatively.

If the device experiences a problem, the Device Status box displays the type of problem. You may see a problem code or number (or both) and a suggested solution. If you call a support line, this number can be useful for determining and diagnosing the problem.

Handling Unknown Devices Listed in Device Manager

When you view device information on your Windows XP computer using the Device Manager, you may see an unknown device listed next to a yellow question mark. Determining the cause of this unknown device can be difficult because there are few indications of what could be creating it.

Some of the possible causes to this problem are

➤ The device does not have a driver.

➤ The driver is for an operating system predating Windows 2000.

➤ The hardware device is unrecognized.

To solve these problems, you must install an updated Windows XP device driver for the hardware device.

Using Storage Devices

Storage devices enable you to save programs, files, or data. They range from floppy disks to Zip drives to DVDs. Each device has its advantages and drawbacks. Review Table 6.2 to compare the different devices.

Table 6.2 Types of Storage Devices	
Storage Device	**Description**
3 1/2 floppy disk	Provides unreliable portable storage. It was the previous standard to transfer information, with a maximum storage space of 1.44MB.
CDR-ROM	Contains data you copy using a CD burner. It may contain company documents or applications written within the company. The maximum storage capacity is 650MB. The CDR-ROM disc can be written to only once. If you have written data to a CD and have an open session, you can copy additional information to the CD when needed. Keep in mind that the information cannot be erased after you copy it to the CD.
CDRW-ROM	Allows you to copy data repeatedly using a CD burner. If you deem the information outdated or unnecessary, you can reformat the CD and delete its contents.
Zip/Jaz drive	Allows up to 100MB storage. These larger-capacity devices have special disks made specifically for them.

Table 6.2 Types of Storage Devices *(continued)*	
Storage Device	**Description**
DVD-ROM	Supports up to seven regular CDs on a single DVD disc. This newer technology is used for large capacity storage and backups.
USB Storage	Plugs directly into the computer's USB port and acts just like another drive. There are no cables or adaptors needed, no power cord and no driver software to install. Currently stores up to 512MB of data.
Hard drive	Contains operating system files, as well as data. Some computers may have multiple hard drives to increase storage space.
Network drive	Provides storage on a hard drive located on another computer on the network. In corporate environments, users are encouraged to store all data in their network drive to prevent data loss and maintain the ability to share information with multiple users.

 Be sure you are know how to troubleshoot storage device problems.

Troubleshooting Storage Devices Within Applications

When you are troubleshooting storage devices, you may encounter a range of problems. For example, a user may be trying to save a document and receive an error that the storage device is unavailable. The device may be unavailable because a network drive is currently offline, or you are not currently connected to that particular drive. Other error messages appear when a storage device has reached maximum capacity or a user does not have appropriate permissions to a network drive.

Addressing Local Storage Device Problems

If a user receives an error indicating insufficient disk space is available, you have several possibilities to consider. For example, the hard disk may be reaching its storage capacity. If this is the case, you should run Disk Cleanup to remove unnecessary temporary files. You can access the Disk Cleanup feature, shown in Figure 6.5, through the General tab from the hard drive properties window.

Figure 6.5 The Disk Cleanup window.

The following steps guide you through using the Disk Cleanup Wizard:

1. From the My Computer window, right-click the hard drive and select Properties.

2. On the General tab of the properties window, click the Disk Cleanup button.

3. To verify the files are unnecessary, select each item in the File to Delete list box and click the View Files button. If you want to delete these files, place a check mark beside the option.

4. Click OK. Click Yes to verify the removal of files.

If you require additional space, you can run additional utilities from the More Options tab of the Disk Cleanup window, as shown in Figure 6.6.

The More Options tab enables you to run three utilities to recover disk space. The first option available is to remove optional Windows components that are not used. To open the Windows Components Wizard, shown in Figure 6.7, click the Clean Up button in the Windows Components section.

The Clean Up button in the Installed Programs section of the Disk Cleanup window opens the Add or Remove Programs window. It allows you to review the programs and remove unused software.

The final Clean Up button located in the *System Restore* section enables you to remove all but the most recent restore point. The Clean Up button opens a confirmation dialog box, as shown in Figure 6.8. To remove the historical restore points, click Yes.

Figure 6.6   The More Options tab of the Disk Cleanup window.

Figure 6.7   The Windows Components Wizard.

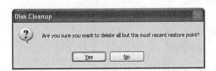

Figure 6.8   The remove system restore point confirmation dialog box.

Troubleshooting Portable Storage Device Media

A user may receive several different error messages when using portable storage devices. It is important to listen to the symptoms of the problem to determine its actual cause. For example, when a user indicates that she is trying to write to a floppy disk and the error message in Figure 6.9 appears, it may indicate the following problems:

➤ The floppy disk is write-protected.

➤ The floppy disk is unreadable or damaged.

Figure 6.9 The floppy disk error window.

To solve the problem, verify that the floppy disk is not write-protected. You can test that the floppy is readable by viewing the contents of the floppy using My Computer. From the My Computer window, you can check the disk's properties window to verify that it has available space. It is important to know whether the file the user is trying to save to the disk will fit on the disk she has selected.

When a user tries to save files using a CD-ROM versus a CD burner, an error message similar to the one in Figure 6.9 appears.

Similar error messages occur when a user tries to send files to a CD-ROM that is not writable. An example of such an error message is displayed in Figure 6.10.

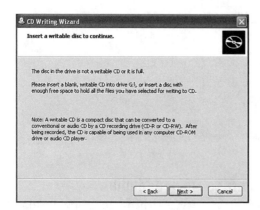

Figure 6.10 The CD-ROM write error window.

The same error message appears if a user has tried to write additional files to a CD-R that has a closed session or is full. You can review the available space in the CD's properties window.

Addressing Network Storage Device Problems

Additional errors, such as connectivity and access permissions, can occur when users work in a network environment. Network access permissions are discussed in Chapter 8, "Configuring and Managing Application Security." The most common problem mobile users encounter is not being able to connect to a network drive. You need to verify that a user has access to other network resources when the error message in Figure 6.11 appears. If the user has access to other network resources, you need to verify that other users can access the network drive. If other users have access to the network drive, you need to verify that the folder the first user is trying to save to has the correct network permissions to do so, as well as the space to save the file.

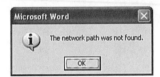

Figure 6.11   The Network Path error window.

 When trying to save to drives locally or on the network, you may encounter problems if you do not have the appropriate permissions. Access permissions are explained in Chapter 8.

Resolving Print Issues

Print issues can be tricky to troubleshoot. You must determine whether hardware, connectivity, or software is causing the print job to fail.

 Make sure you are familiar with installing and troubleshooting *printers.*

Installing Local and Network Printers

To install a printer driver locally on a Windows XP computer, follow these steps:

1. Point to Start, select Control Panel, and then click Printers and Other Faxes.

2. Click the Add Printer link to open the Add Printer Wizard. Click Next to start the wizard.

3. Select Local Printer, click to clear the Automatically Detect and Install check box, and then click Next.

4. Select the port the printer is attached to from the Use the Following Port drop-down list, as shown in Figure 6.12. Click Next.

Figure 6.12 The Select a Printer Port dialog box.

5. Select the manufacturer and your printer model. If you have the device driver disk, select Have Disk. If you want Windows to locate the driver, click Next.

6. In the Name Your Printer dialog box, shown in Figure 6.13, type the name of the printer in the Printer Name text box. Select Yes if you want the new printer to be the default printer. Then click Next.

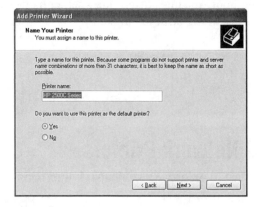

Figure 6.13 The Name Your Printer dialog box.

7. In the Printer Sharing dialog box, shown in Figure 6.14, select the Share Name option to share the printer and enter the name of the printer in the Share Name text box. Click Next.

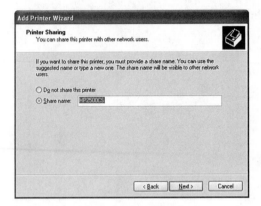

Figure 6.14   The Printer Sharing dialog box.

8. Enter the location and comment information to assist users in finding the exact printer location. Click Next.

9. Select Yes to print a test page. Then click Next.

10. Click Finish to complete the wizard. The device drivers are installed, and the test page is printed.

If you need to install a network printer, follow the preceding steps with some revisions. Instead of choosing Local Printer, choose the Network Printer option in the Local or Network Printer dialog box. To locate the network printer, select the Browse for a Printer option and click Next to view the available printers on your network. After locating the correct printer, you can complete the wizard steps as indicated here.

You also can connect to a corporate printer using the company's intranet. You can type a URL in the Web browser to navigate to the printer; this step makes the Add a Printer Wizard unnecessary. After you have connected to the printer, the correct printer drivers are automatically copied to the client computer.

Troubleshooting Printer Drivers

When you remove a printer from the Printers folder or Print Manager, the printer driver file is not removed from the hard drive. Follow these steps to remove and re-create a printer so that the driver file is reinstalled:

1. Point to Start and then click Printers and Faxes.

2. On the File menu, click Server Properties. The Print Server Properties dialog box opens.

3. On the Drivers tab, shown in Figure 6.15, click the printer driver that you want to delete and then click Remove.

Figure 6.15 The Drivers tab of the Print Server Properties dialog box.

Ensure that you can troubleshoot problems with printer drivers for local and network printers.

Troubleshooting Printers and Print Jobs

Some general troubleshooting steps are applicable to most but not all printers. The simple set of procedures and a logical approach included in the following section guide you through your printer problems. Table 6.3 summarizes the general problem areas when troubleshooting printer problems.

Table 6.3	Troubleshooting Questions
Things to Check	**Explanation**
Power	Verify that the printer is turned on and has power. Check the power bar and the outlet the printer is plugged into.
Connectivity	Check the cable connections to both the printer and computer. Verify that the printer is not working offline, it is not paused, and the print queue isn't causing a problem.

Table 6.3 Troubleshooting Questions *(continued)*	
Things to Check	**Explanation**
Hardware	Verify that the printer does not have any flashing lights indicating error messages.
Paper	Verify that you don't have a paper jam and paper is available in the paper tray.
Device Drivers	Verify that the printer has a digitally signed device driver. Check to see whether the correct device driver is installed.
Test Page	Try printing a test page to rule out hardware failure.
Test Print	Try printing from a different application to verify that the printing error is local to a single application.

 Be sure you can identify issues with printers and problematic print jobs.

Troubleshoot Printing Problems at the Application Level

Users may identify several common printing problems from their Office applications. Some of these problems are as follows:

➤ When a user prints a document or envelope, nothing happens.

➤ When a user prints a document, a blank page is printed at the end of the document.

➤ When a user prints multiple documents, he cannot print property information.

➤ Word stops responding when printing.

Each problem has its own solution—for example, when a user tries to print and nothing happens. Because printing is primarily controlled by Microsoft Windows, you can run through the print troubleshooter. If the print settings appear to be in order, verify the Word print settings to make sure that the printer listed in the program matches your default printer. To view the Print Settings dialog box, select Print from the File menu. You should also verify that the page range specified matches the pages you want to print.

When troubleshooting why a blank page is printed at the end of a printed document, you should verify that no extra blank lines appear at the end of the document. To view the paragraph marks, click the Show/Hide button on the Standard toolbar. Remove all the extra paragraph markers. Select the Print Preview option to verify that the blank page has been removed.

With previous versions of Word, you could print multiple documents including the file properties. However, with the latest version of Word XP, you cannot print the file properties of multiple files. Word still includes the capability to print file properties, but you must print them on an individual file basis.

When a user reports that the application is asking for a paper size she does not have, the file may have been created with a different language version of Word and formatted to a different paper size. To adjust the document's paper size, open the Print dialog box from the File menu. In the Zoom section, select the paper size you want to use in the Scale to Paper Size box. Word then automatically scales the document to fit the selected paper size.

In worst-case scenarios, Word stops responding during print requests. The most suitable solution is to reinstall the print driver. It is best to verify whether the manufacturer has released an updated driver for the printer. Most manufacturers' Web sites contain driver updates that you can download directly.

Exam Prep Questions

Question 1

A user receives the following error message when he attempts to save a spreadsheet to the corporate share drive. What could be the possible problems? Choose two correct answers.

☐ A. The user is not connected to the network.

☐ B. The remote computer is off.

☐ C. The remote computer does not have available storage space.

☐ D. The remote computer is read-only.

Answers A and B are correct. The user is most likely not connected to the network, or the remote computer is off. Answer C is incorrect because the error does not indicate that the drive is full. Answer D is incorrect because the error message indicates that the remote computer is unavailable.

Question 2

A user reports that her system was recently upgraded to Windows XP. Before the upgrade, her DVD-ROM drive functioned normally. However, since the new operating system was installed, she has not been able to view DVDs. What should you check first?

○ A. Verify no hardware conflicts exist by using the Add Hardware Wizard.

○ B. Check the vendor for an updated Windows XP DVD-ROM device driver.

○ C. Verify that the device is functioning by using the Device Manager.

○ D. Reinstall Windows XP.

Answer C is correct. Your first step in troubleshooting the hardware problem should be to verify that the device is functioning. You can do so using the Device Manager. Answer A is incorrect because you cannot use the Add Hardware Wizard to verify that a device is functioning. Answer B is also incorrect. Before looking for a new device driver, you should verify the status of the device. Answer D is incorrect. You should try troubleshooting the hardware problem before reinstalling the operating system.

Question 3

A user indicates that he has recently installed a new modem, but since the installation he has not been able to log in to the network. What is the problem? Choose two correct answers.

❏ A. The modem driver has corrupted the network driver.

❏ B. The modem and network interface card are using the same resources.

❏ C. A conflict exists with the modem and network card.

❏ D. The network card is disabled.

Answers B and C are correct. Because the problem appeared after the new modem was installed, this may indicate that a hardware conflict exists between the modem and network card. Answer A is incorrect because a corrupted network driver would not cause a hardware conflict. Answer D is also incorrect. The question does not indicate that the user disabled the network card at any time.

Question 4

You have recently updated your video driver. Unfortunately, it has caused a problem with the display. What should you do to correct the problem?

○ A. Reinstall the driver.

○ B. Use the System Restore feature.

○ C. Locate and install an updated driver from the vendor's Web site.

○ D. Remove the device using Device Manager.

Answer B is correct. The best option in this situation is to use the System Restore feature to restore the operating system to its state before the device driver was installed. Answer A is incorrect. Reinstalling the existing driver will not correct the problem. Answer C is also incorrect. Although you may want to locate an updated driver for the device, you should correct the problem before installing it. Answer D is incorrect because removing the device would result in no display.

Question 5

A user indicates that she cannot log on to the network. She has logged on to her system locally. You have tried to ping the system, but your efforts are unsuccessful. The network cable has been connected correctly to both the wall and computer. The network card LEDs are lit. You checked the Device Manager, and a red X appears next to the network adapter. What is the problem?

- ○ A. The user is logging on with an incorrect username and password.
- ○ B. TCP/IP is not initialized on the local computer.
- ○ C. The network card is disabled.
- ○ D. The network card is conflicting with another device.

Answer C is correct. A red X on a device within Device Manager indicates that the device is disabled. Therefore, answers B and D are incorrect. Answer A is incorrect because an incorrect username and password would result in authentication errors.

Question 6

You are the desktop support technician for a small insurance company. A user calls to report that he is unable to print a document in Microsoft Word. You verify that the printer is online and it has paper. The problem is not affecting any other users. What should you do next to troubleshoot the problem?

- ○ A. Attempt to print a test page from the user's computer.
- ○ B. Reinstall the printer driver.
- ○ C. Reboot the printer.
- ○ D. Delete all documents in the print queue.

Answer A is correct. To troubleshoot the problem, attempt to print a test page from the user's computer. Because the printer is online and the problem is not affecting any other users, answers B, C, and D are incorrect.

Question 7

A user is trying to save a Word document to a CDR-ROM. She receives an error message. This message did not appear when she performed the same steps the previous day. However, she closed the window before documenting what the message stated. You verify that no changes have been made to the computer in the past day. What could be some possible causes for the problem? Choose two correct answers.

- ❑ A. The user is trying to save to a CD that is not rewritable.
- ❑ B. There is a hardware conflict.
- ❑ C. No free space is available on the rewritable CD.
- ❑ D. The driver for the device needs to be updated.

Answers A and C are correct. Because no changes have been made to the computer, you can rule out a problem with the device driver and a hardware conflict. The error message is more than likely occurring because the user is trying to save to a CD that is not rewritable or trying to save to a rewritable CD that has no available free space. Therefore, answers B and D are incorrect.

Question 8

Which of the following utilities can you use to return the operating system to a previous state?

- ○ A. Device Manager
- ○ B. System Restore
- ○ C. Add Hardware Wizard
- ○ D. Disk Cleanup

Answer B is correct. You can use the System Restore feature to return the operating system to a previous state. Answer A is incorrect because you use the Device Manager to manage and troubleshoot hardware devices. Answer C is incorrect because you use the Add Hardware Wizard to add hardware devices. Answer D is incorrect because you use Disk Cleanup to free disk space.

Question 9

A user is attempting to save a file to his hard disk. However, he receives an error message that not enough space is available. The user calls to report the problem. What should you do to resolve the problem?

- ○ A. Delete all the files and format the hard drive.
- ○ B. Open the properties for the hard drive and use the Disk Cleanup feature.
- ○ C. Use the System Restore feature to restore the operating system to a previous state.
- ○ D. Verify that there are no hardware conflicts by using Device Manager.

Answer B is correct. If the user is receiving an error message that not enough space is available when he attempts to save a document, you can use the Disk Cleanup feature to free disk space. Therefore, answer A is incorrect. Answers C and D are incorrect because the problem is not hardware related.

Question 10

A user is trying to print a document in Microsoft Word. When she retrieves her document from the printer, the characters are garbled. The printer is locally attached to the user's workstation. What should you do?

- ○ A. Stop and restart the print spooler.
- ○ B. Reboot the printer.
- ○ C. Delete all the documents in the print queue.
- ○ D. Reinstall the printer driver.

Answer D is correct. If the characters in a document come out garbled, there is a problem with the printer driver. Answers A and C are incorrect because the user can successfully print a document. Answer B is incorrect. Taking the printer offline and restarting it will not fix the driver problem.

Configuring and Troubleshooting Network Connectivity

. . . .

Terms you'll need to understand:

- ✓ Firewall
- ✓ Internet Connection Firewall (ICF)
- ✓ Domain Name System
- ✓ NetBIOS
- ✓ TCP/IP
- ✓ **ping**
- ✓ **tracert**
- ✓ **ipconfig**
- ✓ Modem
- ✓ Network interface card

Techniques you'll need to master:

- ✓ Identify and troubleshoot network connectivity problems
- ✓ Troubleshoot hardware problems
- ✓ Use **ping** and **tracert** to troubleshoot network connectivity problems
- ✓ Use **ipconfig** to resolve IP addressing issues
- ✓ Identify and resolve issues related to routing and remote access
- ✓ Troubleshoot name resolution problems
- ✓ Understand Internet Connection Firewall
- ✓ Troubleshoot problems related to ICF

Identifying and Troubleshooting Network Problems

Network problems can fall under a number of different categories. Problems can be related to malfunctioning hardware, cabling issues, incorrect protocol configurations, or a network device. The following sections look at some of the network problems you may encounter as well as ways to diagnose and resolve them.

Troubleshooting Hardware Problems

If users report that they are unable to communicate on the network, one of the first things you should do is verify that a network connection is present. For example, if users report they cannot connect to the Internet when using hyperlinks in a Word document, you should begin troubleshooting by identifying whether the problem is hardware related.

 Microsoft publishes a Hardware Compatibility List (HCL) for its operating systems. Hardware devices on the HCL are guaranteed to work with the given operating system. When troubleshooting hardware problems, you should verify that the device appears on this list. Microsoft guarantees only that devices appearing on the list will function correctly under the operating system.

Network Interface Cards

When you are troubleshooting, start with the most obvious to eliminate it as the source of the problem. To verify the network connection, begin by checking the physical network connection. Are the link lights flashing on the network adapter card? Is the network cable securely attached? Is the correct network protocol being used?

Although this check may seem trivial, one of the first things you should do when troubleshooting network problems is to check the physical connections. Make sure the *network interface card* is properly seated and the cables are securely fastened. The network cable should be inspected for any damage. Trying a different cable may also be worthwhile to eliminate it as the source of the problem.

 Keep in mind the hardware problem may be with another network device such as a hub or router.

If users are unable to establish a network connection using a network adapter, consider the following points when troubleshooting the problem:

➤ The network adapter may be conflicting with another hardware device. You can use Device Manager to determine whether this is the case. Device Manager can also provide you with the device's status information (functioning or not functioning).

➤ Make sure the network cable is properly connected and the network card is not loose.

➤ Try using a different network cable to ensure the existing one is not faulty, thereby causing the loss of network connection.

➤ Verify that the correct device driver is installed.

 A lack of network connection can affect applications in a number of ways, such as a user not being able to send or receive email, access shared documents on the network, or use hyperlinks in a Word document.

Modems

Because network access may be made through a *modem* (for example, a cable modem, ISDN, or ADSL), you need to look for some common issues when troubleshooting network connectivity. One of your first tasks should be verifying that the modem has power, it is properly connected to the computer, and any cables are securely in place.

Because the problem may also be with the cabling, you should also inspect it for any damage. (Again, you should try a different cable to eliminate this as being the problem.) Cycling the power may also be worthwhile, either by using an external modem or by restarting the local computer if the modem is internal.

 If you suspect a problem with the hardware on the local computer, you can use Device Manager to determine whether the device is functioning correctly.

If you suspect a problem with an internal modem, you can use the modem diagnostics to test the hardware. To access this feature, open the Phone and Modem Options applet within the Control Panel. On the Modems tab, select the modem you want to test, click Properties, and click Diagnostics. Click the Query Modem button shown in Figure 7.1.

Figure 7.1 Using the Phone and Modems Options applet to test a modem.

If the modem appears to be working, but you still cannot establish a connection, check the modem's configuration. For example, if a user is trying to establish a connection with an ISP, she should consult the documentation or consult the ISP for the correct modem settings.

One common message that users may encounter when trying to establish a connection is that the port is in use by another application. In this case, you can try a number of different approaches to resolve the problem, such as rebooting the computer, verifying that a connection is not already established, or using a different port.

To assist in troubleshooting modem problems, you can enable logging of modem commands through the Phone and Modem Options applet. The default location for the log file is **%systemroot%\system 32\ModemLog_*model.txt***.

Troubleshooting LAN Problems

Troubleshooting a LAN problem can be difficult because several different components can be the source of the problem. For example, the problem can be with a specific computer, another hardware device, the configuration, or even authentication.

If users are experiencing network connectivity problems on a local area network, one of the more common causes is a misconfiguration of network protocols. The default protocol installed with Windows XP is *TCP/IP* (the most common protocol used). It is also the protocol that requires the most configuration and can therefore be difficult to troubleshoot. So after you've eliminated any problems with the hardware, you should ensure TCP/IP is not the source of the problem.

Troubleshooting TCP/IP

TCP/IP requires considerable configuration either on individual clients or centrally on a server. Many issues can appear—for example, incorrect Internet Protocol (IP) parameters on a client or a nonresponsive DHCP server. To successfully implement TCP/IP and DHCP on a network, you must have a general understanding of some of the common issues that can arise as well as ways to troubleshoot them. The following sections describe some of the more common problems that you may encounter on a TCP/IP network.

Diagnosing and Resolving Issues Related to Automatic Private IP Addressing

Automatic Private IP Addressing (APIPA) was introduced in Windows 98, second edition. It is enabled by default and supported by the following clients:

➤ Windows 98, second edition

➤ Windows ME

➤ Windows 2000 (all platforms)

➤ Windows XP

➤ Windows Server 2003

Clients that support this feature are able to self-assign an IP address in the following situations:

➤ A DHCP client is unable to contact a DHCP server, or no DHCP server is available on the network.

➤ A DHCP client's attempt to renew its IP address leased from a DHCP server fails.

In both cases, the client assigns itself an IP address in the range of 169.254.0.1–169.254.255.254 (see Figure 7.2). You can use the `ipconfig` command-line utility to verify that APIPA is enabled and that an IP address within the specific range has been assigned. Remember that APIPA is enabled by default. However, this feature can be disabled through the registry or with the use of Group Policy Objects (GPOs).

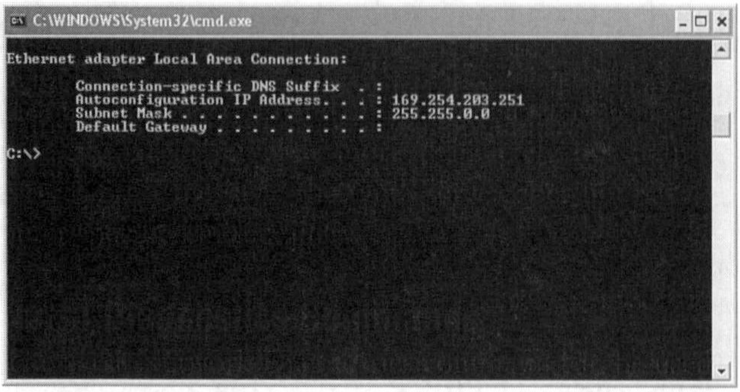

Figure 7.2 Automatic Private IP Addressing.

If your network consists of multiple subnets, clients using APIPA can communicate only with hosts on their local subnet. APIPA does not include optional parameters. Clients assign themselves only an IP address and a subnet mask. Without the IP address of the default gateway and *Domain Name System (DNS)* server, communication outside the local subnet will fail.

Diagnosing and Resolving Issues Related to Incorrect TCP/IP Configuration

You can use several command-line utilities to test and diagnose incorrect TCP/IP configurations. To do so, open the Command Prompt window and type ipconfig. Using the /all parameter brings up more detailed configuration information, as shown in Figure 7.3. Table 7.1 outlines some of the common parameters you can use with the ipconfig command.

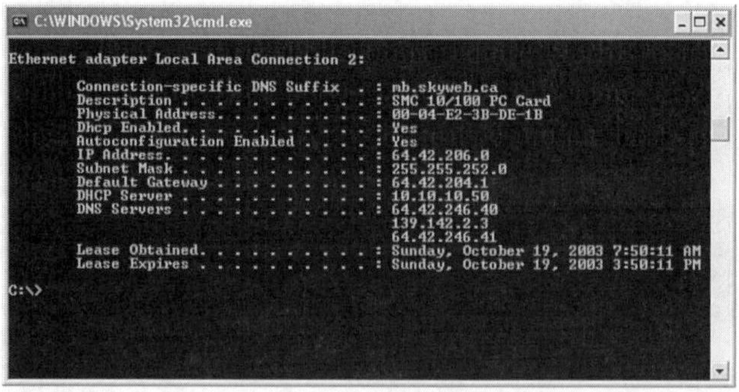

Figure 7.3 Verifying TCP/IP configuration using the **ipconfig /all** command.

Table 7.1	Parameters for Use with the ipconfig Command
Parameter	**Description**
/all	Displays detailed IP configuration information
/release	Releases the IP address for the specified adapter
/renew	Renews the IP address for the specified adapter
/flushDNS	Purges the entries in the DNS cache
/registerDNS	Refreshes all leased IP addresses and reregisters DNS names
/displayDNS	Displays the contents of the DNS cache

Troubleshooting with the `ping` Command

If the communications themselves are at fault, you should look at your software, the path between your system and the remote host, and the remote host itself. Start with the remote host and work back to your local system. The best practice in general is to first ping the remote system to see whether it is online. Test other systems located in the same general area as well (somewhere else on the Internet). As long as you use a handful of hosts, you should be able to determine the source of the problem.

If you are unable to ping only a single host, you can deduce that the host is offline, it does not respond to pings, or the path to the host is interrupted. If multiple hosts—but not all—fail to ping, a router is at fault somewhere in the chain, or a serious network overload is occurring. If all hosts fail to ping, your Internet connection may be at fault.

If you've determined that a network connection is present, the problem may be with a another device on the network such as a router. You can use the `ping` command to ensure that the network connection is not being interrupted.

The `ping` command-line utility is useful in verifying connectivity with another TCP/IP host. Connectivity on the network is verified by sending Internet Control Message Protocol (ICMP) echo requests and replies. When the `ping` command is issued, the source computer sends echo request messages to another TCP/IP host. The remote host, if reachable, then responds with four echo replies. The `ping` command is also issued at the command prompt, along with the TCP/IP address or domain name of the other TCP/IP host, as follows:

```
C:> ping 124.120.105.110
C:> ping www.contoso.com
```

To determine whether TCP/IP is initialized on the local computer, issue the **ping** command and specify the loopback address 127.0.0.1. The loopback address is the address used to route outgoing packets back to the local computer. It is used for testing purposes.

The general steps for troubleshooting TCP/IP using the `ping` command are as follows:

1. Ping the loopback address 127.0.0.1 to ensure TCP/IP is initialized on the local computer. This step does not test any connectivity with other hosts.

2. If successful, ping the IP address assigned to the local computer. This step determines whether the IP address of the computer was successfully added to the network.

3. Ping the IP address of the default gateway. If this step fails, verify that the IP address of the default gateway is correct and the gateway is operational.

4. Ping the IP address of a host on a remote network. If this step is unsuccessful, verify that the remote host is operational, verify the IP address of the remote host, and verify that all routers and gateways between the local computer and remote computer are operational.

A quick way of verifying TCP/IP connectivity is to complete step 4 of the preceding routine. If you can successfully ping the IP address of a remote host, steps 1 through 3 will be successful.

Two other utilities that you can use for TCP/IP troubleshooting are `tracert` and `pathping`. The `tracert` command determines the route taken to a specific destination. You may want to use the `tracert` command if you cannot successfully ping the IP address of a remote host. The results of the `tracert` command indicate whether a problem exists with a router or gateway between the local computer and the remote destination.

The `pathping` command is basically a combination of the `ping` and `tracert` commands. When the command is issued, packets are sent to each router between the local computer and a remote computer. The results determine which routers and gateways may be causing problems on the network.

If the problem is indeed related to the network connection, the actions outlined in this section should help you locate the cause of the problem.

Troubleshooting Routing and Remote Access Configuration Problems

Troubleshooting is a major part of an administrator's job. Issues can arise related to connection problems or the ability to access resources beyond the remote access server. If the remote access server is configured as a router, you may encounter problems related to demand dialing. The following section outlines some of the more common problems you may encounter with a remote access server.

Diagnosing and Resolving Issues Related to Establishing a Remote Access Connection

One of the most common problems you may find yourself troubleshooting is related to establishing a remote access connection with a server. It may be a remote access server on your private network or with an ISP. In the event such connection problems occur, use the following tips to start troubleshooting:

➤ Verify that the modem installed is working and correctly configured (refer to the section "Troubleshooting Hardware Problems" earlier in the chapter).

➤ Verify the number the user is dialing. Also consider that the problem may exist with the phone line.

➤ Verify the credentials the user is providing.

➤ If the user is dialing into a remote access server on your network, check that the remote access service is enabled and started on the server.

➤ On the server side, verify the availability of ports. If necessary, disconnect any idle sessions or increase the number of available ports.

➤ If you are using remote access policies to control remote access connections, verify that the remote access policy is not prohibiting the connection.

 If a user receives an **access denied** message when attempting to establish a remote access connection, check the credentials the user is providing and verify that the user has indeed been granted remote access permissions.

Identifying and Troubleshooting Name Resolution Problems

Each machine on a computer network is assigned a unique network address. Computers communicate with each other across networks by connecting to these network addresses. These numbers, also known as *IP addresses*, are 12 digits long and difficult for people to remember. To solve this dilemma, a system was developed whereby people can use "friendly" names that are then translated into the network addresses the computers use to locate each other and to communicate. These names are called *hostnames*, and each machine is assigned one. Groups of hosts form a domain. The software that translates these names to network addresses is called the *Domain Name System (DNS)*.

Domain Name Servers have been in use on the Internet for many years. Prior to DNS, HOSTS files were used for name resolution, but as the Internet quickly grew in size and popularity, maintaining HOSTS files and keeping them up to date became impossible. When the Internet community realized a need for a more manageable, scalable, and efficient name resolution system, DNS was created.

Prior to the introduction of Windows 2000, *Network Basic Input/Output System (NetBIOS)* names were used to identify computers, services, and other resources on Windows-based machines. In the early days of Windows networks, LMHOSTS files were used for NetBIOS name resolution. Later, these names were often resolved to Internet Protocol (IP) addresses using a NetBIOS Name Server (NBNS).

The following sections identify some of the common name resolution problems you may encounter and the tools you can use to troubleshoot name resolution problems.

Troubleshooting DNS

As already mentioned, DNS is required to resolve hostnames or fully qualified domain names (FQDNs) to IP addresses. DNS name resolution problems usually occur in the following two areas:

➤ A user receives no response when attempting to resolve a hostname.

➤ A successful response is received from a DNS server, but the information returned is incorrect.

One of the more common errors that you will encounter in regards to name resolution is a `server not found` error. This error indicates a problem with name resolution that can be related to incorrect parameters on the client or the DNS server not being online. If an error message of this type is reported (and you have eliminated the hardware and network connection as the source of the problem), verify that the user is configured with the correct IP address of a DNS server. You can do so through the properties of the Internet or LAN connection if static IP addressing is used. You can use the `ipconfig` command to check DNS settings when dynamic IP addressing is being used.

DNS can support both static and dynamic entries. An administrator can manually add resource records to the database, thereby creating static entries. Conversely, through Dynamic DNS, DNS clients can create and update their own resource records. This capability is particularly useful if dynamic IP addressing is used.

When dynamic IP addresses are assigned to computers, problems may occur if the DNS server stores static entries in the DNS database. The static entries contain the IP address and hostname of the computer. With this information, the DNS server answers name resolution requests for computers located on the network. Problems that can occur include the IP address of a computer being changed but the record in the DNS database not being updated or the DNS server having incorrect information within the DNS cache. If the DNS server has incorrect information, it causes name resolution errors to occur.

You can update the DNS database with new and correct IP information by using the **ipconfig /registerdns** command.

As simple as it sounds, you should verify that the user is referencing the correct domain name. A simple typing mistake can return a **server not found** error.

NSLOOKUP

One of the commands you can use to diagnose DNS problems on the network is nslookup. For example, you can use the command to query a specific DNS server to resolve the computer name registered for a given IP address. The following parameters are available with the command:

➤ subcommands—Allows you to specify additional subcommands to be used with nslookup.

➤ Computertofind—Queries the default DNS server for information about the computer specified. This can be an IP address or a computer name.

➤ server—Specifies which DNS server to query.

If you issue the command and receive a No response from server error message, the DNS server is more than likely not online. If you receive a No records error message, the DNS server does not have a record for the computer specified in the query.

Netsh Diagnostics Commands

The Netsh Network Diagnostics command can be used to troubleshoot network services including DNS from the command line.

You can use the following commands to troubleshoot DNS:

➤ ping dns—Verifies connectivity with DNS servers configured through the TCP/IP Properties dialog box.

➤ show dns—Lists the DNS servers configured for a given interface. If no parameters are used, DNS servers configured for all adapters are displayed.

The **Netsh diag** context is a new feature of Windows XP. It is not supported by previous versions of Windows.

Troubleshooting NetBIOS Name Resolution

Some clients and/or applications require NetBIOS names to communicate with other hosts on a network. A NetBIOS name is a 16-character name in which the first 15 characters identify a unique host, and the 16th character identifies a service or application running on the host such as the Workstation or Server service.

As with domain names, NetBIOS names must be resolved to an IP address before two hosts can communicate. Numerous methods are available for name resolution, and the method employed depends on the environment. For example, some networks may use Windows Internet Naming Service (WINS), whereas others may opt to rely on broadcasts for name resolution.

If your network uses both NetBIOS and DNS, you may need to identify where name resolution is failing. If an application is generating name resolution errors, you should determine whether the application uses NetBIOS or DNS. If the application uses Window Sockets (for example, Internet Explorer and Telnet), the error is related to hostname resolution. Name resolution errors generated by applications using NetBIOS are obviously related to NetBIOS name resolution.

The most common error message you will probably encounter with NetBIOS name resolution is a `computer not found` message. Often this error may be the result of a user typing in the incorrect NetBIOS name. You can easily determine whether name resolution is failing by using the `ping` command. A successful ping to the computer's IP address will indicate that the computer is online and eliminate network issues as the source of the problem. How you troubleshoot the problem depends on the method of name resolution used on the network. For example, if a WINS server is being used, verify that an entry for the computer appears in the WINS database, or if an LMHOSTS file is used, verify that a mapping exists for the computer.

You can use numerous methods to resolve NetBIOS names. Windows Internet Naming Service (WINS) is one of the most common. A WINS server is similar to a DNS server. It maintains dynamic database mappings for NetBIOS names and their corresponding IP addresses. An LMHOSTS file may be used; it is a static text file containing mappings for NetBIOS names and IP addresses. Alternatively, some networks may rely on broadcast messages for name resolution.

Nbtstat Command

The `Nbtstat` command can be used to troubleshoot NetBIOS-related problems. The output of the command can display NetBIOS over TCP/IP protocol statistics, the NetBIOS name tables for a local or remote computer, as well as the contents of the NetBIOS name cache. Table 7.2 summarizes the parameters available for use with the command.

Table 7.2	Nbtstat Command-Line Parameters
Parameter	**Description**
-a *remotename*	Displays the NetBIOS name table of the computer specified. The *remotename* portion is the NetBIOS name of the computer.
-A *ipaddress*	Displays the NetBIOS name table of the computer specified. The *ipaddress* portion is the IP address assigned to the computer.
-c	Displays the contents of the NetBIOS name cache.
-r	Displays NetBIOS name resolution statistics.
-R	Purges the contents of the NetBIOS name cache and reloads the #pre-tagged entries from the LMHOSTS file.
-RR	Releases and refreshes NetBIOS names for a local computer that are registered with a WINS server.

Troubleshooting Name Resolution and Applications

When troubleshooting name resolution within applications, you must watch out for certain issues. For example, when a hyperlink identifies a file on a mapped drive S, the user who is trying to access the link must have the same network drive mapped to the same drive letter. If the user has the wrong drive mapped to drive S, the link produces an error that the file is not found. All links within files should use the UNC path, so regardless of which drive mappings the user has on his system, he can locate the destination file.

Figure 7.4 displays the common error message that appears when a hyperlink uses an unavailable drive mapping.

Figure 7.4   Cannot open specified file error message.

Hyperlinks are not the only problem. Shortcuts located on desktops or within folders should also use the UNC path to files. The same reasoning applies. If a drive is mapped to the wrong network drive or has been remapped to a different letter, it generates the same error shown in Figure 7.4.

Identifying and Troubleshooting Network Connectivity Problems Caused by the Firewall Configuration

Most home users and businesses have expanded beyond the borders of their local intranet; the Internet has become a powerful tool for them. However, expanding beyond the local intranet makes private networks vulnerable to security attacks. Opening the door for users on the intranet to access the Internet in turn opens a door for attackers to your private network. So as more and more home users and businesses connect to the Internet, security becomes crucial. Providing Internet access for users also means looking for ways to secure your private network from Internet attacks. One of the ways in which you can secure your private network is to deploy a firewall.

What Is a Firewall?

A *firewall* can be hardware or software based. The purpose of a firewall is to create a barrier between the Internet and your private network. It allows users on the intranet to access Internet resources and at the same time restricts Internet access to your private network.

A firewall can protect your network from Internet attacks such as viruses and Denial of Service attacks. It can also ensure that Internet users do not have access to confidential information stored on your network. Table 7.3 describes some of the common attacks from which a firewall can protect your network.

Table 7.3 Common Internet Attacks	
Internet Attack	**Description**
Ping of Death	A remote computer continuously sends ping requests larger than 64KB to overflow the internal buffer on another computer.
All Port Scan Attack	A remote computer accesses more than the available number of ports to look for a weakness.
Land Attack	This attack is a form of spoofing in which the source IP address is changed to appear as though it is the same as the destination IP address.
Denial of Service	This attack is designed to hinder normal use of a computer or network.

Table 7.3 Common Internet Attacks *(continued)*	
Internet Attack	**Description**
UDP Bomb attack	UDP packets containing invalid values for various fields are sent.
Worms	This malicious software replicates itself to other computers usually via email.
Virus	This program or malicious code secretly replicates itself by attaching to a medium such as another program, the boot sector, a partition sector, or a document that contains macros.
Trojan horse	This virus is designed to compromise security, such as stealing passwords. The purpose of a Trojan horse is to trick users into believing they are doing one thing when in fact they are doing something else.

Here, reference is made to a firewall being able to protect a network from any external intrusion. However, even if you have only a single computer, you should still deploy a firewall if the computer has an Internet connection.

As already mentioned, a firewall can be hardware or software based. In either case, the firewall examines and filters packets from the Internet going to the local computer or private network. A firewall can also operate at different layers of the OSI Model. A firewall that operates at the Network layer inspects incoming packets and grants or denies access based on source and destination IP address as well as port numbers. A firewall that functions at the Application layer provides more sophisticated functions such as granting or denying access based on applications.

Although some firewalls can be very complex to configure, the idea behind them is relatively straightforward. A firewall creates a barrier between the Internet and your private network by intercepting all inbound packets before they reach the private network. The firewall inspects the information within a packet's header and grants or denies access based on configured rules. For example, all FTP traffic for port 23 can be granted access, whereas all other traffic is denied.

Firewalls come in many different shapes and sizes. The type of firewall you implement is largely determined by the level of security you require. Fortunately, if you are looking for a simple and easy-to-use solution, you can implement the Internet Firewall Component included with Windows XP.

Internet Connection Firewall

Windows XP includes a software-based firewall component called *Internet Connection Firewall (ICF)*. It allows you to safely connect your computer or network to the Internet. Once enabled, ICF restricts the flow of packets between the Internet and your private network.

If you have ever worked with or configured various firewall solutions, you know that many of them are difficult to install and properly configure. Fortunately, Windows XP offers a firewall solution that is simple to enable and requires little or no configuration. You can enable ICF to secure a single computer with an Internet connection, or you can enable it on a computer that has a shared Internet connection.

So, how exactly does ICF work? ICF inspects each packet destined for the private network. It maintains a table to determine which incoming traffic was initiated on the local network—for example, a user on the private network accessing an FTP server on the Internet. Any incoming traffic resulting from this request is allowed through the firewall. If an inbound request was not initiated by the local computer or a computer on the private network, it is not allowed through the firewall.

ICF uses the following methods to determine which packets to allow through the firewall and which packets to drop:

➤ Any incoming packets that match a request initiated on the private network are allowed through the firewall.

➤ Any incoming packets that do not match a request initiated on the private network are not allowed to pass through the firewall.

➤ Those incoming packets that will create a new entry in the table are allowed through the firewall.

In some cases, you may need to make resources on the private network available to users on the Internet. In other words, a certain type of traffic initiated on the Internet is allowed to pass through the firewall. You can do so by creating static rules that allow traffic on a specific port to pass through the firewall. For example, if you have an FTP server on the private network, you can open port 21.

ICF can be used to filter incoming traffic. If you want to filter outgoing traffic, you need to implement a more sophisticated firewall solution.

Enabling ICF

The ICF component of Windows XP can be enabled in a number of different ways. For example, you can enable it using the Network Setup Wizard. ICF can also be enabled manually using the Network Connection applet in the Control Panel.

You can use the following steps to enable ICF:

1. Click Start, point to Settings, and click Control Panel.

2. Within the Control Panel, double-click the Network Connections applet. The Network Connections folder opens.

3. Select the Internet connection you want to protect and click Change Settings of This Connection under the list of Network Tasks. An alternate method is to right-click the Internet connection and click Properties.

4. Within the properties window for the Internet connection, click the Advanced tab.

5. Click the box beside the option Protect My Computer and Network by Limiting or Preventing Access to This Computer from the Internet (see Figure 7.5). Click OK.

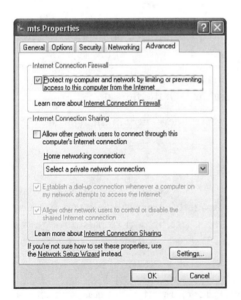

Figure 7.5 Enabling Internet Connection Firewall.

After enabling ICF, you can select the Settings button on the properties window's Advanced tab to control the flow of data. This topic is covered in the following section.

Controlling the Flow of Data

By default, ICF blocks all inbound packets that do not match an entry in the connection table. However, if you have services running on the private network you want to make available to Internet users, you can create a port mapping.

 NOTE Port mappings can redirect incoming traffic to another computer on the private network. To do this, Internet Connection Sharing must also be enabled.

After ICF is enabled, certain predefined port mappings are created as well (see Figure 7.6). If you want to allow certain types of traffic through the firewall, place a check mark beside the appropriate protocol type (such as FTP) in the Advanced Settings dialog box and click OK. You can also create new port mappings by selecting the Add button on the Services tab.

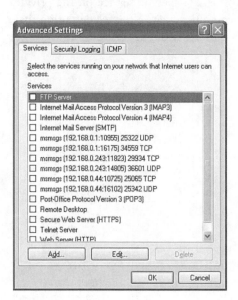

Figure 7.6 Configuring port mappings for Internet Connection Firewall.

Common Firewall Configuration Problems

Because many home offices and businesses are now opting to implement firewalls to secure their network, you need to be familiar with some of the common configuration problems that can arise and ways to troubleshoot them.

After you enable ICF, you may encounter problems browsing the network and sharing the files on your computer with other users. If this situation occurs, verify the connection where ICF has been enabled. ICF should be enabled only on an Internet connection, not the connection used for the LAN. When ICF is enabled, it closes the ports.

One of the most common problems you will encounter when using ICF is that an application does not work through the firewall. The cause of this problem is more than likely the service definitions. You need to enable or create a new service definition that will allow the application to function through the firewall. Doing so requires that you know what protocol and ports the application uses.

Another common problem you may encounter is Internet users not being able to access a server, such as a Web server, on the private network. This is normal behavior because ICF blocks all traffic that does not correspond to an entry in the connection table. To make a specific service on the private network available to Internet users, you must create a service definition that allows the specific type of traffic through the firewall.

Exam Prep Questions

Question 1

You are the help desk support technician for an Internet service provider. A user calls to report that she is unable to establish a connection. When the user attempts to dial into the ISP, she receives an **access denied** error message. What should you do?

- ○ A. Have the user open the Phone and Modem applet to run diagnostics on the modem.
- ○ B. Tell the user to verify that the cable is securely in place.
- ○ C. Check the credentials the user is providing.
- ○ D. Check that the hardware configuration for the modem matches those of the remote access server.

Answer C is correct. An access denied error message indicates a problem with authentication. One of the first things you should check is that the user is providing the correct username and password. A hardware problem or a problem with the configuration of the modem would result in a different error message. Answer A is incorrect because a different error would appear if it was hardware related. Answer B is incorrect because a connection has been established, but authentication with the server is failing. Answer D is incorrect because the problem is not hardware related.

Question 2

You are the desktop support technician for a small insurance company. The IP-based network hosts approximately 20 workstations. All workstations are members of the same domain. A user on the network reports that he is unable to access any network resources. The problem did not occur the previous day. You have verified that the problem does not exist with the network card or cable. When you issue the **ipconfig** command, you receive the output shown in the following figure.

```
C:\WINDOWS\System32\cmd.exe                                    _□×

Ethernet adapter Local Area Connection:

        Connection-specific DNS Suffix  . :
        Autoconfiguration IP Address. . . : 169.254.203.251
        Subnet Mask . . . . . . . . . . . : 255.255.0.0
        Default Gateway . . . . . . . . . :

C:\>
```

What is most likely causing the problem?

- ○ A. The client is configured with the incorrect IP address of the DNS server.
- ○ B. The client is unable to obtain an IP address from a DHCP server.
- ○ C. The network interface card is not functioning.
- ○ D. A domain controller is not available to authenticate the user.

Answer B is correct. The figure above indicates that Automatic Private IP Addressing (APIPA) is being used. If a DHCP server is unavailable, DHCP clients self-assign an IP address until the DHCP server is available. Therefore, answers A, C, and D are incorrect.

Question 3

A user reports that she is unable to access resources on another computer. When you use the UNC path to the remote computer, you receive the error shown in the following figure.

The user can successfully access other computers on the network. How should you begin troubleshooting the connectivity problem?

- ○ A. Replace the network cable to the network adapter.
- ○ B. Issue the **ipconfig** command to ensure TCP/IP is properly configured on the local computer.
- ○ C. Update the device driver for the network card.
- ○ D. Use the **ping** command to test connectivity between the two computers.

Answer D is correct. You can use the ping command to test connectivity between two hosts. You should use this command to verify that the remote computer is responding. If you receive an unsuccessful response, the remote computer may be offline. Because the user can access other computers on the network, you can eliminate the network card or cable as being the cause of the problem. This would also indicate that TCP/IP is properly configured on the local computer. Therefore, answers A, B, and C are incorrect.

Question 4

A user is having problems related to NetBIOS name resolution. You want to purge the contents of the local NetBIOS name cache. Which command must you use?

O A. **ipconfig**

O B. **net diag**

O C. **nbtstat**

O D. **nslookup**

Answer C is correct. You can use the nbtstat command to purge the contents of the local NetBIOS name cache. Answer A is incorrect because ipconfig can be used to view and manipulate IP parameters. Answers B and D are incorrect because neither of these commands allows you to empty the contents of the NetBIOS name cache.

Question 5

You have just updated a static record in the DNS database for Computer1. A user now reports that he is unable to access resources on this computer. You suspect an incorrect mapping in the user's DNS resolver cache. Which of the following commands can you use to purge the contents of the cache on the user's computer?

O A. **ipconfig /renew**

O B. **ipconfig /flushdns**

O C. **ipconfig /release**

O D. **ipconfig /displaydns**

Answer B is correct. Each DNS client maintains a cache of recently resolved hostnames. You can use ipconfig /flushdns to purge the contents of the cache. Therefore, answers A, C, and D are incorrect.

Question 6

A user calls to report that she is unable to establish a dial-up connection with her ISP. You discover that the modem does not make any noise when the user attempts to establish the connection. What two steps should the user perform to begin troubleshooting the problem? Choose two correct answers.

❏ A. The user should check that the modem is properly seated in the computer.

❏ B. The user should contact the modem's manufacturer for an update.

❏ C. The user should verify she is using the correct username and password for authentication.

❏ D. The user should check that the phone line is properly connected to the modem and phone jack.

Answers A and D are correct. Before having the user update the device driver for the modem, have the user check that the modem is properly seated inside the computer and that the phone line is properly connected. If neither method solves the problem, you can then begin looking at reinstalling or updating a device driver. Because the modem is not dialing out, authentication can be eliminated as the cause of the problem. Therefore, answer C is incorrect. Answer B is incorrect. Although this step may be necessary later, other simple troubleshooting steps should be performed first.

Question 7

You are the desktop support technician for a small consulting firm. A user calls to report that he is unable to access a shared folder on another computer. The user is trying to access the share using a mapped drive but receives an error message that the computer is not found. The user can successfully access other computers on the network. How should you troubleshoot the issue?

○ A. Use the **ipconfig** command to check the TCP/IP configuration of the user's computer.

○ B. Check the user's permission on the shared folder.

○ C. Verify that the user has a network connection.

○ D. Check to see that the remote computer is online.

Answer D is correct. If the user is unable to connect to the shared folder and is receiving a message that the computer cannot be found, verify that the remote computer is online. Because the user can successfully access other shares on the network, this eliminates TCP/IP and the user's network connection as the source of the problem. Therefore, answers A and C are incorrect.

Answer B is incorrect because a permission problem would result in an `access denied` message.

Question 8

A user is not able to communicate on the network. You have verified that the network adapter installed in the user's computer is on the HCL for Windows XP. You want to check the status of the device to see whether it is functioning correctly. What should you do?

○ A. Open the properties window for the network adapter within Device Manager.

○ B. Open the Phone and Modems Option applet and use the Diagnostics tab.

○ C. Open the Command Prompt window and use the **ping** command with the loopback address.

○ D. Open the Command Prompt window and use the **ipconfig /all** command.

Answer A is correct. By opening the properties window for the network adapter within Device Manager, you can view the status of the device to determine whether it is functioning. Answers C and D are incorrect because these commands are used to diagnose TCP/IP problems. Answer B is incorrect because you use the Diagnostics tab located within the Phone and Modem Options applet to diagnose modem problems.

Question 9

You are the help desk support technician for an ISP. A user calls to report that she is unable to send email. You verify that the user can successfully receive email. However, the user also indicates that she receives a **host not found** message when attempting to send email. You also have determined that the user can successfully browse the Internet with the dial-up connection. What should you do?

○ A. Have the user **ping** the IP address of an Internet host.

○ B. Open the properties for the email account and verify the correct spelling of the username.

○ C. Open the properties for the email account and verify that the user has entered the correct name for the POP server.

○ D. Open the properties for the email account and verify the user has entered the correct name for the SMTP server.

Answer D is correct. An SMTP server is used for sending email. If the user receives a message that the host cannot be found, open the properties for the email account and verify that the user has put in the correct name of the SMTP server. Answer C is incorrect because a POP server is used for receiving mail. The user is not having a problem receiving email messages. Answer B is incorrect. If the user had an authentication problem, a different error message would appear. Answer A is incorrect because you have already established that the user can successfully browse Web pages on the Internet.

Question 10

Two hosts on your network are not able to communicate. You suspect that a problem may exist with one of the routers between the computers. What command can you use to determine which router may be causing the problem?

○ A. **ipconfig /all**

○ B. **tracert**

○ C. **ping 127.0.0.1**

○ D. **ipconfig /renew**

Answer B is correct. You can use the tracert command to trace the path a packet will take to reach a destination host. The results tell you if one of the routers is not responding. Answer A is incorrect because the ipconfig /all command enables you to view the IP configuration on a computer. Answer C is incorrect because this command enables you to test whether TCP/IP is initialized on the local computer. Answer D is incorrect because you use this command to renew an IP address obtained from a DHCP server.

Configuring and Managing Application Security

Terms you'll need to understand:

✓ NTFS permissions
✓ Access Control List (ACL)
✓ Share permissions
✓ Effective permissions
✓ Audit
✓ Macro
✓ Digital IDs (certificates)

Techniques you'll need to master:

✓ Configure NTFS and Share permissions
✓ Troubleshoot NTFS and Share permissions
✓ Configure auditing of files, folders, and printers
✓ Configure application security settings

Identifying and Troubleshooting Problems Related to Security Permissions

When you create files, you must ensure the data is secure. For example, the Accounting department certainly would not share company financial information with everyone on the network. You set resource security on files and folders within the NT File System (NTFS) by using *NTFS permissions.* You need to have a good grasp of how these permissions affect users on the network.

 You must have a thorough understanding of NTFS file and folder permissions.

Understanding NTFS File Permissions

A *permission* is a rule associated with an object to regulate which users can gain access to that object and in what manner. Permissions that can be used only on NTFS-formatted partitions or volumes are commonly called NTFS permissions.

NTFS file permissions enable you to control the access a user, group, or application has to files. This access includes everything from reading a file to modifying and executing it.

The five NTFS file permissions are listed in Table 8.1 with a description of the access allowed to a user or group when each permission is assigned. The permissions are listed in a specific order because they all build on each other.

Table 8.1 NTFS File Permissions	
NTFS File Permission	**Allowed Access**
Read	Allows a user or group to read the file and view its attributes, ownership, and assigned permissions.
Write	Allows a user or group to overwrite the file, change its attributes, view its ownership, and view the assigned permissions.
Read & Execute	Allows a user or group to run and execute the application. In addition, the user or group can perform all duties allowed by the Read permission.

Table 8.1 NTFS File Permissions *(continued)*	
NTFS File Permission	**Allowed Access**
Modify	Allows a user or group to modify and delete a file. In addition, the user or group can perform all the actions permitted by the Read, Write, and Read & Execute NTFS file permissions.
Full Control	Allows a user or group to change permissions on the folder, take ownership, and perform all activities included in all other permissions.

If a user needs access to a file to do anything except take ownership or change its permissions, you can grant the Modify permission. The access allowed by the Read, Write, and Read & Execute permissions is automatically granted within the Modify permission. Assigning it saves you from assigning multiple permissions to a file or group of files.

Understanding NTFS Folder Permissions

NTFS folder permissions determine what access is granted to a folder and the files and subfolders within that folder. These permissions can be assigned to a user or group. Table 8.2 displays a list of the NTFS folder permissions and the access granted to a user or group when each permission is applied.

Table 8.2 NTFS Folder Permissions	
NTFS Folder Permission	**Allowed Access**
Read	Allows a user or group to view the files, folders, and subfolders of the parent folder. It also allows the viewing of folder ownership, permissions, and attributes.
Write	Allows a user or group to create new files and folders within the parent folder, as well as view folder ownership and permissions and change folder attributes.
List Folder Contents	Allows a user or group to view the files and subfolders contained within the parent folder.
Read & Execute	Allows a user or group to navigate through all files and subfolders. In addition, the user or group can perform all actions allowed by the Read and List Folder Contents permissions.
Modify	Allows a user to delete the folder and perform all activities included in the Write and Read & Execute NTFS folder permissions.
Full Control	Allows a user or group to change permissions on the folder, take ownership of it, and perform all activities included in all other permissions.

The only major difference between NTFS file and folder permissions is the List Folder Contents NTFS folder permission. By using this NTFS folder permission, you can limit a user's ability to browse through a tree of folders and files. This capability is useful when trying to secure a specific directory such as an application directory. A user must know the name and location of a file to read or execute it when this permission is applied to its parent folder.

Using Access Control Lists

Windows XP stores an *Access Control List (ACL)* with every file and folder on the NTFS partition or volume. The ACL includes all the users and groups that have access to the file or folder. In addition, it indicates what access or specifically what permissions each user or group is allowed to that file or folder. Whenever a user tries to access a file or folder on an NTFS partition or volume, the ACL checks for an Access Control Entry (ACE) for that user account. The ACE indicates what permissions are allowed for that user account. The user is granted access to that file or folder, provided that the access requested is defined within the ACE. In other words, when a user wants to read a file, the Access Control Entry is checked in that file's Access Control List. If the Access Control Entry for that user contains the Read permission, the user is granted access to read that file.

 If a user does not have an entry in the ACL, she is denied access to that file or folder.

Applying Multiple NTFS Permissions

Multiple permissions can be assigned to a single user account. They can be assigned to the user account directly or to a group in which the user account is a member. When multiple permissions are assigned to a user account, unexpected things can happen.

First, you must understand that NTFS permissions are cumulative. This means that a user's *effective permissions* are the result of combining the user's assigned permissions and the permissions assigned to any groups in which the user is a member. For instance, if a user is assigned Read access to a folder, and a group in which the user account is a member has the Write permissions assigned, the user is allowed the Read and Write NTFS permissions to that folder.

NTFS file permissions override or take priority over NTFS folder permissions. A user account having access to a file can access that file even though it does not have access to the parent folder of that file. However, a user would not be able to navigate to the file through the folder. The user would require the List Folder Contents permission. When the user tries to access the file, he must supply the full path to it. The full path can be either the logical file path (**F:\MyFolder\ MyFile.txt**) or the Universal Naming Convention (UNC). If the user has access to the file but does not have an NTFS folder permission to browse for that file, the file is invisible to the user and he must supply the full path to access it.

Using Deny to Override All Other Permissions

The concept of permission denial has not changed through the evolution of the Microsoft Windows operating systems and NTFS. If a user is denied an NTFS permission for a file, any other instance in which that permission has been allowed is canceled. Microsoft does not recommend using permission denial to control access to a resource. For instance, if a user has access to a file or folder as being a member of a group, denying permission to that user stops all other permissions that the user might have to the file or folder. Troubleshooting this situation can be very hard on a large network with thousands of users and groups.

Managing Inherited Permissions

By default, when NTFS permissions are assigned to a parent folder, all the same permissions are applied or propagated to the subfolders and files of that parent folder. However, the automatic propagation of these permissions can be stopped.

Subfolders and files inherit NTFS permissions from their parent folder. As the Windows XP administrator, you assign NTFS permissions to a folder. All current subfolders and files with that folder inherit the same permissions. Any new files or subfolders created within that parent folder also assume the same NTFS permissions of that parent folder.

You can prevent NTFS permission inheritance so that any files and subfolders in a parent folder do not assume the same NTFS permissions of their parent folder. The directory or folder level on which you decide to prevent the default NTFS permission inheritance becomes the new parent folder for NTFS permission inheritance.

Planning NTFS Permissions

A Windows XP network should be well thought out and planned. Not only should you spend time planning the Active Directory and Windows domain infrastructure, but you also need to plan for NTFS permissions. You should plan the NTFS permissions in advance before implementing the Windows network.

Having a plan for NTFS permissions on your Windows network will save your organization time and money. You will also find that a network with well-planned NTFS permissions is easier to manage. Use the following guidelines to help you plan NTFS permissions on your Windows network. Notice that some steps are not directly related to NTFS permissions themselves, but they help organize the data on your network. This way, you can manage the resources on your Windows network more easily and make sure those resources are secure.

1. Assign each user only the level of access required. If a user needs only to read a file, grant only the Read permission to the resource that she requires access to. This precludes the possibility of a user damaging a file, such as modifying an important document or even deleting it.

2. When a group of users requires the same access to a resource, create a group for those users and make each a member of that new group. Assign the NTFS permissions required to that resource to the group. If at all possible, avoid assigning NTFS permissions to users and assign them only to groups.

3. When assigning permissions to folders with working data, use the Read & Execute NTFS folder permission. You should assign it to a group containing the users who need to access this folder and to the Administrators group. This way, you allow the users to work with the data but also prevent them from deleting any important files in the folder.

4. When assigning NTFS permissions to a public data folder, use the following criteria as guidelines:

   ➤ Assign the Read & Execute and Write NTFS permissions to the group containing the users who need access to the public data folder.

   ➤ Assign the Full Control NTFS permission to the *Creator Owner* of the folder. Any user on the network who creates a file, including one in a public data folder, is by default the Creator Owner of that file.

   ➤ After that file has been created, the Windows administrator can grant NTFS permissions to other users for file ownership.

➤ If the Read & Execute and Write NTFS permissions are assigned to a group of users who need access to the public data folder, they have Full Control to all files that they create in the public data folder and can modify and execute files created by other users.

5. Try to avoid using the Deny NTFS permission. Using this permission to manage resources on a Windows network is not recommended because NTFS permissions assigned for that resource elsewhere for the user or group are automatically canceled. This can cost a great deal of time and cause a great deal of frustration when you are troubleshooting permission problems.

Working with NTFS Permissions

After a newly created volume is formatted with the NTFS 5.0 file system in Windows XP, by default the Full Control NTFS permission is granted to the Administrator. The Users group is assigned the following permissions:

➤ Read and Execute

➤ List Folder Contents

➤ Read

You can change the permissions to meet your requirements by using the Security tab from the folder's or file's Properties dialog box.

 If the Security tab is not visible, your system is probably configured to use simple file sharing. To enable the Security tab, open the Folder Options dialog box from the Tools menu in the My Computer window. On the View tab, remove the check mark from the Use Simple File Sharing (Recommended) option.

To access permissions, follow these steps:

1. Right-click the Start button and select Explore from the pop-up menu. The Windows Explorer opens.

2. Click the plus sign to the left of an NTFS volume that you would like to view.

3. Find a folder and right-click it.

4. Select Properties from the pop-up menu.

5. Select the Security tab. Figure 8.1 displays the Security tab of the Documents and Settings Properties dialog box.

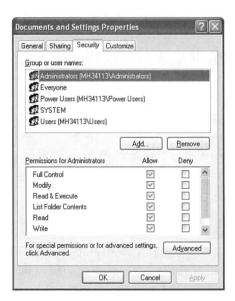

Figure 8.1 Security tab with assigned permissions.

The Security tab displays the permissions currently assigned to the selected user or group. Table 8.3 lists the options available on the Security tab and describes briefly what they are used for.

Table 8.3 Security Tab Options	
Option	**Description**
Group or user names	Displays a list of users who currently have access to the selected resource. You can highlight an object in the list and either change that object's current NTFS permission or select Remove to remove it from the list.
Permissions	Contains a list of all the NTFS permissions. To allow or deny an NTFS permission to the user or group selected in the Names list box, click the appropriate check box.
Add	Opens the Select Users, Computers, or Groups dialog box. There, you can select which users or groups to add to the Names list box.
Remove	Enables you to remove users or groups from the Names list box. To do so, you select a user or group and then click Remove.

Clicking the Advanced command button near the bottom of the Security tab displays the Advanced Security Settings dialog box, which you use to assign special access permissions. Here, you can also find the check box to allow inheritable permissions from the parent to propagate to this object, as discussed earlier. By default, when a folder is created on an NTFS volume, this option is set. To turn it off, clear the check box on the Permissions tab. Figure 8.2 displays the message box displayed when you clear this option. If you click Remove, the permissions that were inherited from the parent folder are removed. Conversely, clicking the Copy button copies the permissions assigned to the parent folder.

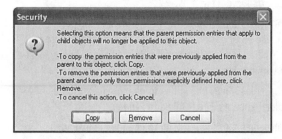

Figure 8.2   Clearing inheritable permissions.

Using Special Access Permissions

NTFS file and folder permissions provide a great way to secure your resources on a Windows network. Special access permissions can be used if the default selections do not give you the required results.

The 14 special access permissions provide the specific level of security to resources on a Windows network that some administrators require. Table 8.4 lists the special access permissions and provides a description of the type of access they allow or deny.

Table 8.4 Special Access Permissions	
Permission	**Description**
Full Control	Allows a user or group to change permissions on a folder, take ownership of it, and perform all activities included in all other permissions.
Traverse Folder/ Execute File	Allows or denies a user to browse through a folder's subfolders and files where he would otherwise not have access. It also allows or denies the user the ability to run programs within that folder.
List Folder/Read Data	Allows or denies a user to view subfolders and filenames in the parent folder. It also allows or denies the user to view the data within the files in the parent folder or subfolders of that parent.
Read Attributes	Allows or denies a user to view the standard NTFS attributes of a file or folder.

Table 8.4 Special Access Permissions *(continued)*	
Permission	**Description**
Read Extended Attributes	Allows or denies a user to view the extended attributes of a file or folder, which can vary because they are defined by the programs themselves.
Create Files/ Write Data	Allows or denies a user the right to create new files in the parent folder. In addition, it allows or denies the user to modify or overwrite existing data in a file.
Create Folders/ Append Data	Allows or denies a user to create new folders in the parent folder. It also allows or denies the user the right to add data to the end of files. This does not include making changes to any existing data within a file.
Write Attributes	Allows or denies a user the ability to change the attributes of a file or folder, such as Read-Only and Hidden.
Write Extended Attributes	Allows or denies a user the ability to change the extended attributes of a file or folder. These attributes are defined by programs and may vary.
Delete Subfolders and Files	Allows or denies a user to delete files and subfolders within the parent folder. The user can delete files and subfolders even if the Delete special access permission has not been granted.
Delete	Allows or denies a user to delete files and folders.
Read Permissions	Allows or denies a user the ability to read the standard NTFS permissions of a file or folder.
Change Permissions	Allows or denies a user the ability to change the standard NTFS permissions of a file or folder.
Take Ownership	Allows or denies a user the ability to take ownership of a file or folder. The owner of a file or folder can change the permissions on the files and folders she owns, regardless of any other permission that might be in place.

It is important to understand how the special access permissions are related to the standard NTFS file permissions. Table 8.5 displays a cross-reference chart of NTFS permissions and special access permissions. Notice that each standard NTFS file permission is actually a group made up of special access permissions. For example, the Write NTFS permission is made up of four special access permissions. The Write NTFS permission is actually made up of the Create Files/Write Data, Create Folders/Append Data, Write Attributes, and Write Extended Attributes special access permissions.

Having these reference tables will be helpful when you decide which special access permissions to use in your organization.

Table 8.5   Special Access Permissions and NTFS Permissions

	Read	Write	List Folder Contents	Read & Execute	Modify	Full Control
Traverse Folder/ Execute File			X	X	X	X
List Folder/ Read Data	X		X	X	X	X
Read Attributes	X		X	X	X	X
Read Extended Attributes	X		X	X	X	X
Create Files/ Write Data		X			X	X
Create Folders/ Append Data		X			X	X
Write Attributes		X			X	X
Write Extended Attributes		X			X	X
Delete Subfolders & Files						X
Delete					X	X
Read Permissions	X		X	X	X	X
Change Permissions						X
Take Ownership						X

Using Change Permissions and Take Ownership Permissions

Two special access permissions are worth special mention: *Change Permissions* and *Take Ownership*.

When using special access permissions, you no longer need to assign users or Windows administrators the Full Control NTFS permission so that they are allowed to change permissions. Using the Change Permissions special access permission, users or Windows administrators can change permissions to a file or folder. However, they do not have access to delete any files or subfolders. That way, the users or Windows administrators can control the access to the data but not delete any of the data itself.

All files and folders on an NTFS volume have an owner. By default, the owner is the person installing the volume and formatting it with the NTFS file system. This person is usually a Windows administrator. File and folder ownership can be transferred to another user or group. You can grant a user account or a user group the ability to take ownership of a file or folder. As an administrator, you have the ability to take control of any files or folders on the NTFS volume.

Two hard-and-fast rules apply here. Remember these rules when thinking about granting someone the ability to take ownership of a file or folder:

1. The owner of a file or folder or any user with the Full Control NTFS permission to a file or folder can assign the Full Control standard NTFS permission or the Take Ownership special access permission, which allows taking control of that file or folder. For instance, if User A has the Full Control standard NTFS permission to D:\Apps and assigns the Take Ownership special access permission to User B, User B can now take ownership of any files or folders in D:\Apps.

2. Windows administrators can take ownership of a file or folder at any time. This is one of their inherited rights. Administrators can then assign the Take Ownership special access permission to another user or group so that they can take control of the files and folders in a parent folder. For instance, if User A leaves the organization for another position, a Windows administrator can assign the Take Ownership special access permission to the former employee's manager for the former employee's files and folders. The manager can then take ownership of those files and folders.

 You can assign the Take Ownership special access permission to a user account or group. The receiving user account or group can then take ownership of the respected resources. However, it cannot assign ownership to a file or folder for a user account or group.

Assigning Special Access Permissions

Special access permissions provide a specific level of security other than the standard NTFS permissions. It is important that you understand how each special permission affects the user.

To set special access permissions to a folder, follow these steps:

1. Right-click the Start button and select Explore. The Windows Explorer opens.

2. Click the plus sign to the left of an NTFS volume that you would like to view.

3. Locate a folder that requires changes. Right-click the folder and select Properties.

4. Select the Security tab.

5. Click the Advanced button to view the Advanced Security Settings dialog box, as shown in Figure 8.3.

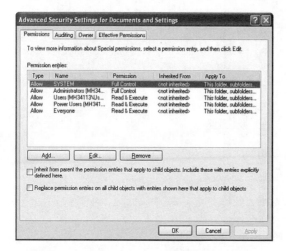

Figure 8.3 Advanced Security Settings dialog box.

6. Click the Add button to open the Select User or Group dialog box, as shown in Figure 8.4.

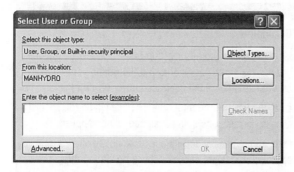

Figure 8.4 Select User or Group dialog box.

7. Select an object and click the Advanced button to modify the special permissions.

8. In the Advanced Security Settings dialog box, select the permission entry you want to modify and click the Edit button, as shown in Figure 8.5.

Figure 8.5 Permission Entry dialog box.

The special access permissions are listed in the Permissions list box of the Permission Entry dialog box. All special access permissions are assigned and denied here. Table 8.6 lists the options and their descriptions.

Table 8.6 NTFS File Permissions	
Permission	**Description**
Name	Lists the user account or group name affected by the special access permissions. Clicking the Change command button can change the user account or group affected.
Apply Onto	Lists the level of the folder hierarchy at which the special access permissions being assigned will be applied.
Permissions	Lists all the special access permissions. To allow a special access permission, click the check box in the Allow column to the right of the permission. Alternatively, to deny a special access permission, click the check box in the Deny column to the right of the special access permission.
Apply These Permissions to Objects Within This Container Only	Allows or denies permission inheritance for the parent folder. To allow permission inheritance for the special access permissions being assigned, select this check box; otherwise, clear it.
Clear All	Clears all the check boxes in the Allow and Deny columns in the Permissions list box.

Taking Ownership of Secure Resources

A Windows administrator working with NTFS file and folder permissions should know how to take ownership of a resource. The Take Ownership special access permission allows users to claim ownership of files and folders.

To take control of a file or folder, the user or group member must have the Take Ownership permission assigned for that file or folder. Then the user or group member must explicitly take ownership of that file or folder. You follow these steps to take ownership:

1. Right-click the Start button and select Explore. The Windows Explorer opens.

2. Click the plus sign to the left of an NTFS volume that you would like to view.

3. Locate the folder that requires changes. Right-click the folder and select Properties.

4. Select the Security tab.

5. Click the Advanced button to view the Advanced Security Settings dialog box.

6. Select the Owner tab to view the current owner of the folder or file.

7. Select your name in the Change Owner To list box.

8. Check the Replace Owners on Sub Containers and Objects check box and click OK.

Copying and Moving Data

When files and folders on an NTFS volume are copied to another volume, the permissions change. For instance, if you copy a file from one NTFS volume to another NTFS volume, the following changes occur if the right criteria are met:

➤ The receiving NTFS volume treats the file as a new file. Like any new file, it gains the permissions of the folder it is created in.

➤ The user account used to copy the file must have the Write NTFS permission in the destination folder on the receiving volume.

➤ The user account used to copy the file becomes the Creator Owner of that file.

Essentially, any permissions assigned to that file before it is copied are lost during the copy itself. If you want to keep those same permissions, they must be reassigned to the destination folder.

When files and folders are copied from an NTFS volume to a FAT partition, the permissions are lost. This happens because FAT partitions do not support NTFS permissions.

When files or folders are moved from an NTFS volume, the permissions might or might not change. This depends entirely on where the destination folder lies. If any files or folders are moved to a FAT partition, the permissions are lost. As stated earlier, a FAT partition does not support NTFS permissions. However, you need to consider other scenarios when moving files and folders from an NTFS volume: moving files and folders within an NTFS volume and moving files and folders to another NTFS volume.

When files and folders are moved within a single NTFS volume, these rules are followed:

1. The files and folders keep the original permissions assigned to them.

2. The user account moving the files and folders must have the Write NTFS permission to the destination folder.

3. The user account moving the file must have either the Modify standard NTFS permission or the Delete special access permission assigned. The reason is that during a file or folder move, the files and folders are deleted from the source directory after they have been copied to the destination folder.

4. The user account used to move the files and folders becomes the Creator Owner of those files and folders.

When files and folders are moved from one NTFS volume to another NTFS volume, these rules are followed:

1. The files and folders being moved inherit the permissions of the destination folder.

2. The user account moving the files and folders must have the Write NTFS permission to the destination folder because a move is really a combination copy/delete.

3. The user account moving the file must have either the Modify standard NTFS permission or the Delete special access permission assigned. The reason is that during a file or folder move, the files and folders are deleted from the source directory after they have been copied to the destination folder.

4. The user account used to move the files and folders becomes the Creator Owner of those files and folders.

Troubleshooting Insufficient User Permissions and Rights

Avoiding permission problems is the first step in troubleshooting permission problems. These preventive measures involve following some basic guidelines:

➤ When assigning NTFS permissions, try to assign only enough access for a user or group of users to perform their job.

➤ Try not to assign any NTFS permissions at the file level. Doing so increases the complexity of managing the permissions. Assign the NTFS permissions at the folder level only. If several files require the same access, move them to a common folder and assign the permissions to that folder.

➤ Application executables should have Read & Execute and Change assigned to the Administrators group. The Users group, on the other hand, should have only Read & Execute. Setting permissions this way prevents users or a virus from modifying the files. When an administrator wants to update the application executables, she can temporarily assign herself Full Control to perform the task.

➤ Assign Full Control to the Creator Owner of public folders and the Read and Write NTFS permissions to the Everyone group. This way, users have full access to the files they create, but members of the Everyone group can only read and create files in the folder.

➤ Try not to deny any NTFS permissions. If you have to do this to a user or group, document it well and state that this is a special case. Instead of denying access to a resource by denying NTFS permissions, don't assign the permissions to gain access.

To help troubleshoot some of the more common NTFS permission problems, Table 8.7 lists the most common problems and solutions.

Table 8.7 Common NTFS Permissions Problems and Solutions	
Problem	**Solution**
A user or group cannot access a file or folder.	Check the permissions assigned to the user or group. Permissions may not be assigned for the selected resource, or permission could be denied. In addition, the permissions could have been changed if the file or folder has been copied or moved.
The administrator assigns access to a group for a selected file or folder, but a user of that group still cannot access the file or folder.	Ask the user to log off and then log back on. When the user logs back on, her NTFS permissions are updated to include the new group that she was added to. Another way to update a user's permissions is to ask her to disconnect the network drive on which the file or folder resides and then reconnect it. This forces the permissions to update on the reconnect of the network drive.
A user with Full Control to files has deleted some files in a folder, and you want to prevent him from doing it again.	Open the Permission Entry dialog box (refer to Figure 8.5) for that folder and remove the Delete Subfolders and Files special access permission for that user.

Determining Effective NTFS Permissions

One of the new features with Windows XP is the ability to view the *effective permissions* on an object for a particular user. Windows XP calculates the net result permissions by looking at all user and group memberships, along with any inherited permissions. This feature allows you to troubleshoot permission problems much faster than previous versions of Windows.

There is one caveat with the effective permissions feature: It calculates the resulting general permissions for a given user, but those permissions may not be exactly correct. What's the scoop? The addition of Implicit Groups can wreak havoc because permissions can be assigned based on group membership that changes depending on how the data is accessed: local to the server, over the network, via a Terminal Server client, and so on. The effective permissions feature takes this into account to the best of its ability, but you should be aware that the connection method may be a contributing factor.

Microsoft has buried the effective permissions feature within a file or folder's Security Properties. To access the Effective Permissions tab, right-click the file, select Properties, and select the Security tab. Click the Advanced button and then click the Effective Permissions tab. From there, you need to select a user or user group, and the resultant special permissions are displayed with a check mark in the box.

Managing Share Permissions

Sharing data is the primary purpose of configuring a company network. The process of enabling shared data is to specifically flag the data as shared. Data access is granted or denied based on a combined set of shared permissions and NTFS permissions.

You create a share by right-clicking the folder and selecting Sharing and Security from the pop-up menu. A Properties dialog box opens, with the Sharing tab in focus. You can also access the Sharing tab by right-clicking the folder, selecting Properties, and then clicking this tab.

Share permissions haven't changed with the times. Although it might be easier for you if the Share permissions were the same as NTFS permissions, this is not the case. Unfortunately, they do use some of the same names, which just serves to confuse the issue:

➤ Full Control allows users to create, delete, modify, and grant Share permissions.

➤ Read allows users to read the contents of a folder but not modify any contents. Users cannot create files either.

➤ Change allows users to create, delete, and modify the contents of a folder. This includes creating documents and subfolders.

When you are first learning about NTFS permissions, confusing Share permissions and NTFS permissions is easy; the result causes a jumble of permissions that not only are impossible to track and document, but also frequently leave security holes wide open.

One hole in particular deals with the Guest account. Anonymous users who don't have a local or domain account on the server are automatically converted to the Guest account and allowed access to any resources the Guest account can access. The solution is to disable the Guest account and create specialized accounts for any real guests who need access to network data. Another solution is to rely on NTFS permissions to stop any transgressions from occurring.

Combining NTFS and Share Permissions

When you mix NTFS permissions with Share permissions, the most restrictive permission between the two rules wins. In other words, if permissions are stacked with the most restrictive on the bottom and the least restrictive on top, the one at the bottom of the stack is the permission you live by.

To determine a user's effective permissions, you start by reviewing the user's NTFS permissions as well as Share permissions. If the user belongs to multiple groups, you need to determine the least restrictive NTFS permissions and the least restrictive Share permissions in effect. After you determine the least restrictive NTFS permission and the least restrictive Share permission, you need to determine which permission is the most restrictive between them. The most restrictive permission is the permission in effect.

When you are dealing with multiple group memberships, you can easily understand why someone may become confused. Consider this: Multiple NTFS permissions are cumulative. They stack up on each other, with the most restrictive on the bottom and the least restrictive on top. The highest permission wins. Share permissions are also cumulative, so you must determine the least restrictive Share permission. When you mix NTFS permissions with Share permissions, the most restrictive permission between the two rules wins. In other words, the one at the bottom of the stack is the permission that is in effect.

Managing Hidden Shares

By default, without your ever touching the system, some shares are configured for you. These shares are called *administrative shares*. For example, shares are automatically created for every drive installed on the system. These shares are called *hidden shares* because they do not show up on a list of shares when you type \\SERVERNAME, the UNC name for the computer. If you look at the share name for a drive on the system, you'll notice that a $ symbol appears after the share name. This symbol indicates that the share is hidden and can be used to hide any share on the system.

The hidden shares can help you gain access to a user's computer if he does not know how to set up a share. It is a great way to transfer files if the user is not familiar with creating his own shared folder.

Sharing Printers

To share a printer, open the Printers and Faxes folder on the computer connected to the printer by following these steps:

1. Click Start and then click Control Panel.

If you are using the Classic Start menu, you need to click the Start button, select Settings, and click Control Panel.

2. Double-click Printers and Faxes.

3. In the Printers and Faxes folder, click the printer's icon and, in the Tasks pane, click Share This Printer. The Printer's Property dialog box is displayed with the Sharing tab in view.

4. Click the Share This Printer option and type the share name for the printer.

5. Click OK.

Auditing User Access of Files, Folders, and Printers

As an administrator of a Windows XP Professional computer, you can configure your computer to *audit* user access to files, folders, and printers. The audit log appears in the security log in Event Viewer. To enable this feature, follow these steps:

1. Click Start, click Control Panel, and double-click Administrative Tools.

If you are using the Classic Start menu, you need to click the Start button, select Settings, and click Control Panel.

2. Open the Local Security Policy.

3. In the left pane, double-click Local Policies to expand it.

4. In the left pane, click Audit Policy to display the individual policy settings in the right pane.

5. Double-click Audit Object Access.

6. To audit successful access of specified files, folders, and printers, select the Success check box.

7. To audit unsuccessful access to these objects, select the Failure check box.

8. To enable auditing of both, select both check boxes.

9. Click OK.

Specifying Files, Folders, and Printers to Audit

After you enable auditing, you can specify the files, folders, and printers that you want audited. To do so, follow these steps:

1. In Windows Explorer, locate the file or folder you want to audit. To audit a printer, locate it by first clicking Start and then clicking Printers and Faxes.

2. Right-click the file, folder, or printer that you want to audit and then click Properties.

3. Click the Security tab and then click Advanced.

4. Click the Auditing tab and then click Add.

5. In the Enter the Object Name to Select box, type the name of the user or group whose access you want to audit. You can browse the computer for names by clicking Advanced and then clicking Find Now in the Select User or Group dialog box.

6. Click OK.

7. Select the Successful or Failed check boxes for the actions you want to audit.

8. Click OK three times to close the open dialog boxes.

Troubleshooting Auditing

Two requirements must be met for auditing to function properly. When troubleshooting, be sure to verify these items first so you can rule them out immediately:

➤ The hard disk must be formatted with the NTFS file system for auditing to work.

➤ If your computer is a member of a domain and the administrator has set domain-level auditing policies, those policies override these local settings.

Managing Application Security Settings

Microsoft Office has several built-in security features designed to ensure the safety of files used within its programs. Each application within the Office Suite contains configuration options to set its security.

You must have a thorough understanding of the security features within Microsoft Office applications.

Managing Security Settings for Office Applications

You can access the security features from the Options dialog box opened through the Tools menu. The Security tab of this dialog box is separated into the following areas:

➤ File Encryption Options for This Document

➤ File Sharing Options for This Document

➤ Privacy Options

➤ Macro Security

Figure 8.6 displays the Security tab located in Microsoft Word.

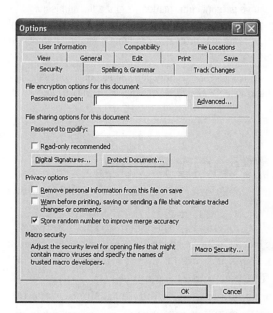

Figure 8.6 The Security tab of the Options dialog box in Word.

The Security tabs are similar for Word, Excel, and PowerPoint. Outlook also has a Security tab; however, the available options are customized to specifically modify email security settings. On the other hand, Access does not have a Security tab in its Options dialog box, but it has its own User and Group Accounts security to determine user-level security for individual databases.

The security options are summarized in Table 8.8.

Table 8.8	Security Settings
Options	**Description**
File encryption	Sets or checks the file encryption for the current document. The Password to Open text box sets the password to view the document. The Advanced button allows you to choose which type of encryption to use.
File sharing	Sets the password for users who will be able to modify the document. You can also set the document to recommend read-only when it is opened. The modify password is not required to use the read-only feature. The Digital Signatures button allows you to add or remove digital signatures. The Protect Document button protects the document for tracked changes, comments, or forms.
Privacy Options	Enable you to remove personal information from the file and issue warnings before printing, sending, or saving documents that contain tracked changes or comments. You also can store a random number to improve merge accuracy.
Macro Security	Allows you to set which level of security you will use on your system for files that contain Visual Basic for Applications (VBA) code and macros.

Configuring Macro Security Settings

In regards to Basic Word, Excel, and PowerPoint, *macro* is a general term that also implies ActiveX controls, COM objects, OLE objects, and any executable that can be attached to a document, worksheet, or email message. However, when you use the term with respect to Outlook, Microsoft Publisher, and Microsoft FrontPage, it is used only for a macro written in Visual Basic for Applications. The macro itself is a mini-program that automates a procedure. It could be as simple as selecting a predefined range in Excel and printing that range or as complex as required.

You can configure macro security using one of three settings: High, Medium, or Low. Figure 8.7 displays the Security dialog box, and Table 8.9 summarizes the security levels available and the result of each configuration.

Figure 8.7   Security dialog box.

Table 8.9	Security Settings
Options	**Description**
High	Allows only signed macros from trusted sources to run.
Medium	Allows the user to choose whether the macro can be executed.
Low	Allows the user to execute all macros without the warning. This setting is not recommended.

Depending on the security configuration, opening a file that contains a macro produces different results. For example, the Medium setting prompts the user to either enable or disable the macros. Figure 8.8 displays the warning message that appears when a file containing a macro is opened.

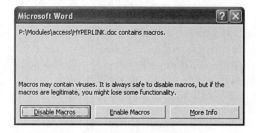

Figure 8.8   Warning message that the macro may contain viruses.

The warning message allows the user to either enable or disable the embedded macros. To avoid this message, you must set the security level to Low.

This message may be annoying to users, but it is to their advantage to endure the pain. The Low security setting does not present the prompt to users, and macros are allowed to run. Any certificates attached to macros run under Low security are not posted to the trusted source list for Office applications. Only when security is set to Medium or High and a user agrees to trust a certificate is a certificate added to Office's trusted source list. This list of security settings does not present the Low security option because Low security is the same for all cases.

After the macro security settings are configured, they are applied to all applications in the Microsoft Office Suite. Even though macro security is the same among these applications, you must consider how each security setting affects associated features in an application. For example, disabling an ActiveX control in Outlook or Excel may limit functionality in each application to different degrees that are acceptable or unacceptable for users.

Macro security is determined by the certificate associated with an application's data file or email message. Attaching a certificate of authenticity to a file requires the user to obtain a certificate from a certificate authority (CA) such as VeriSign. You can contact VeriSign at `http://www.verisign.com`.

Under all security-setting levels, if an antivirus service compatible with the Microsoft XP antivirus API is installed, and you open a document that contains macros, the antivirus service scans the document for known viruses.

You can use two types of antivirus services with Office. The first type reviews the file as it arrives either from a disk or from over the network; the second type reviews the file each time an application opens it. An antivirus service compatible with the Office antivirus API examines the file when the application opens it.

If a virus is found, the user is notified prior to the file being activated, and a message is displayed in the work area of the application. Virus services compatible with the Office antivirus API and installed on the computer are noted at the bottom of the application's Security dialog box. If the computer does not have an antivirus service compatible with the API, the `No virus scanner installed` message appears at the bottom of the Security dialog box, as shown in Figure 8.9.

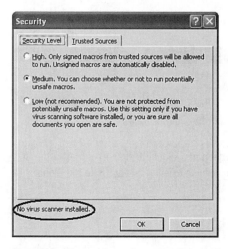

Figure 8.9   The antivirus software installation indicator on the Security dialog box.

Configuring Outlook Security Settings

The Security tab in Outlook's Options dialog box is significantly different from the Security tabs in other programs in the Office Suite, as you can see in Figure 8.10.

Figure 8.10   Outlook's Security tab.

Table 8.10 summarizes the features found in Outlook's Security tab.

Table 8.10 Outlook Security Settings	
Options	**Description**
Secure Email	Allows a user to configure incoming and outgoing messages
Secure Content	Allows a user to set the security zone when viewing HTML messages
Digital IDs (Certificates)	Allows a user to get a new digital ID, import and export existing *digital IDs,* or publish existing digital IDs to the Global Address List (GAL)

Exam Prep Questions

Question 1

A user has indicated that she used to have a shortcut on her desktop to a database called SAMI. The database is located on the company shared drive at the following location: **\\mobilebugs\SharedDocs\Databases\SAMI.mdb**. The user has tried to navigate to the database but receives the error message shown in the following figure. What is the problem?

○ A. The user has been denied access to the database.

○ B. The user does not have the List Folders special access permission.

○ C. The database has been moved to a new file location.

○ D. The user does not have Read access to the database file.

Answer B is correct. The user was able to open the database from her shortcut but cannot browse to the database file. Answer A is incorrect because the user was able to open the database from the shortcut on her desktop. Answer C is incorrect because there is no indication that the database file was moved. Answer D is incorrect because the user is able to open the file from the shortcut on her desktop.

Question 2

A user has been granted the NTFS Modify permission to a folder called Corporate Data. The same user also has Read permission assigned using Share permissions. When the user accesses the file locally from the Corporate Data folder, he can save changes to files within the folder; however, when he opens files across the network, they are read only. What is the problem?

○ A. The effective permissions are Read.

○ B. The effective permissions are Write.

○ C. The NTFS permissions have not propagated to subfolders.

○ D. The Share permissions are not applied when accessed locally.

Answer A is correct. When a user has a combination of NTFS and Share permissions, the most restrictive permission is applied. The most restrictive permission is Read; therefore, the user cannot save changes to any files within the Corporate Data folder. Answer B is incorrect because the effective permission is the most restrictive, Read. Answer C is incorrect because the NTFS permissions not being propagated to subfolders is not an issue in this situation. Answer D is incorrect because the Share permission is Read.

Question 3

A user indicates that she can create and modify documents in a parent folder named Corporate Data; however, in the subfolder named Accounting, she cannot create new files. Why is this problem occurring?

- ○ A. Automatic propagation has been stopped.
- ○ B. The user has been denied access to the Accounting subfolder.
- ○ C. The user has only the Read permission.
- ○ D. The user has Modify permission but has been denied the Create New Files permission.

Answer A is correct. The parent folder Corporate Data has not propagated the permissions to the child folders. Answer B is incorrect because the user is able to view the contents of the Accounting folder. Answers C and D are incorrect because the user has Modify permission in the parent folder.

Question 4

You have three files in a folder named Marketing to which you want to restrict access from the users in the Users group. What can you do to restrict access to these files but allow the Users group to still read the other files in the Marketing folder?

- ○ A. Deny access to the three files at the file level.
- ○ B. Move the files into their own folder and do not grant the Users group access to the folder.
- ○ C. Deny access to the Marketing folder.
- ○ D. Add the Users group to the Deny policy.

Answer B is correct. You should avoid using the Deny option to assist in troubleshooting permissions problems. Applying permissions at the file level also is not recommended. Answer A is incorrect because you should avoid using Deny, especially at the file level. Answer C is also incorrect because you should avoid using Deny. Answer D is incorrect because there is not a Deny policy.

Question 5

You suspect a user is accessing a folder that he should be prevented from accessing. This might mean that the permissions need to be modified. You first need to verify that the user is accessing this folder. How can you do this?

○ A. NTFS file activity logging

○ B. Event auditing

○ C. Event Viewer

○ D. Account lockout

Answer B is correct. Event auditing tracks the activity on the folder and the users who access the folder. Answer A is incorrect because NTFS file activity logging is a feature used to verify who accesses the folder when it is enabled. Answer C is incorrect because the Event Viewer is used to view the security log created by the auditing system but is not the feature that does the actual tracking. Answer D is incorrect because account lockout is used to prevent compromised accounts from being used.

Question 6

Which of the following is not a folder or file standard permission?

○ A. Read

○ B. List

○ C. Create Folder

○ D. Write

Answer C is correct. Create Folder is not a permission. Answers A, B, and D are valid file or folder permissions.

Question 7

A user indicates that she opened a document containing macros from an untrusted source but did not receive a macro warning. She is also able to execute the macro without any problems. What is her current macro security setting?

- ○ A. Low
- ○ B. Medium
- ○ C. High
- ○ D. Restricted

Answer A is correct. When a file from an untrusted source is received without a warning message indicating the file has macros, the security setting is Low. Answer B is incorrect because the Medium setting warns the user if the file contains macros from an untrusted source. Answer C is incorrect because the file would open, but the macros would be disabled. Answer D is incorrect because this option does not exist.

Question 8

A user has a Windows 98 system with several shared folders. He set up each shared folder with Read access. However, since he set up the shares, several files have been deleted. What happened?

- ○ A. The NTFS permissions allowed users to delete the files.
- ○ B. Another user accessed the system locally and deleted the files.
- ○ C. The files were moved to a subfolder.
- ○ D. The folder has the Delete special access permission.

Answer B is correct. A user would need to have local access to the files to delete them. The Share permissions do not apply when accessing the files locally. Answers A and D are incorrect because the user cannot have NTFS permissions on a Windows 98 system. Answer C is incorrect because there is no indication that the files have been moved.

Question 9

A user has requested that a file available on the company network should prompt her to see whether she wants to read the file or open it to modify its contents. What feature needs to be enabled?

- ○ A. Set the open password.
- ○ B. Set the modify password.
- ○ C. Check the Read-Only Recommended check box.
- ○ D. Protect the document.

Answer C is correct. Any user who opens the file is prompted to open the file as read-only. If she refuses, the file still opens for modifications without a password. Answers A and B are incorrect because they only restrict access to the file. Answer D is incorrect because it prevents the file from being modified.

Question 10

How can the NTFS permission settings of a file be changed, altered, or modified? Select two correct answers.

- ❑ A. Delete the file.
- ❑ B. Move the file to a new partition.
- ❑ C. Use the Security tab on the Properties dialog box.
- ❑ D. Take ownership of the file.

Answers B and C are correct. When a file is moved to a new NTFS partition, it inherits the NTFS permissions of the destination folder; therefore, answer B is correct. Answer C is correct because using the Permissions button on the Security tab is the most common method to modify the NTFS permissions. Answer A is incorrect because the file permissions are not modified, but the file is removed. Answer D is incorrect because taking ownership of a file does not alter the permissions on a file.

Identifying and Responding to Security Incidents

Terms you'll need to understand:

✓ Virus
✓ Trojan horse
✓ Critical update
✓ Antivirus software
✓ Microsoft Baseline Security Analyzer
✓ Worm
✓ Automatic Updates
✓ Windows Update

Techniques you'll need to master:

✓ Identify different types of security attacks
✓ Respond to security attacks
✓ Protect against viruses
✓ Identify critical updates for Windows XP and Office applications
✓ Apply critical updates to a computer
✓ Configure Automatic Updates
✓ Use Microsoft Baseline Security Analyzer

Identifying and Responding to Security Events

As a desktop support technician, you must be ready to identify and respond to security events. One of the most common types of security events you will encounter is a virus attack. Although some viruses cause little harm, some can bring down an entire system or network. In any case, you should be able to identify the signs that a computer has been infected by a virus, the steps to take in removing a virus, and ways to protect a computer or network from such attacks. These topics are discussed in the following sections.

Identifying Attacks

Unfortunately, viruses come in many different forms, with some being more harmful than others. New viruses are introduced daily. It is impossible to know everything about every virus. However, knowing the different categories of viruses and the ways they affect a computer can alert you to the signs that a computer may be infected with one. The three general categories of viruses are

➤ Worms

➤ Viruses

➤ Trojan horses

Worms

A *worm* is a form of malicious software that makes copies of itself. For example, after the worm is received, it can copy itself from one hard drive to another or spread by attaching itself to email. One of the most common ways of acquiring and spreading a worm is through email attachments. However, with the growing popularity of Internet chat programs, they also are becoming a medium of transferring a worm to other computers. Worms are often referred to as viruses, which are discussed in the next section.

 A worm tends to consume resources. If you see a sudden decrease in computer or network performance, this change could be an indication that the computer or network has been infected with a worm. Worms are also known to delete data.

An example of a worm is W32/KLEZ. This worm was able to replicate itself to network shares, thereby affecting other computers on the network. It also mailed itself to email addresses within the Windows Address Book and other addresses extracted from the user's computer.

Viruses

A *virus* is a program or malicious code that secretly replicates itself by attaching to a medium such as another program, the boot sector, a partition sector, or a document that contains macros.

 Many viruses today are macro viruses. A macro is a piece of code that can be embedded into a document such as an Excel document. A macro virus therefore exists as a macro in a data file.

Trojan Horses

Unlike a virus or worm, a *Trojan horse* does not replicate nor make copies of itself. The main purpose of a Trojan horse is to compromise security such as stealing passwords. The Trojan horse tricks users into believing they are doing one thing when, in fact, they are doing something else.

To a user, a Trojan horse is difficult to identify because it may seem to be a legitimate program. However, the program may contain a hidden function designed to compromise security. For example, a user may receive email with a Trojan horse as an attachment. When the user runs what appears to be a legitimate program, a hidden function may steal passwords stored on the computer and email them to another recipient.

A Trojan horse does not cause any harm until the user runs the required program. After the program is run, code is usually added to the computer's startup functions so the virus is loaded each time the computer is restarted.

An example of a Trojan horse virus is BackOrifice. This Trojan horse allowed remote users to connect to a computer with the virus and have complete control over the computer.

Identifying Ways Viruses Affect a Computer

Now that you have a general idea of the different types of viruses, let's look at the ways a virus can affect a computer. Again, knowing the signs to look for can make it much simpler to identify when a computer has acquired a virus.

You may encounter these common signs that a computer is infected with a computer virus:

➤ Applications do not function properly.

➤ You cannot access your hard drive.

➤ New icons appear on the desktop.

➤ Unusual error messages appear.

➤ Unusual sounds unexpectedly come from your speakers.

➤ You experience a decrease in performance.

➤ Your computer has an unusually high level of disk drive activity.

➤ Data is missing.

➤ Your antivirus software is disabled and cannot be restarted.

 Some virus symptoms may resemble symptoms produced by Windows—for example, if you attempt to start Windows but receive an error message that a critical system file is missing. Therefore, some viruses may be more difficult to detect than others.

Protecting Against Virus Attacks

Some viruses cause little damage or no damage at all. However, other viruses can cause serious damage, such as formatting your hard drive, resulting in a loss of data. Therefore, protecting against such attacks is extremely important. You can take a number of different steps to secure your computer against virus attacks:

➤ Install antivirus software.

➤ Keep signature files up to date.

➤ Educate users about viruses.

➤ Use an Internet firewall.

➤ Install the latest critical updates.

➤ Use Security features in Outlook Express.

 Microsoft recommends the following three steps to secure a computer and protect it from virus attacks: use an Internet firewall, keep your computer up to date with the latest critical updates, and use up-to-date antivirus software.

Antivirus Software

One of the most important measures you can take to prevent viruses from infecting your computer is to install *antivirus software*.

Antivirus software is a program designed specifically to detect and remove viruses. Two of the most popular programs are Norton Antivirus and McAfee Virusscan. After you install antivirus software, it scans your computer and deletes any viruses it finds.

Because new viruses are constantly being created, the makers of antivirus software have to constantly update their database with new fixes for detecting and removing them. So, installing antivirus software does not necessarily mean your system is secure. You have to make sure you update the signature files for the antivirus software so it can detect and remove new viruses. Generally, you can update the signature files over the Internet.

 Signature files contain the latest virus updates. Therefore, you need to keep the signature files up to date. You can do so by downloading the latest files from the vendor's Web site. Not keeping the signature files up to date defeats the purpose of installing antivirus software because your computer is not protected against the latest viruses.

Internet Firewall

A firewall is a piece of software that runs on a computer with an Internet connection and acts as a barrier between your computer and Internet users. It allows traffic from the local network or computer to pass through but blocks traffic initiated by Internet users. The benefit of using a firewall is that it can protect your computer from malicious users as well as computer viruses.

Windows XP has a built-in firewall component called the Internet Connection Firewall (ICF). You should enable this feature on any computer that has a direct Internet connection. Those computers that have Internet access through a shared connection do not need to have the firewall component enabled. You can enable the firewall component by using the following steps:

1. Click Start and click the Control Panel option. If you are using the Classic Start menu, click Start, point to Settings and then click the Control Panel option.

2. Open the Network Connections applet.

3. Right-click the Internet connection and click Properties.

4. Select the Advanced tab, as shown in Figure 9.1.

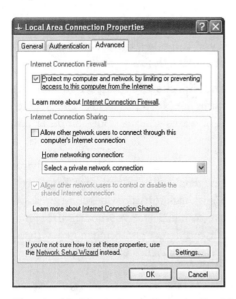

Figure 9.1 Enabling the Internet Connection Firewall.

5. Under Internet Connection Firewall, check the box beside the option named Protect My Computer and Network by Limiting or Preventing Access to This Computer from the Internet.

 You can configure the Internet Connection Firewall component to allow certain types of traffic to pass through to the private network. For example, if you have an FTP server on the private network, you can make it accessible to Internet users by allowing FTP traffic.

Educating Users

Another way in which you can protect your network against virus attacks is to educate users. This includes educating them about how viruses can enter the network and how they are spread.

Viruses can be acquired in a number of different ways, including email attachments or programs downloaded from unknown Internet sources. For example, users can unknowingly introduce a virus onto their system and possibly a network by opening an email attachment. To prevent virus outbreaks, do the following:

➤ Educate users about the different ways in which viruses can be spread.

➤ Alert users to the common signs of viruses. These signs can include a decrease in system performance, unusual messages, or programs not behaving as they normally would.

➤ Educate users to the dangers of bringing in floppy disks from outside sources. Many organizations discourage this practice. If it is allowed, users should be encouraged to scan all floppy disks for viruses before opening or copying any files onto their computer or a network share.

➤ Emphasize the importance of using antivirus software and keeping the signature files up to date.

Understanding Outlook Express Security Features

As already mentioned, one of the most common ways in which viruses are spread is via email. Outlook Express 6, therefore, has some built-in security features to protect against viruses.

Security zones in Outlook Express determine whether active content can be run from within an HTML message. You can configure the security zone for Outlook Express by using the following steps:

1. Click Start and select Outlook Express. Conversely, if you are using the Classic Start menu, click Start, point to Programs, and click Outlook Express.

2. Within Outlook Express, click the Tools menu and click Options.

3. From the Options dialog box, select the Security tab.

4. Under Virus Protection, select Restricted Sites Zone (see Figure 9.2). This option should be selected by default in Outlook Express 6. Previous versions of Outlook Express used the Internet zone, which is less secure because it allows most active content to run.

Outlook Express can also be configured to read all email messages in plain text. The benefit of this approach is that no active content contained within the message is run. The disadvantage is that some HTML emails are not displayed correctly in plain text. To enable Outlook Express to read all messages in plain text, repeat steps 1 and 2 from the preceding set of steps. Then, from the Options dialog box, select the Read tab and check the option Read All Messages in Plain Text (see Figure 9.3).

 Not all email clients support HTML. The result of sending an HTML message to a recipient using an email client that does not support this feature is a message that may appear in small print, a message that arrives as an attachment, or even a message with no text. So, using plain text not only increases security, but it may also increase functionality.

Figure 9.2 Configuring security zones in Outlook Express.

Figure 9.3 Configuring Outlook Express to read all messages in plain text.

Some viruses are capable of exploiting your Outlook Express contact list. They can spread themselves by sending copies of email messages containing the viruses to all your Outlook Express contacts.

Outlook Express can be configured to notify you before another application can send an email message without your knowledge. You can configure Outlook Express to do so using the Security tab from the Options dialog box and selecting the option Warn Me When Other Applications Try to Send Mail as Me. This option is enabled by default in Outlook Express 6.

Many users are often unable to differentiate between those attachments that are safe and those that are potentially harmful. Outlook Express can be configured to block attachments with certain extensions. You can do so by selecting the option Do Not Allow Attachments to Be Saved or Opened That Could Potentially Be a Virus. With this option enabled, Outlook Express uses Internet Explorer's unsafe file list and the settings configured using the Folder Options applet to determine which attachments should be blocked. Typically, Internet Explorer considers any attachments containing script or code to be unsafe. You can configure which file types are unsafe by using the Folder Options applet within the Control Panel. When Outlook Express receives an email message with an attachment considered to be unsafe, a message appears notifying you that the attachment has been blocked.

Managing Critical Updates

Often after a vendor releases an operating system or application, security issues are identified and reported. Most vendors, including Microsoft, release updates that can normally be downloaded from their Web sites. These updates are released to fix known issues and security vulnerabilities with an operating system or software program. A *critical update* is one considered critical to the normal operation of your computer.

Windows XP Updates

Windows XP makes it relatively simple to identify any critical updates that should be installed on your computer. By using the *Windows Update* Web site, you can have your computer scanned to determine the critical updates that are missing.

You can easily access the Windows Update Web site by clicking Start, pointing to All Programs, and clicking Windows Update. You are immediately connected to the Windows Update Web site (see Figure 9.4).

To begin scanning your system for missing updates, select the Scan for Updates option (refer to Figure 9.4). When the scan is complete, you are notified whether any updates for your system were detected. Click the Review and Install Updates option (see Figure 9.5) to browse through the updates found.

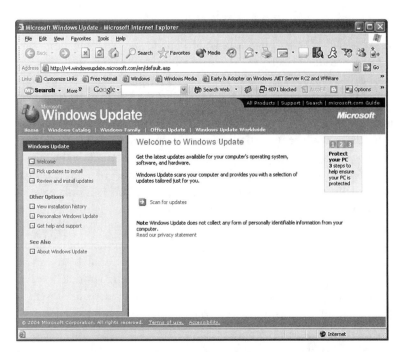

Figure 9.4 Using the Windows Update Web site.

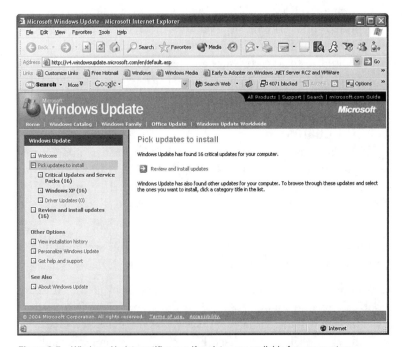

Figure 9.5 Windows Update notifies you if updates are available for your system.

Windows Update lists any critical updates you should install on your system. You can review the updates and click the Install Now button, shown in Figure 9.6, to begin downloading and installing the updates. You also have the option of selecting the specific updates you want to install.

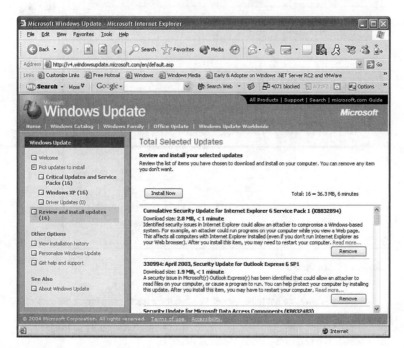

Figure 9.6 Installing critical updates.

 Windows Update alerts you to those updates critical to the normal operation of your system. Therefore, it is recommended that you download and install all those updates considered critical.

Office Application Updates

Not only does Microsoft release critical updates for the various versions of Windows, but it also releases critical updates for Office applications. Again, critical Office updates are designed to improve the stability and security of your applications.

You can access the Microsoft Office Update Web site by selecting the Check for Updates option available from the Help menu within an Office application. After you select this option, you are connected to the Office Update Web site, as shown in Figure 9.7.

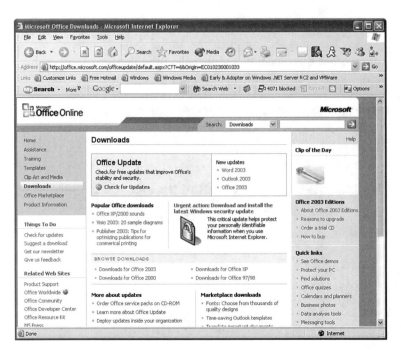

Figure 9.7 Installing Office Updates.

 Security is always a hot topic, especially when it comes to exam topics. Be sure you are familiar with the different ways of keeping a system up to date and secure. Securing your computer refers not only to the operating system but also to additional software components such as Microsoft Office.

Automatic Updates

You can configure Windows XP to keep your system up to date without your intervention by using the *Automatic Updates* feature. With Automatic Updates, you no longer need to search for critical updates pertinent to your computer. Instead, Windows detects when you have an Internet connection and uses the connection to automatically connect to the Windows Update site. If any updates are found, an icon is displayed in the notification area alerting you of the updates.

You do have the ability to control the Automatic Updates feature. For example, you can have Windows automatically download any updates it finds and install them on the schedule you specify. Conversely, you can configure Automatic Updates such that you are notified before any updates are downloaded.

To access and configure Automatic Updates, follow these steps:

1. Click Start and select the Control Panel. If using the Classic Start menu, click Start, point to Settings, and click Control Panel.

2. Within the Control Panel, open the System applet. The System Properties dialog box appears.

3. Select the Automatic Updates tab, as shown in Figure 9.8.

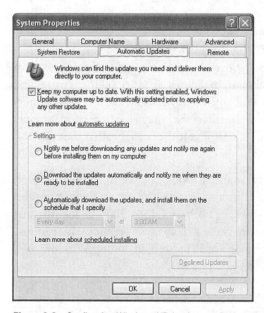

Figure 9.8   Configuring Windows XP for Automatic Updates.

As you can see in Figure 9.8, different options allow you to control the behavior of Automatic Updates. These options are summarized here:

➤ *Keep My Computer Up to Date*—Select this option to enable Automatic Updates on a computer. This option is selected by default.

➤ *Notify Me Before Downloading Updates and Notify Me Again Before Installing Them on My Computer*—If you select this option, Windows notifies you twice: once before downloading the updates from the Windows Update Web site and again before installing the updates.

➤ *Download the Updates Automatically and Notify Me When They Are Ready to Be Installed*—When you select this option, Windows automatically downloads any updates. You receive notification when the updates are ready to be installed.

➤ *Automatically Download the Updates, and Install Them on the Schedule That I Specify*—When you select this option, Windows automatically downloads any updates and installs them based on the schedule that you specify.

When it comes to deploying Automatic Updates, another technology you can use is Software Update Services. This free tool from Microsoft allows updates to be downloaded onto a server on your private network. You can then test the updates and approve them before deploying them to computers.

Microsoft Baseline Security Analyzer

Ensuring that a computer is up to date is crucial in protecting the system against any security attacks, including malicious software such as viruses and worms. Any misconfigurations with software can also leave a system vulnerable. Because identifying misconfigurations that may lead to security vulnerabilities can be difficult, an administrator can use a tool called the *Microsoft Baseline Security Analyzer (MBSA)*.

The Microsoft Baseline Security Analyzer tool, available from the Microsoft Web site, can be used to scan a computer to identify any misconfigurations with the operating system or software such as Office 2000 to identify any misconfigurations. The tool can be used to scan computers running Windows XP as well as other versions of Windows, including Windows NT 4.0, Windows 2000, and Windows Server 2003.

You can use MBSA to scan remote computers. In other words, you can run MBSA on your computer and use it to scan other computers on the network.

After you download and install the Microsoft Baseline Security Analyzer, you can use it to scan a system for misconfigurations as well as determine which security updates are missing (see Figure 9.9).

By selecting the Scan a Computer option, you open a window in which you can specify which computer you want to scan. By default, the local computer is scanned (see Figure 9.10). When you are ready, you can select the Start Scan option.

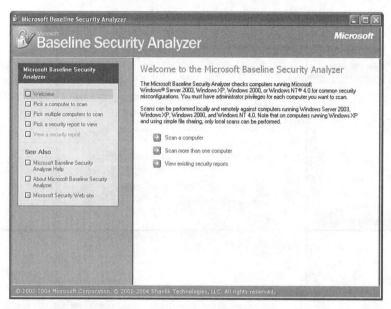

Figure 9.9   Using the Microsoft Baseline Security Analyzer.

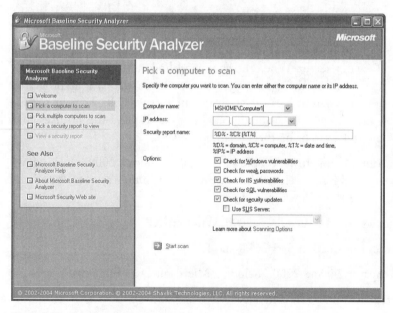

Figure 9.10   Selecting a computer to scan.

MBSA scans the operating system, Internet Explorer, and other desktop applications such as Microsoft Office (it also scans programs such as IIS and SQL).
The results alert you to any critical updates that are missing as well as configuration changes that should be changed to increase security (see Figure 9.11).

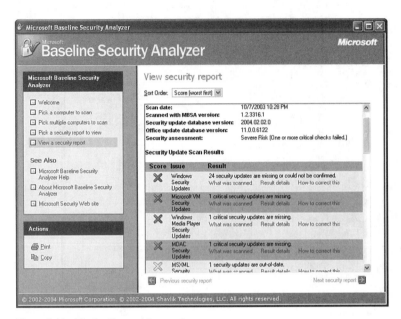

Figure 9.11 Viewing the security report.

Hfnetchk.exe Utility

You can use the Hfnetchk.exe utility to determine the hotfixes that might be required for your server. When the command-line utility is run, it scans the system to determine the operating system, service packs, and programs installed. It then determines the security patches available for your system based on the components running. Hfnetchk.exe displays the hotfixes that should be installed to bring the system up to date.

You can run Hfnetchk from Windows NT 4.0, Windows 2000, or Windows XP systems, and it scans either the local system or remote systems for patches available for the following products:

➤ Windows NT 4.0, Windows 2000, Windows XP

➤ Internet Information Server 4.0 and 5.0

➤ SQL Server 7.0 and 2000 (including Microsoft Data Engine)

➤ Internet Explorer 5.01 and later

The system requirements to run the utility are as follows:

➤ Windows NT 4.0, Windows 2000, or Windows XP

➤ Internet Explorer 5.0 or later (an XML parser is required and one is included with Internet Explorer 5.0)

Exam Prep Questions

Question 1

> A user calls to report that he is unable to open an attachment within Outlook Express. You determine that Outlook Express has blocked the attachment. What should you do to allow the user to download attachments with a specific file extension?
>
> ○ A. From the Options dialog box within Outlook Express, click the Security tab and deselect the option Do Not Allow Attachments to Be Saved or Opened That Could Potentially Be a Virus.
>
> ○ B. Using the Folder Options applet within the Control Panel, locate the file extension and deselect the option Confirm After Download.
>
> ○ C. From the Options dialog box within Outlook Express, click the Read tab and deselect the option Read All Messages in Plain Text.
>
> ○ D. From the Options dialog box within Outlook Express, click the Security tab and change the security zone to Internet zone.

Answer B is correct. When Outlook Express is configured to block attachments, it will not allow a user to open any attachments that may contain viruses. To enable a user to open attachments with a specific file extension, open the Folder Options applet, locate the file extension from the File Types tab, and deselect the option Confirm After Download. Answer A is incorrect. Deselecting this option means Outlook Express will not block any attachments that may compromise security. Answer C is incorrect. Configuring Outlook Express to read all messages in plain text ensures that any HTML messages that contain code will not be run. Answer D is also incorrect. If you change the security zone to Internet zone, security may be compromised because active content contained in email messages may be run.

Question 2

> You are the desktop support technician for a small company. A user calls to report that her computer is suddenly slow to respond. Upon investigation, you discover that several applications are no longer behaving correctly. What should you do?
>
> ○ A. Reinstall the applications that are not functioning as they should.
>
> ○ B. Reinstall the operating system and all applications.
>
> ○ C. Scan the computer with antivirus software.
>
> ○ D. Apply the latest critical updates.

Answer C is correct. If a computer experiences a sudden decrease in performance and applications are not functioning as they should, these symptoms may be an indication that it has a computer virus. The first thing you should do before reinstalling the operating system or the applications is scan for any viruses. Therefore, answers A and B are incorrect. Before applying any critical updates, you should determine the cause of the problem. Therefore, answer D is incorrect.

Question 3

You have configured a computer running Windows XP Professional as shown in the following figure.

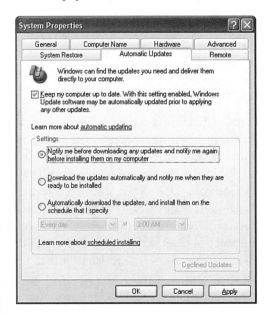

Which of the following statements is true regarding the configuration of the computer?

○ A. Updates will be installed every day at 3 a.m.

○ B. You will receive notification when updates are downloaded and again when they are installed.

○ C. You will receive notification when updates are downloaded but not when they are installed.

○ D. You will not receive notification when updates are downloaded but will be notified when they are installed.

Answer B is correct. Based on the configuration of the computer, you will receive notification before updates are downloaded from the Windows Update Web site. You will receive notification again when the updates are ready to be installed. Therefore, answers A, C, and D are incorrect.

Question 4

A recent virus outbreak on your network has forced you to take additional security precautions. You tracked the virus to an email attachment from an unknown source. All users currently use Outlook Express as their email client. You want Outlook Express to block any email attachments that may be harmful. What should you do?

- O A. From the Options dialog box within Outlook Express, select the Security tab and configure Outlook Express to block attachments that may be harmful.
- O B. Open the Folder Options applet within the Control Panel and configure Windows to block harmful attachments.
- O C. From the Options dialog box within Outlook Express, select the Read tab and configure Outlook Express to block attachments that may be harmful.
- O D. From the Internet Options dialog box within Internet Explorer, select the Security tab and configure Outlook Express to block attachments that may be harmful.

Answer A is correct. Outlook Express can be configured to block email attachments that may be harmful to a computer. You can configure this option by opening the Options dialog box within Outlook Express and selecting the Security tab. Therefore, answers B, C, and D are incorrect.

Question 5

What type of malicious software does not typically replicate itself?
- O A. Worm
- O B. Virus
- O C. Macro virus
- O D. Trojan horse

Answer D is correct. A Trojan horse does not typically replicate itself. A Trojan horse appears to be a legitimate program such as a game. When the program is run, a hidden function within the program normally compromises the security of the computer. Therefore, answers A, B, and C are incorrect.

Question 6

You are the desktop support technician for a consulting company that has 10 computers running Windows XP. You are responsible for ensuring all computers have the latest critical updates. You do not want to manually download and install the updates. You also do not want updates installed between the business hours of 8 a.m. and 6 p.m. What should you do?

○ A. Windows XP does not support this feature. You must connect to the Windows Update site and manually download and then install all critical updates.

○ B. Install the Microsoft Baseline Security Analyzer and scan each computer. Connect to the Windows Update site and download the necessary critical updates.

○ C. Open the System applet within the Control Panel and configure Automatic Updates to download updates automatically and install them at 12 a.m.

○ D. Nothing more needs to be done. Windows XP will, by default, automatically download and install critical updates every day at 3 a.m.

Answer C is correct. You can configure Automatic Updates using the System applet within the Control Panel. Configure Automatic Updates to download automatically and set the schedule anytime between 6 p.m. and 8 a.m. Therefore, answers A and D are incorrect. Answer B is incorrect because MBSA is used to scan a computer to detect holes in the configuration, such as missing updates or misconfigurations.

Question 7

You are the desktop support technician for a small insurance company. Each computer runs Windows XP. Antivirus software is installed on each computer. A firewall has been configured, and the Automatic Updates feature is enabled on all computers. Updates are downloaded and installed at midnight each day. A month later users complain that their systems are slow. Upon investigation, you discover all the computers are infected with a virus you read about two weeks earlier. You took all the necessary security precautions. What is most likely the reason for the virus outbreak on your network?

○ A. You did not install the necessary critical updates.

○ B. Outlook Express is not configured to display email in plain text only.

○ C. Outlook Express is not configured to block unsafe attachments.

○ D. You did not update the signature files for the antivirus software.

Answer D is correct. After a new virus is discovered, vendors who produce antivirus software update their database with fixes to remove the virus. If you have antivirus software installed, you have to keep the signature files up to date to protect your computer from recent viruses. The signature files have more than likely not been updated. Therefore, answers A, B, and C are incorrect.

Question 8

You are securing your network against security attacks. You have enabled the Internet Connection Firewall on the computer with a shared Internet connection. All the computers have been configured for Automatic Updates. What else should you do to physically protect the computers from virus attacks?

- ○ A. Install antivirus software on all computers.
- ○ B. Run the Microsoft Baseline Security Analyzer.
- ○ C. Visit the Windows Update site and download any critical updates.
- ○ D. Inform users of the implications of opening attachments from unknown sources.

Answer A is correct. Microsoft recommends these three steps to securing a computer against virus attacks: use a firewall, install the latest critical updates, and use up-to-date antivirus software. Therefore, you need to install antivirus software on all computers. Answer B is incorrect because MBSA will scan a computer and identify holes in the security. It does not actually protect a computer from viruses. Answer C is incorrect because all computers are enabled to use Automatic Updates. Answer D is incorrect. Although users should be educated about viruses, this knowledge will not physically secure the computers against viruses.

Question 9

A user calls to report that some of the email messages he received in Outlook Express are not being displayed correctly. Some messages are received with distorted text, and others contain only an attachment. What could be causing the problem?

- ○ A. Outlook Express is blocking the attachments.
- ○ B. The email messages contain viruses.
- ○ C. Outlook Express is configured to display all messages in plain text.
- ○ D. The security zone is set to Internet zone.

Answer C is correct. If Outlook Express is configured to display all email messages in plain text, any HTML messages may not be displayed properly. Configuring Outlook Express to display all messages in plain text increases security because any functions with the email will not run. Answers A, B, and D are incorrect because these options would not cause the message to be displayed improperly.

Question 10

Which of the following type of security attack attempts to disguise itself as a legitimate program?

O A. Virus

O B. Macro virus

O C. Worm

O D. Trojan horse

Answer D is correct. A Trojan horse is a type of security attack that attempts to disguise itself as a legitimate program. The program contains some type of hidden function designed to compromise the security of the computer. Therefore, answers A, B, and C are incorrect.

Practice Exam #1

Question 1

A user has a multiboot system with two partitions on her hard disk. Windows 95 is installed on drive C. Windows XP is installed on drive D. When she boots into Windows 95, she is unable to access the D partition. What is most likely causing the problem to occur?

- ○ A. The user does not have Read permission to access the drive.
- ○ B. The partition has been formatted with NTFS.
- ○ C. The partition is on a dynamic disk.
- ○ D. The hard disk has been converted to a basic disk.

Question 2

A user reports that the Windows XP taskbar contains two arrows that, when clicked, display the remaining shortcuts on the Quick Launch toolbar. He has tried to resize the toolbar to see all the icons available but cannot resize it. What steps are required to fix the user's taskbar?

- ○ A. Unlock the taskbar and resize the Quick Launch toolbar.
- ○ B. Open the Quick Launch toolbar and delete unused icons.
- ○ C. Resize the Quick Launch toolbar and set the taskbar to Autohide.
- ○ D. Set the taskbar to Autosize in the Taskbar Properties dialog box.

Question 3

Jane has recently started a work-share program with Barbara. They will be sharing the same computer. During Barbara's training, they used Jane's login to help Barbara understand how to navigate to the files they will be using. When Barbara started work, she reported that she could not find the network resources using her login. What do you need to do so the same shortcuts are available for Barbara?

- ○ A. Using the Taskbar tab from the Taskbar and Start Menu Properties dialog box, create a new submenu and add shortcuts to the appropriate programs.
- ○ B. Using the Start Menu tab from the Taskbar and Start Menu Properties dialog box, create a new submenu and add shortcuts to the appropriate programs.
- ○ C. Right-click the Start button and click Open All Users. Then create a new folder and add shortcuts to the appropriate programs.
- ○ D. Right-click the Start button and click Explore All Users. Then locate Barbara's Start Menu folder and copy it into Jane's profile.

Question 4

A multiboot system has Windows 95 installed on drive C and Windows XP on drive D. A user processed a request to have Office XP installed. After the installation, the user reports that Office XP is sometimes unavailable. What is the problem?

- ○ A. Office XP was not published to both operating systems.
- ○ B. The application was installed on an NTFS network drive.
- ○ C. Office XP was installed only on the Windows XP drive.
- ○ D. The NTFS permissions must be adjusted to Read and Execute on the Office XP program folder.

Question 5

When troubleshooting a file access problem on a user's system, you notice the contents of the Windows System folder are visible. It is a company standard to hide the System files. What steps should be taken to resolve this problem?

- ❑ A. From the Folder Options window, choose Deny Access to System Files and Folders.
- ❑ B. From the Folder Options window, choose Do Not Show Hidden Files and Folders.
- ❑ C. From the Control Panel, open the Files and Folders applet and choose Deny Access to System Files and Folders.
- ❑ D. From the Control Panel, open the Files and Folders applet and choose Do Not Show Hidden Files and Folders.

Question 6

The new corporate standard is to use Microsoft Word for all word processing documents. All file conversion from WordPerfect to Word has been completed. The WordPerfect software has been removed, so as a safety measure, all historical documents will be set to open in Microsoft Word. What steps should you take to prevent users from trying to open word processing documents in WordPerfect?

- ○ A. Use the File Association Wizard to set all WordPerfect documents to open using Microsoft Word.
- ○ B. Uninstall Microsoft Word.
- ○ C. Run Microsoft Word in compatibility mode.
- ○ D. Remove Microsoft Word as a shortcut from the Start menu.

Question 7

A user indicates that her dates are being displayed as *yyyy/mm/dd*. She wants to change the default date format. What should you tell her?

- ○ A. The user must format the date in each program she uses.
- ○ B. The user must edit the settings using the Folder Options applet within the Control Panel.
- ○ C. The user must reinstall Windows XP.
- ○ D. The user must edit the settings using the Regional and Language Options within the Control Panel.

Question 8

A user needs to run an application designed for Windows 95. His system is currently running Windows XP. After the installation, the user tries to run the program and receives an error message indicating that the program in not compatible with Windows XP. What should you do?

- O A. Nothing. The application is not supported under the Windows XP operating system.
- O B. Multiboot the computer with Windows 95 and install the application under this operating system. Advise the user that he must boot into Windows 95 to use this program.
- O C. Install the application using the Program Compatibility Wizard.
- O D. Contact the vendor of the application for a Windows XP–compatible version of the application.

Question 9

A _____ is the default Web page opened each time your Web browser is opened.

- O A. Security zone
- O B. Home page
- O C. Cookie
- O D. Proxy server

Question 10

A user reports that she had difficulty logging in to her laptop, so she used the local administrator account to log in to the system. The user indicates that her home page is stale, and she is having trouble accessing the links there. What is the problem?

- O A. The Web server is down.
- O B. The exchange server is down.
- O C. The user does not have access to network resources.
- O D. The user's home page is not a valid address.

Question 11

A new user reports that since he configured Outlook Express to send and receive email, he receives a prompt for his password whenever checking for new messages. What steps should you advise the user to take so he can stop the prompts?

- ○ A. Change the security zone using the Security tab from the Outlook Express Options dialog box.

- ○ B. Open the properties window for the email account and select the Remember Password option on the Servers tab.

- ○ C. Open the properties window for the email account and select the Servers tab. Click the My Server Requires Authentication option.

- ○ D. Open the Options dialog box for Outlook Express. From the General tab, select the Automatically Log On to Windows Messenger option.

Question 12

You are working as a help desk support technician for a small insurance company. A user indicates that he continually receives messages that his Inbox is full. The user is required to delete his messages before he can send or receive mail. What do you suggest to prevent loss of information?

- ○ A. Archive historical messages on a weekly basis.

- ○ B. Clear the deleted items on exit.

- ○ C. Move important messages to the C drive.

- ○ D. Set up a rule that organizes the user's messages into Custom Mail folders.

Question 13

You are the help desk technician for a small consulting firm. One of the users recently received an email message with an executable attachment. You want to prevent users from opening attachments that could be potentially harmful. What should you do to configure Outlook Express from restricting file attachments?

- ○ A. Have users forward all email messages with attachments to you before opening them.

- ○ B. Change the program used to open executables to Outlook Express.

- ○ C. Using the Options window, configure Outlook Express to block attachments that could be potentially harmful.

- ○ D. Using the Options window, configure Outlook Express to notify you when another program attempts to send an email.

Question 14

A user calls to indicate that she has been recently receiving a large amount of unwanted email in her Inbox from an unsolicited sender. The user indicates that throughout the day she must manually delete these messages. She is concerned that some of the emails may contain viruses and does not want to receive them anymore. What should you do?

- ○ A. Create a rule that will place all email from the sender into another folder.
- ○ B. Configure Outlook Express to automatically empty the contents of the Deleted Items folder when it is closed.
- ○ C. Block the sender's email address.
- ○ D. Create a rule to place all incoming email from the sender into the Deleted Items folder.

Question 15

You are the support technician at an accounting firm. A user reports that he can successfully send and receive email. However, he would like assistance configuring Outlook so he can view the content of received messages without having to open each one in a new window. What do you recommend?

- ○ A. Open the Windows Layout Properties window and enable the preview pane.
- ○ B. Enable the preview pane from the View menu for Outlook.
- ○ C. Open the Options window for Outlook and enable Outlook to display folders with unread messages.
- ○ D. Create a new rule to display the preview pane for all received messages.

Question 16

Users in your company currently use Outlook Express. However, all users are being migrated to Microsoft Outlook. You want to move email messages from Outlook Express into Microsoft Outlook. What should you do?

- ○ A. Use the Export function within Outlook Express and then import the PST file into Outlook.
- ○ B. Use the Save As function within Outlook Express, save all messages into a PST file, and then import the PST file into Outlook.
- ○ C. Import the messages into a PST file and then import the messages into Microsoft Outlook.
- ○ D. Back up the mail messages and restore them in Microsoft Outlook.

Question 17

You are setting up a new laptop for a Microsoft Office power user. What steps should you take to ensure that all Office customizations will be transferred from the user's old computer to his new system?

○ A. Run the Save My Settings Wizard on the user's current system and then run it on the new laptop.

○ B. Copy Normal.dot, presentation.pot, and xluser.xlt from the user's existing system and replace the existing copies on the new laptop.

○ C. Re-create the customized settings on the new laptop.

○ D. Copy the user's profile from the existing system onto the new laptop.

Question 18

A power user indicates that some features are missing from her current installation of Microsoft Word. You have verified that the thesaurus is unavailable. What steps should you take to solve this problem?

○ A. Repair the Office XP installation.

○ B. Customize the Office XP installation to include the missing features.

○ C. Reset the Format menu.

○ D. Reset the Standard toolbar.

Question 19

You are working as a support technician for an accounting firm. A user reports that the Undo button is missing from the Standard toolbar. What should you do?

○ A. Verify that the user has not applied any customization to the Standard toolbar and then reset the toolbar from the Customize dialog box.

○ B. Reset the Standard toolbar.

○ C. Open the Customize dialog box and drag the Undo button onto the Formatting toolbar.

○ D. Inform the user to press Ctrl+Z because the Undo button is gone.

Question 20

A user calls and reports that whenever someone tries to use the Get External Data feature in Access, the program stops responding. After further investigation, the user indicates that Access has had other performance problems. What should you do?

- ○ A. Remove the Access application.
- ○ B. Install the Get External Data feature.
- ○ C. Use the Detect and Repair feature from the Help menu.
- ○ D. Remove the Office installation and perform a custom installation.

Question 21

A user reports that her system was rebuilt approximately a month ago. She has not had any problems with her Windows XP system. However, today she opened Microsoft Outlook and found that several menu options are unavailable. What is the problem?

- ○ A. The Office XP product key has expired.
- ○ B. The user has a virus.
- ○ C. The user's permissions have been customized with a domain policy to restrict access to some Office features.
- ○ D. The Office XP installation has not been activated.

Question 22

A user indicates that whenever he opens Word, a file he was working on last week is automatically opened. You ask the user to verify the filename on the toolbar, but it is says Document1. Each time the user clicks the New button on the Standard toolbar, the same text appears. What should be done?

- ○ A. The Normal.doc template should be re-created.
- ○ B. The Normal.dot template should be edited to remove the unwanted text.
- ○ C. The Normal.dot template should be re-created.
- ○ D. The Blank.dot template should be edited to remove the unwanted text.

Question 23

A user reports that the Office XP installation window periodically appears on her screen while she is using the Office programs. The user indicates that she already has the suite installed and thinks her system is broken. What is occurring?

○ A. The Office XP installation is set to Auto Detect and Repair.

○ B. The most common features are installed; however, the remaining features are set to Install on First Use.

○ C. The Office installation needs to be repaired.

○ D. A domain policy is applying software patches.

Question 24

A user has recently been upgraded to Office XP. He reports that his menus are shorter than those in the previous version. After hovering the mouse on the menu for a while, he notices that it automatically expands to display additional options. What is the problem?

○ A. The Personalized menus are turned on.

○ B. The Customized menus are turned on.

○ C. The Personalized toolbars are turned on and cause the menus to show only the buttons displayed on the toolbars.

○ D. The Customized toolbars are turned on and cause the menus to show only the buttons displayed on the toolbars.

Question 25

A user tries to use the bullets and numbering button and realizes that the Formatting toolbar is not in view. How do you guide the user to reactivate the Formatting toolbar?

❏ A. Click the Tools menu and select Toolbar.

❏ B. Click the View menu and select Toolbars and then Formatting.

❏ C. Click the View menu and select Toolbars and then Activate Default Toolbars.

❏ D. Right-click any active toolbar and select Formatting from the menu.

Question 26

A user indicates that she is responsible for receiving her supervisor's email. When the user creates new messages, the default account used to send messages is her supervisor's email address. She can select her personal account from the accounts list when she sends the message, but she finds it cumbersome. What can you do to help this user? Select three correct answers.

- ❑ A. The user is already accomplishing the task, and there are no other options.
- ❑ B. Configure the default email address to the generic company account using the Set as Default button from the Email accounts dialog box.
- ❑ C. Configure the Reply Email address to the user's company account.
- ❑ D. Configure the Forward Email address to the user's company account.

Question 27

A user reports that he receives hundreds of messages daily. He is having difficulty keeping track of his incoming messages. What steps would you suggest to assist the user in managing his email?

- ○ A. Set up Custom Mail folders and rules to organize the messages by priority or sender.
- ○ B. Set up rules for high-priority messages only.
- ○ C. Suggest an auto-reply message to indicate that the user is busy and may be slow to respond.
- ○ D. Use the Out of Office assistant to indicate that the user is away.

Question 28

A user is reading through her archived messages in Outlook and has indicated that some messages do not contain the message text. What should you do?

- ○ A. Restore the user's Archive.pst file to its original location.
- ○ B. Run the Inbox Repair Tool.
- ○ C. Reboot the user's system.
- ○ D. Apply the latest patches to the Office XP software.

Question 29

A user reports that when a new appointment is created, the reminder appears 24 hours before the appointment. He wants to change the default reminder to appear 10 minutes before the appointment. How do you resolve this problem?

- ○ A. From the Options dialog box, select the Other tab and adjust the default reminder to 10 minutes.

- ○ B. From the Options dialog box, select the Calendar tab and adjust the default reminder to 10 minutes.

- ○ C. From the Options dialog box, select the Preferences tab, click the Calendar Options button, and change the default reminder to 10 minutes.

- ○ D. From the Options dialog box, select the Preferences tab and modify the default reminder to 10 minutes.

Question 30

A user reports that she is having a problem with managing the number of messages in her Inbox. You suggest she archive messages older than 30 days. The user wants Outlook to automatically perform this function. How can you configure the user's Outlook settings to accomplish this task?

- ○ A. Archive dialog box
- ○ B. AutoArchive dialog box
- ○ C. Data File Management dialog box
- ○ D. Backup dialog box

Question 31

You receive a call indicating that a user cannot open an attachment within Outlook Express. You determine that Outlook Express has blocked the attachment. The user indicates he is exchanging macro files with a coworker. What should you do to allow the user to download the required attachments with a specific file extension?

- ○ A. From the Options window within Outlook Express, click the Security tab and deselect the option Do Not Allow Attachments to Be Saved or Opened That Could Potentially Be a Virus.

- ○ B. Using the Folder Options applet within the Control Panel, click the File Types tab, locate the file extension, and deselect the Confirm After Download option.

- ○ C. From the Options window within Outlook Express, click the Receipts tab and deselect the Read All Messages in Plain Text option.

- ○ D. From the Options window within Outlook Express, click the Security tab and change the security zone to Internet zone.

Question 32

You are the desktop support technician for a small company. A user calls to report that her computer is suddenly slow to respond. During your investigation, you find that many applications are not functioning properly. What should you do?

- ○ A. Reinstall the applications that are not functioning as they should.
- ○ B. Rebuild the user's system starting with the operating system and all necessary applications.
- ○ C. Scan the computer with antivirus software.
- ○ D. Apply the latest Windows XP updates.

Question 33

A user indicates that after he modified the Options dialog box, email messages he received in Outlook Express are not being displayed correctly. Some messages contain distorted text, and some messages contain only an attachment. What configuration is causing the problem?

- ○ A. Outlook Express is blocking the attachments.
- ○ B. The email messages contain viruses.
- ○ C. Outlook Express is configured to display all messages in plain text.
- ○ D. The security zone is set to Internet zone.

Question 34

Which of the following type of virus attack attempts to disguise itself as a legitimate program?

- ○ A. Virus
- ○ B. Macro virus
- ○ C. Worm
- ○ D. Trojan horse

Question 35

Your company has its own Web server on the corporate network. You need to add the intranet site to a security zone. Which zone should you choose?

- ○ A.   Internet
- ○ B.   Local Intranet
- ○ C.   Trusted Sites
- ○ D.   Restricted Sites

Question 36

A user has returned from a one-year sabbatical and indicates that her Outlook data is missing. The user indicates that her login name has been changed since her return. She requires the contact information that was previously stored in the Outlook.pst file. How can you resolve this problem?

- ○ A.   Locate the user's Archive.pst file and import the data.
- ○ B.   Re-enable the user's old login so she can access her previous PST file.
- ○ C.   Import the user's Outlook.pst file from the old profile.
- ○ D.   The information is lost and cannot be corrected.

Question 37

A user has been granted the NTFS Modify permission to a folder named Marketing. The same user also has the Read permission assigned using Share permissions. When he accesses files locally from the Marketing folder, he can save changes to those files within the folder, but when opening files across the network, he cannot modify them. What is the problem?

- ❏ A.   The effective permissions are Read.
- ❏ B.   The effective permissions are Write.
- ❏ C.   The NTFS permissions have not propagated to subfolders.
- ❏ D.   The Share permissions are not applied when accessed locally.

Question 38

How can the NTFS permission settings of a file be changed, altered, or modified? Select two correct answers.

- ❑ A. Delete the file.
- ❑ B. Move the file to a new partition.
- ❑ C. Use the Security tab on the properties window.
- ❑ D. Take ownership of the file.

Question 39

You are a support technician for an accounting firm. A manager wants all users to be prompted to open a specific file in read-only format. She does not want to distribute a password for the particular file. However, she indicates that she does not want to restrict users from being able to make changes to the file when they deem it necessary. What feature do you recommend for the file?

- ○ A. Set the Open password.
- ○ B. Set the Modify password.
- ○ C. Enable the Read-only recommended option.
- ○ D. Protect the document.

Question 40

Whenever a user opens a document that contains macros from an untrusted source, he does not receive a macro warning. He is also able to execute all macros within the files. What is the user's current macro security setting?

- ○ A. Low
- ○ B. Medium
- ○ C. High
- ○ D. Restricted

Question 41

You are a support technician for a private law firm where there is some suspicion that a user is accessing files that she should be prevented from accessing. You suspect that there is a permissions problem. You need to verify that the user is accessing the folder. How can you do this?

- ○ A. NTFS file activity logging
- ○ B. Event auditing
- ○ C. Event Viewer
- ○ D. Account lockout

Question 42

A user can create and modify documents in a parent folder named XP Migration, but in the subfolder named Software Training, he is not able to create new files. Why is this occurring?

- ○ A. Automatic propagation has been stopped.
- ○ B. The user has been denied access to the subfolder named Software Training.
- ○ C. The user has only Read permission.
- ○ D. The user has Modify permission but has been denied the Create New Files permission.

Question 43

You are a help desk technician, and you receive a request to assist a user access the corporate database. After further investigation, you find out that this user previously had a shortcut to the database on her desktop. The file is located on the Corporate Data server in the Client Database folder. The user has tried to navigate to the database but receives an error message. You have checked the database file, and the user has the appropriate permissions to open the file. What is the problem?

- ○ A. The user has been denied access to the Client Database folder.
- ○ B. The user does not have the special List Folders permission.
- ○ C. The database has been moved to a new file location.
- ○ D. The user does not have Read access to the database file.

Question 44

A user has a Windows 95 system with several shared folders. He set up each shared folder with Read access. However, since he has set up the shares, the user indicates that several files have been deleted. Under what circumstances could the files have been deleted?

○ A. The NTFS permissions allowed users to delete the files.

○ B. The files were accessed locally and then deleted.

○ C. The files were moved to a subfolder.

○ D. The folder has the Delete special permission.

Question 45

You have several files that you need to restrict access to in a folder named Project Development. The files are currently located on the public drive that the entire company has access to. What can you do to restrict access to these files?

○ A. Deny access to the files at the file level.

○ B. Move the files into their own folder and grant access only to the required users or groups.

○ C. Deny access to the Project Development folder.

○ D. Copy the files to users' local drives to prevent public access to them.

Answer Key for Practice Exam #1

Answer Key

1. B	**16.** A	**31.** B
2. A	**17.** A	**32.** C
3. C	**18.** B	**33.** C
4. C	**19.** A	**34.** D
5. B and D	**20.** C	**35.** B
6. A	**21.** D	**36.** C
7. D	**22.** B	**37.** A and D
8. C	**23.** B	**38.** B and C
9. B	**24.** A	**39.** C
10. C	**25.** B and D	**40.** A
11. B	**26.** B, C, and D	**41.** B
12. A	**27.** A	**42.** A
13. C	**28.** B	**43.** B
14. C	**29.** D	**44.** B
15. B	**30.** B	**45.** B

Question 1

Answer B is correct. Windows 95 operating systems cannot read NTFS partitions. Answer A is incorrect because NTFS permissions do not apply; the disk is unreadable from the Windows 95 operating system. Answer C is incorrect because Windows 95 cannot be installed on a dynamic disk. Answer D is incorrect because Windows 95 must be installed on a basic disk, so booting into Windows 95 is not possible if the disk has been converted.

Question 2

Answer A is correct. If the taskbar is locked, the user cannot resize the Quick Launch toolbar. To begin, unlock the taskbar by right-clicking a blank area on the Start menu; then select the Lock Taskbar option. Selecting this option sets the toggle option so the check mark beside it is removed. At this point, resize the Quick Launch toolbar so all the icons are visible. Answer B is incorrect because the user did not indicate that there are unused icons. Answer C is incorrect because you cannot resize the Quick Launch toolbar until the taskbar has been unlocked. Answer D is incorrect because there is no Autosize feature in the Taskbar Properties dialog box.

Question 3

Answer C is correct. To customize the Start menu for all users who log in to the computer, you must right-click the Start button and click Open All Users. Answers A and B are incorrect because you cannot add submenus from the Taskbar and Start Menu Properties dialog box. This dialog box is used to configure view properties for both the Start menu and the taskbar. Answer D is incorrect because Barbara does not have the shortcuts required. If Jane's Start Menu folder were copied into Barbara's profile, any shortcuts would be visible with Barbara's login.

Question 4

Answer C is correct. If you are multibooting a computer, an application must be installed under each operating system. If not, the application will be available only under the operating system on which the application was installed. Answer A is incorrect because the installation was not performed to both operating systems. Answer B is incorrect because Windows 95 cannot view NTFS drives. Installing Office XP on an NTFS drive would not be possible. Answer D is incorrect because NTFS permissions would not be applicable with Windows 95.

Question 5

Answers B and D are correct. You can hide the system files and folders using the Folder Options window, which you can access from the Control Panel or from the Windows Explorer window through the Tools menu. When you select the option Do Not Show Hidden Files and Folders, program and system files are not displayed. Answers A and C are incorrect because they are not valid options.

Question 6

Answer A is correct. File extensions are associated with certain programs. When a file is opened from Windows Explorer, the program automatically launches based on the file extension. More than likely, the file association has been changed so WordPad launches instead of Microsoft Word. Answer B is incorrect because this would prevent the user from opening the files in Microsoft Word. Answer C is incorrect because the compatibility mode is used when older software is run on new operating systems. Answer D is incorrect because the Word shortcut will not prevent users from opening word processing files with WordPerfect.

Question 7

Answer D is correct. The user can change the default date using the Regional and Language Options applet within the Control Panel. Answer A is incorrect because the dates would revert to the default setting from the Regional and Language Options window. Answer B is incorrect because the date format is not available from the Folder Options applet. Answer C is incorrect because the user does not need to reinstall Windows XP. During the installation, the user would be able to set the default date settings; however, the same window is available for modification after installation. She would need to reinstall all applications and back up all local data. This option would cause more problems than it would solve.

Question 8

Answer C is correct. If the application will not run under the Windows XP operating system, you should install the application using the Program Compatibility Wizard. Answer A is incorrect because Windows XP can run older programs after the compatibility settings have been configured. Answer B is incorrect because multibooting the computer is not necessary. Answer D is also incorrect. You might need to contact the vendor for updated software; however, you should try running the Compatibility Wizard first to avoid purchasing updated software.

Question 9

Answer B is correct. The home page is the Web page displayed each time the Web browser is opened or when the Home button is selected. Answer A is incorrect because security zones are used to group Web sites for the purpose of applying security settings. Answer C is incorrect because a cookie is a small text file that may store information such as your preferences for an Internet site or personal information such as your email address. Answer D is incorrect because a proxy server retrieves Web content on behalf of computers on the private network and blocks unwanted Internet traffic from reaching the intranet.

Question 10

Answer C is correct. The user indicated that she logged on to her system using the local administrator logon and does not have access to network resources, which includes the Internet. Answers A and B are incorrect because the user does not have access to these servers; she used the local administrator account to log in. Answer D is incorrect because the user does not have access to an Internet connection to test whether the address is valid.

Question 11

Answer B is correct. Outlook Express can be configured to remember the password for an email account so the user is not prompted to type it in when

Outlook Express checks for email. The user can configure this setting in the properties window for the email account by selecting the Servers tab and clicking the Remember Password option. Answer A is incorrect because a security zone is used to apply security settings. Answer C is incorrect because this option is selected if the outgoing mail server requires authentication. Answer D is incorrect because this option is used to configure Outlook Express to automatically log on the user to Windows Messenger.

Question 12

Answer A is correct. Outlook allows you to archive data to a file called Archive.pst, which places the user's oldest data into the file. The Archive.pst file removes items from the Inbox and therefore does not count toward mailbox size. Answer B is incorrect because it will clear only the items that have been deleted. It will also cause loss of data. Answer C is incorrect because moving individual items to the C drive will not allow the user to view data from the Outlook Express window. Answer D is incorrect because moving messages to Custom folders within the Inbox will still count toward mailbox size.

Question 13

Answer C is correct. Outlook Express can be configured to block attachments that can be potentially harmful to a computer. This option can be enabled using the Security tab within the Options window. Therefore, answers A and B are incorrect. Answer D is incorrect because this option is used to prevent viruses from sending email to contacts in your address book.

Question 14

Answer C is correct. If the user does not want to receive any email from a particular sender, the sender's email address can block any future messages from delivery. Answer A is incorrect because it will allow the message to be received and placed into another folder. Answers B and D are incorrect because the messages are received but are moved directly to the Deleted Items folder.

Question 15

Answer B is correct. To display the preview pane, you must enable it using the View menu. Therefore, answers A and C are incorrect. Answer D is incorrect because rules are used to configure how Outlook Express handles incoming email.

Question 16

Answer A is correct. You can use the Export function within Outlook Express to copy all mail messages (as well as the address book) into Microsoft Outlook. Therefore, answers B, C, and D are incorrect.

Question 17

Answer A is correct. To prevent the loss of customized settings, you can create a backup file that contains the user's customized settings, including menu, toolbar, and template modifications. Store the file on the company network and reapply the user's customizations on the new system. Answer B is incorrect because it will copy only a portion of the user's settings to the new system. Answer C is incorrect because some settings may be missed or require many hours to re-create if complex macros are involved, so it is not a viable solution. Answer D is incorrect because it will copy only some of the customized settings from the Windows environment, such as the Favorites and some customized settings for Office applications.

Question 18

Answer B is correct. The Typical Office XP installation does not contain the thesaurus. You must customize the installation to include such features. For power users, you should perform a full installation or configure the additional features to install on first use. Answer A is incorrect because the installation is not damaged. Answers C and D are incorrect because the menus and toolbars have not been customized.

Question 19

Answer A is correct. You can reset the toolbar using the Customize dialog box. If any other changes have been made, they will be fixed by resetting the toolbar. Answer B is incorrect because you need to verify that the user has not applied customizations to the toolbar. Answer C is incorrect because the Undo button is located on the Standard toolbar. Answer D is also incorrect. Although the user can press the Ctrl+Z key combination, it does not solve the issue of the missing Undo button.

Question 20

Answer C is correct. The Office installation should be repaired using the Detect and Repair option from the Help menu. You can also repair the installation from the Add/Remove Programs applet. Answer A is incorrect because removing the Access application will not solve the problem with the current Access installation. Answer B is incorrect because the Get External Data feature is currently installed. Answer D is incorrect because it is not necessary to remove the entire Office installation and reinstall. This step may be necessary if the Detect and Repair feature cannot solve the installation problem. However, you should do so after you try to use the Detect and Repair feature.

Question 21

Answer D is correct. The Office XP installation requires the product to be activated before unlimited usage is permitted. The user can open the Office applications 50 times before activation is required. When the user exceeds this number, the programs will allow her to view files but not create new files or modify existing files. Answer A is incorrect because the product key does not expire. Answer B is incorrect because no known virus disables Office features. Answer C is incorrect because there is no mention that a domain policy has been applied. It is also not possible for a domain policy to disable features within Office.

Question 22

Answer B is correct. The Normal.dot template file stores several customized settings as well as the text. To ensure that no loss of customizations is experienced, you should edit the Normal.dot file to remove the text. Answers A and D are incorrect because the blank template is named Normal.dot. Answer C is incorrect because when the Normal.dot template is re-created, it loses all configuration settings the user has modified.

Question 23

Answer B is correct. The Office XP installation window will appear as features are used for the first time. The feature is automatically installed and immediately available after the installation is complete. Answer A is incorrect because the Office XP installation cannot automatically detect and repair the installation. Answer C is incorrect because the Office installation is intact. Answer D is incorrect because there is no indication that a domain policy has been applied.

Question 24

Answer A is correct. The Personalized menus automatically customize menus and toolbars based on how often you use the commands. When you first start an Office program, only the basic commands appear. As the user accesses features from the menus and toolbars, they adjust so that only the commands and toolbar buttons he uses most often appear. Answer B is incorrect because the feature is called Personalized menus. Answers C and D are incorrect because the buttons used on the toolbar do not affect the menu commands in view in the program menus.

Question 25

Answers B and D are correct. To activate the Formatting toolbar, you can right-click on an active toolbar and select Formatting; or you can click the View menu, select the Toolbars submenu, and then select the Formatting option. Answers A and C are incorrect because they do not open the Formatting toolbar.

Question 26

Answers B, C, and D are correct. To help the user set up her email account to automatically reply using her personal company address, set the Reply Email address on the General tab of the Internet Email Setting dialog box. You can also set the default mail account to the user's personal email address using the Set as Default button in the Email Accounts dialog box. You can access this dialog box by using the Tools menu and selecting Email Accounts. Answer A is incorrect because some configurations do allow automation to occur.

Question 27

Answer A is correct. The user should set up custom mail folders and rules to organize the messages into the new folders. Answer B is incorrect because this approach will deal only with high-priority messages. Not all messages will be received with a high priority, and some messages may require imme-diate attention based on the sender rather than the high-priority indicator. Answer C is incorrect because the user is trying to organize the incoming messages. Answer D is incorrect because the user is not trying to configure an out of office message.

Question 28

Answer B is correct. The Inbox Repair Tool will try to repair the header of the PST file. Answer A is incorrect because the user did not indicate that he moved the Archive.pst file. Answer C is incorrect because rebooting will not affect the data in Outlook. Answer D is incorrect because the latest patches to the Office XP software will not affect the data.

Question 29

Answer D is correct. The default reminder is located on the Preferences tab in the Options dialog box. Answers A, B, and C are incorrect because they do not contain the default reminder setting.

Question 30

Answer B is correct. The AutoArchive dialog box is available from the Other tab in the Options dialog box. The AutoArchive button displays the configuration options available with the AutoArchive feature. Answer A is incorrect because it is used to initiate the Archive feature manually. Answer C is incorrect because it is used to manage the PST files configured in Outlook. Answer D is incorrect because it is not a valid feature.

Question 31

Answer B is correct. If Outlook Express is configured to block attachments, the user is not able to open any attachments that may contain viruses. To allow the user to open attachments with a specified file extension, open the Folder Options applet, locate the file extension from the File Types tab, and open the Advanced options to deselect the Confirm After Download option. Answer A is incorrect. Deselecting this option means Outlook Express will not block any attachments, which will allow all file attachments to be opened regardless of their file extension. Answer C is also incorrect. Configuring Outlook Express to read all messages in plain text ensures that any HTML messages that contain code will not be run. Answer D is incorrect. If you change the security zone to Internet zone, security may be compromised because any ActiveX content contained in email messages may be run.

Question 32

Answer C is correct. If a computer suddenly shows a dramatic decrease in performance and applications are not functioning properly, the system may be infected with a computer virus. You should always scan for viruses before reinstalling the operating system. Therefore, answers A and B are incorrect. Answer D is incorrect because before applying Windows XP updates, you should determine the cause of the problem.

Question 33

Answer C is correct. If Outlook Express is configured to display all email messages in plain text, some HTML messages may not be displayed properly. Using the plain text configuration increases security because any ActiveX controls that may contain macros cannot be executed. Answers A, B, and D are incorrect because these options would not cause the message to be displayed improperly.

Question 34

Answer D is correct. A Trojan horse is a type of security attack that tries to disguise itself as a valid program. The program contains some type of hidden function designed to compromise the security of the computer. Therefore, answers A, B, and C are incorrect.

Question 35

Answer B is correct. You use the Local Intranet security zone to group the sites that exist within the corporate network. Therefore, answers A, C, and D are incorrect.

Question 36

Answer C is correct. The information is located in the user's old profile and needs to be imported into her new profile. Answer A is incorrect because the user indicated that her data was stored in the Outlook.pst file. Answer B is incorrect because the PST file needs to be imported into the user's new profile. Answer D is incorrect because data is not active and has not been tested to verify its integrity.

Question 37

Answers A and D are correct. When a user has a combination of NTFS and Share permissions, the most restrictive permission is applied. Therefore, the most restrictive permission is Read, so he cannot save changes to any files within the Marketing folder. The Share permissions are also not applied when the user accesses the folder from a local computer, which explains why he can modify the files from the local system but not when the shared folder is accessed across the network. Answer B is incorrect because the effective permission is the most restrictive, which is Read. Answer C is incorrect because NTFS permissions not being propagated to subfolders are not an issue in this situation.

Question 38

Answers B and C are correct. When a file is moved to a new NTFS partition, it will inherit the NTFS permissions of the destination folder. You can also modify the NTFS permissions using the Security tab. Answer A is incorrect because the file permissions are not modified when a file is deleted. Answer D is incorrect because taking ownership of a file does not alter the permissions on a file.

Question 39

Answer C is correct. Any user who opens the file will be prompted to open the file as read-only. If that user refuses, the file will still open for modifications without a password. Answers A and B are incorrect because these approaches will only restrict access to the file, and passwords would need to be distributed to the users. Answer D is incorrect because it will prevent the file from being modified.

Question 40

Answer A is correct. When a user receives a file from an untrusted source and no warning message indicating the file has macros, the security setting is low. Therefore, answers B, C, and D are incorrect.

Question 41

Answer B is correct. Event auditing will track the activity on the folder and the users who access the folder. NTFS file activity logging is a feature used to verify who accesses a folder when it is enabled. Answer A is incorrect because the Event Viewer is used to view the security log created by the auditing system but is not the feature that does the actual tracking. Answer C is incorrect because you can view the log file in the Event Viewer. Answer D is incorrect because you use account lockout to prevent compromised accounts from being used.

Question 42

Answer A is correct. The parent folder named XP Migration has not propagated the permissions to the child folders. Answer B is incorrect because the user is able to view the contents of the Software Training folder. Answers C and D are incorrect because they allow Modify permission in the parent folder.

Question 43

Answer B is correct. The user was able to open the database from the shortcut on her desktop but cannot browse to the database file. Answer A is incorrect because the user was able to open the database from the shortcut on her desktop. Answer C is incorrect because there is no indication that the database file was moved. Answer D is incorrect because the user can open the file from the old shortcut on her desktop.

Question 44

Answer B is correct. A user would need to have local access to the files to delete them. The Share permissions do not apply when accessing the files locally. Answers A and D are incorrect because the user cannot have NTFS permissions on a Windows 95 system. Answer C is incorrect because there is no indication that the files have been moved.

Question 45

Answer B is correct. You should avoid using the Deny option to assist in troubleshooting permissions problems. Applying permissions at the file level also is not recommended. Answers A and C are incorrect because, in practice, you should avoid using the Deny option. Answer D is incorrect because it would create multiple copies of the same files.

Practice Exam #2

Question 1

A user has a multiboot system. Windows XP Professional is installed on partition D. Windows 98 has been installed on partition C. The user selects Windows XP Professional as the boot menu and proceeds to install Microsoft Office 2000. When he restarts the computer and selects Windows 98 from the boot menu, he is unable to run the Office applications. How should he resolve the problem?

- ○ A. Boot into Windows XP Professional and edit the permissions for the application executables.
- ○ B. Install Microsoft Office 2000 under Windows 98.
- ○ C. Create a third partition and reinstall Microsoft Office 2000 on the new partition.
- ○ D. Format partition C with NTFS.

Question 2

Your company has a single Internet connection that is shared among users. A user on the network has informed you that she receives an error message when opening Web pages that contain Java or ActiveX controls. All other Web pages are successfully displayed. What is most likely the cause of the problem?

- ○ A. ICF has been enabled on the computer with the Internet connection.
- ○ B. The user does not have permission to access the Web site.
- ○ C. The security level for the Internet zone is too high.
- ○ D. Internet Explorer has not been configured to access the Internet through a proxy server.

Question 3

A user reports that he is receiving an error message indicating that the C partition is running low on disk space. The user indicates that he has not installed any new programs but has been accessing a large number of new Internet sites lately. You discover that the Temporary Internet Files folder is taking up a large amount of disk space. You purge the contents of the folder. What else should you do?

- ○ A. Delete the Temporary Internet Files folder.
- ○ B. Inform the user that he must reduce the number of Internet sites he accesses.
- ○ C. Move the Temporary Internet Files folder to another hard drive.
- ○ D. Reduce the amount of disk space available to the Temporary Internet Files folder.

Question 4

You are the help desk support technician for Contoso, Ltd. A user from the Sales department calls to report that she is unable to view any Web pages. The user receives a **Web pages not found** message. You verify that the problem is not affecting any other users on the network. You can successfully ping the user's computer. What could be causing the problem?

- ○ A. The user does not have network connectivity.
- ○ B. The IP address of the computer is not configured correctly.
- ○ C. Internet Explorer has not been configured with the correct connection settings.
- ○ D. The user does not have permission to view the Web pages.

Question 5

A user has just configured an email account through Outlook Express. The user calls to report that he is unable to send email. You verify that the user can successfully receive email. Upon further investigation, you discover the user is receiving a **server not found** error message. What should you do?

- ○ A. Ping the IP address of the computer to verify connectivity.
- ○ B. Have the user open the properties window for the email account and verify the name typed in for the SMTP server.
- ○ C. Have the user open the properties window for the dial-up networking account and verify the user has typed in the correct phone number.
- ○ D. Have the user open the Options window within Outlook Express and verify Outlook Express is not configured to block attachments.

Question 6

You are the desktop support technician for a real estate company. The network hosts an intranet Web server. Users soon report that the Web server is slow to respond to requests. You suspect a problem with one of the routers on the intranet. How can you easily identify whether a router is causing the problem?

- ○ A. Use **tracert** to follow the path a packet will take to reach the Web server.
- ○ B. Ping the IP address of each router.
- ○ C. Physically inspect each router.
- ○ D. Use the **ipconfig** command to test network connectivity with each router.

Question 7

A computer running Windows XP Professional is unable to access the company intranet Web server on another subnet. You want to verify the default gateway the computer is configured with. Which command can you use?

- ○ A. **ping**
- ○ B. **tracert**
- ○ C. **ipconfig**
- ○ D. **winipcfg**

Question 8

A user indicates that she is unable to connect to the Internet. All Internet access takes place through a shared Internet connection. What should be your first step in troubleshooting the problem?

- ○ A. Check the TCP/IP connectivity.
- ○ B. Check the configuration of the network adapter.
- ○ C. Check that the computer has network connectivity.
- ○ D. Check whether the computer with the Internet connection is online.

Question 9

You are running Outlook Express as your email client. Which protocol can be used to download email from the mail server at your ISP?

- ○ A. POP3
- ○ B. SMTP
- ○ C. HTTP
- ○ D. FTP

Question 10

You are unable to access your company Web site that is hosted by your ISP. You have verified that the Web server is online. This problem is also affecting other users. You can successfully access other Web sites. You suspect a problem with DNS. What should you do to determine whether the problem is DNS related? Choose two correct answers.

- ❑ A. Ping the IP address of the Web server.
- ❑ B. Ping the DNS name of the Web site.
- ❑ C. Use the **ipconfig** command to verify the DNS settings configured on your local computer.
- ❑ D. Ping the IP address of a local computer.

Question 11

One of the users on your network cannot access any network resources. He is unable to open any of his mapped network drives on one of the servers. You open Device Manager and verify that the network adapter is functioning. However, when you ping the loopback address, you receive a **destination host unreachable** error message. What is causing the problem?

- ○ A. The driver for the network adapter is corrupted.
- ○ B. TCP/IP is not installed correctly.
- ○ C. The computer is configured with incorrect IP settings.
- ○ D. The server is not online.

Question 12

You are taking precautions to protect your network from virus attacks. Aside from installing antivirus software on all computers, what is the most important step in keeping your computers secure?

- ○ A. Configure Outlook Express to block email attachments.
- ○ B. Educate users about ways to avoid viruses.
- ○ C. Disable Internet access for all users on the network.
- ○ D. Update the signature files for the antivirus software.

Question 13

A user on your network reports that he is unable to print from Microsoft Word. When he sends a document to the printer, nothing happens. You have verified that both the computer and printer have network connectivity. What should be your next step in troubleshooting the problem?

- ○ A. Ping the IP address of the computer.
- ○ B. Update the printer driver on the computer.
- ○ C. Try printing from a different program.
- ○ D. Recycle the power on the printer.

Question 14

A user calls to report that she is unable to establish a dial-up connection with the company's remote access server. The user can successfully connect to her local ISP. You discover that when the user attempts to connect, she hears a ring, but nothing happens. Which of the following may be causing the problem? Choose two correct answers.

- ❏ A. The user's modem is not functioning correctly.
- ❏ B. The remote access server is not online.
- ❏ C. The user does not have sufficient permissions to establish a remote access connection.
- ❏ D. The dial-up networking account is configured to dial the wrong number.

Question 15

A user indicates that Internet Explorer is often slow when loading Web pages
that have previously been viewed. What can you do to improve performance?

- ○ A. Decrease the number of days Internet Explorer will keep track of pages
  in the user's History folder.
- ○ B. Decrease the maximum size of the Temporary Internet Files folder.
- ○ C. Delete the contents of the Temporary Internet Files folder.
- ○ D. Increase the amount of disk space allocated to the Temporary Internet
  Files folder.

Question 16

A user calls to indicate that each time he opens a file with a **.doc** extension, the
file opens in WordPad. The user wants Microsoft Word to open when he opens
a file with this extension in Windows Explorer. What should you do?

- ○ A. Change the file association using the Folder Options applet.
- ○ B. Tell the user to open Microsoft Word and use the Open command from
  the File menu and search for the file to open.
- ○ C. Uninstall WordPad.
- ○ D. Use the Detect and Repair feature to repair the installation of Microsoft
  Word.

Question 17

Users are reporting errors when trying to resolve certain hostnames. You need
to determine whether the problem is DNS related. Which command can
you use?

- ○ A. **nslookup**
- ○ B. **ipconfig**
- ○ C. **tracert**
- ○ D. **ipconfig /registerdns**

Question 18

You are deploying antivirus software on your company network to reduce the risk of virus attacks. On which of the following should you install the software? Choose two correct answers.

❑ A. Workstations

❑ B. Routers

❑ C. Servers

❑ D. Printers

Question 19

Users on your company network are reporting that there is no incoming email. The problem did not occur yesterday. After further investigation, you discover that the problem is affecting all users. Users can still browse the Internet, and there is no problem with sending email. Given this, what is most likely the cause of the problem?

○ A. The POP3 server is offline.

○ B. The proxy server is not available.

○ C. Clients are configured with incorrect email settings.

○ D. The SMTP server is not responding.

Question 20

You are the desktop support technician for a small insurance company. A user calls to report that she is having Internet problems but is unable to provide any more details about the problem. From the user's workstation, you can success-fully access the Internet. However, when you attempt to access the Web server the user was trying to connect to, you receive an error message. You can con-nect to the Web server using the IP address. What is most likely causing the problem?

○ A. The Web server is offline.

○ B. There is an incorrect DNS entry.

○ C. The workstation does not have connectivity.

○ D. NetBIOS name resolution is failing.

Question 21

All computers on your network are members of the same workgroup. Some computers are shared among multiple users. One user has a Windows 98 system that has several shared folders. He set up each shared folder with Read access. However, a week later, the user discovered that some of the files within the shared folders had been changed. What caused the problem to occur?

- ○ A. The user configured incorrect Share permissions.
- ○ B. A user with Local access changed the file contents.
- ○ C. The NTFS permissions were not configured for each folder.
- ○ D. Read access allows users to change the contents.

Question 22

Computers on your network are configured in a workgroup. All computers are running Windows 98. One of the computers has a folder that all other users require access to. However, users should not be able to change the contents of the folder. What should you do?

- ○ A. Share the folder and append a dollar sign to the end of the share name.
- ○ B. Assign NTFS permissions so users have only Read access.
- ○ C. Share the folder and assign the Share permission of Read.
- ○ D. Share each individual file within the folder and assign users Read permission to each file.

Question 23

You are the help desk support technician for an ISP. A user calls to report that she is unable to establish a dial-up connection. The user reports that the modem does not make any noise when she attempts to dial a connection. You need to assist the user in troubleshooting the problem. What two steps should you have the user perform first? Choose two correct answers.

- ❏ A. Check the dial-up account settings.
- ❏ B. Check to see that the modem is properly connected to the phone line.
- ❏ C. Check to see that the modem is properly seated inside the computer.
- ❏ D. Run the modem diagnostics using the Phone and Modem Options applet.

Question 24

You are the support technician for a small company. A single Internet connection is shared among all users. Internet Connection Firewall is enabled on the computer with the shared connection. An FTP server located on your intranet must be accessible to users in another branch office. You soon discover that no one outside your local intranet is able to access the FTP server. Users on your intranet have no problem accessing Internet resources. What should you do?

○ A. Disable ICF on the computer with the shared Internet connection using the Advanced tab from the properties window for the Internet connection.

○ B. Using the Advanced tab from the properties window for the Internet connection, enable the FTP service.

○ C. Disable ICF on the computer with the shared Internet connection using the Advanced tab from the properties window for the LAN connection.

○ D. Using the Advanced tab from the properties window for the LAN connection, enable the HTTP service.

Question 25

A user has attached a print device to his workstation. When he attempts to print a document through Microsoft Word, the characters are garbled on the page. The user calls and reports the problem. The same problem occurs when printing from other applications. What should you do?

○ A. Reinstall the printer driver.

○ B. Empty the contents of the print queue.

○ C. Repair the installation of Microsoft Word.

○ D. Install the print device on another workstation.

Question 26

A user is trying to save a Word document to a CD using her CD burner. The user has not encountered problems saving before. She is vague in her description of the error message received. You can successfully save the document to another CD. What could be causing the problem? Choose two correct answers.

❑ A. The CD is rewritable but has no free space available.

❑ B. The CD the user is trying to save to is not rewritable.

❑ C. The CD burner is conflicting with another device.

❑ D. The user does not have permission to write to the CD.

Question 27

A user reports that Outlook Express always prompts him to enter a password. The user does not want to be prompted for his password each time he launches Outlook Express. What should you tell him to do?

- ○ A. Within Outlook Express, open the properties window for the email account. On the Connection tab, select Remember Password.

- ○ B. Within Outlook Express, open the properties window for the email account. On the General tab, select Remember Password.

- ○ C. Within Outlook Express, open the properties window for the email account. On the Servers tab, select Remember Password.

- ○ D. Within Outlook Express, open the properties window for the email account. On the Security tab, select Remember Password.

Question 28

A user calls to indicate that Outlook Express will not allow her to view email attachments. What should you tell the user to do?

- ○ A. Open the Options window in Outlook Express. Select the Read tab and remove the check beside Do Not Allow Attachments to Be Saved or Opened That Could Potentially Contain a Virus.

- ○ B. Open the Options window in Outlook Express. Select the General tab and remove the check beside Do Not Allow Attachments to Be Saved or Opened That Could Potentially Contain a Virus.

- ○ C. Open the Options window in Outlook Express. Select the Connection tab and remove the check beside Do Not Allow Attachments to Be Saved or Opened That Could Potentially Contain a Virus.

- ○ D. Open the Options window in Outlook Express. Select the Security tab and remove the check beside Do Not Allow Attachments to Be Saved or Opened That Could Potentially Contain a Virus.

Question 29

You are the desktop support technician for Litware, Inc. A user calls to report that he is unable to access the Internet. When he opens Internet Explorer, he receives a message stating the page cannot be found. You verify that the problem isn't affecting other users, and the proxy server is not reporting any errors. What should you do?

○ A. Open the Internet Options window within Internet Explorer and check the settings configured on the Connection tab.

○ B. Open Internet Explorer, and from the Internet Options window, verify the security level configured for the Internet zone on the Security tab.

○ C. Open Internet Explorer, and from the Internet Options window, verify the size of the Temporary Internet Files folder on the General tab.

○ D. Open Internet Explorer, and from the Internet Options window, verify the privacy level configured for the Internet zone using the Privacy tab.

Question 30

A user is trying to install a legacy application on her desktop running Windows XP. She receives an error that the program is not compatible with Windows XP. What should the user do?

○ A. Obtain an updated version of the program.

○ B. Run the Program Compatibility Wizard.

○ C. Multiboot the computer with a legacy operating system.

○ D. Nothing. Windows XP does not support legacy applications.

Question 31

Users on your network access the Internet through a proxy server. They report that it is sometimes slow accessing Web servers on the intranet using Internet Explorer. You want to improve performance. What should you do?

○ A. Within Internet Explorer, open the Internet Options page and configure the browser not to use a proxy server using the Connections tab.

○ B. Within Internet Explorer, open the Internet Options window and increase the amount of space available for the Temporary Internet Files folder using the General tab.

○ C. Within Internet Explorer, open the Internet Options window and increase the number of days Internet Explorer will keep pages in the History folder using the General tab.

○ D. Within Internet Explorer, open the Internet Options page and clear the check box beside the option to bypass the proxy server for local addresses using the Connections tab.

Question 32

You are the desktop support technician for a small company. All users access the Internet through a shared Internet connection. A user calls to report that each time she opens Internet Explorer her default home page is no longer displayed. The user indicates that she can successfully browse other Web sites. Which of the following could be causing this problem to occur? Choose two correct answers.

- ❑ A. The default Web page is currently not available.
- ❑ B. The computer with the shared Internet connection is offline.
- ❑ C. The settings configured on the Connection tab from the Internet Options window are incorrect.
- ❑ D. The user has configured Internet Explorer to use a blank Web page as the home page.

Question 33

You are the desktop support technician for a small real estate company. One of the users wants to move all his email from Outlook Express into Microsoft Outlook. What should you tell him to do?

- ○ A. Tell the user to use the Import function within Outlook Express to import messages to Outlook.
- ○ B. Tell the user to use the Save As function in Outlook Express and save all the messages into a PST file.
- ○ C. Tell the user to use the Export function within Outlook Express to move messages into Outlook.
- ○ D. Back up all the email messages and restore them into Outlook.

Question 34

You are the desktop support technician for an ISP. A user calls to report that she can no longer receive email after changing some of the email account properties. The user is unable to indicate the error message she received. The email account properties are shown in the the following figure. What should you tell the user to do?

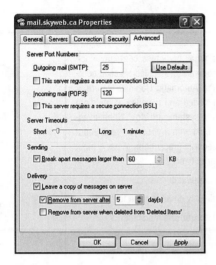

- ○ A. Use the Servers tab and check the name configured for the SMTP server.
- ○ B. Change the POP3 port number back to 110.
- ○ C. Deselect the option to leave a copy of the message on the server.
- ○ D. Increase the Server Timeouts value.

Question 35

Your network consists of 10 computers in a workgroup. You want any critical updates to be downloaded to workstations on your network and installed during nonbusiness hours. Any updates should be installed after 5 p.m. What should you do?

- ○ A. Manually connect each computer to the Windows Update site and download updates during nonbusiness hours.
- ○ B. Using the Automatic Updates tab from the System Properties window, configure critical updates to be downloaded automatically and installed between the hours of 8 a.m. and 5 p.m.
- ○ C. Using the Automatic Updates tab from the System Properties window, configure critical updates to be downloaded automatically and installed between the hours of 5 p.m. and 6 a.m.
- ○ D. Using the Automatic Updates tab from the System Properties window, configure automatic updates to notify you when updates are ready to be installed and installed between the hours of 5 p.m. and 6 a.m.

Question 36

You are the desktop support technician for a small insurance company. Each computer is running Windows XP. Antivirus software is installed on each computer. A firewall has been configured, and the Automatic Updates feature is enabled on all computers. Updates are downloaded and installed at midnight each day. A month later users complain that their systems are slow. Upon investigation, you discover the systems are all infected with a virus you read about two weeks earlier. You took all the necessary security precautions. What is most likely the reason for the virus outbreak on your network?

○ A. You did not install the necessary critical updates.

○ B. Outlook Express is not configured to display email in plain text only.

○ C. Outlook Express is not configured to block unsafe attachments.

○ D. You did not update the signature files for the antivirus software.

Question 37

A user indicates that when he receives messages from his home office, they do not appear in his Inbox when he returns to his office computer. The user indicates that mail received on one computer is not available on the other computer. What should you do?

○ A. Configure the delivery of the messages to be retained on the mail server.

○ B. Modify the server timeouts to allow the messages to be downloaded.

○ C. Verify the user's Internet connection in his home office.

○ D. Modify the user's account to use a Mandatory profile.

Question 38

You are the desktop support technician for a small company. A user calls to report that her computer is suddenly slow to respond. Upon investigation, you discover that several applications are no longer behaving correctly. What should you do?

○ A. Reinstall the applications that are not functioning as they should.

○ B. Reinstall the operating system and all applications.

○ C. Scan the computer with antivirus software.

○ D. Apply the latest critical updates.

Question 39

A user indicates that the blank template in Word contains part of a file he was working on the previous day. Each time he creates a new file, the text appears. What should be done?

- ○ A. The Normal.doc template should be re-created.
- ○ B. The Normal.dot template should be edited to remove the unwanted text.
- ○ C. The Normal.dot template should be re-created.
- ○ D. The Blank.dot template should be edited to remove the unwanted text.

Question 40

Your company hosts a Web server on the internal network. To which security zone should the site be added?

- ○ A. Internet
- ○ B. Local Intranet
- ○ C. Trusted Sites
- ○ D. Restricted Sites

Question 41

You are securing your network against security attacks. You have enabled the Internet Connection Firewall on the computer with a shared Internet connection. All the computers have been configured for automatic updates. What else should you do to physically protect the computers from virus attacks?

- ○ A. Install antivirus software on all computers.
- ○ B. Run the Microsoft Security Baseline Analyzer.
- ○ C. Visit the Windows Update site and download any critical updates.
- ○ D. Inform users of the implications of opening attachments from unknown sources.

Question 42

You are the desktop support technician for a consulting company. Ten computers are running Windows XP. You are responsible for ensuring all computers have the latest critical updates. You do not want to manually download and install the updates. You also do not want updates installed between the business hours of 8 a.m. and 6 p.m. What should you do?

- ○ A. Windows XP does not support this feature. You must connect to the Windows Update site and manually download and then install all critical updates.
- ○ B. Install the Microsoft Baseline Security Analyzer and scan each computer. Connect to the Windows Update site and download the necessary critical updates.
- ○ C. Open the System applet within the Control Panel and configure Automatic Updates to download updates automatically and install them at 12 a.m.
- ○ D. Nothing more needs to be done. Windows XP will, by default, automatically download and install critical updates every day at 3 a.m.

Question 43

Which of the following tools can you use to scan a computer to determine whether any configuration changes should be made to increase security?

- ○ A. Microsoft Security Baseline Analyzer
- ○ B. Windows Update
- ○ C. Automatic Update
- ○ D. Event Viewer

Question 44

A user calls to report that some of the email messages received are not displayed correctly. Many of the messages contain distorted text. Others contain only email attachments. Outlook Express is configured as shown in the following figures. What should you tell the user to do to have all messages displayed correctly?

○ A. Change the Internet Explorer security zone to Internet zone.

○ B. Clear the option Read All Messages in Plain Text.

○ C. Clear the option Warn Me When Other Applications Try to Send Mail as Me.

○ D. Clear the option Do Not Allow Attachments to Be Saved or Opened That Could Potentially Be a Virus.

Question 45

You are the desktop support technician for a small branch office. A recent virus outbreak within your office has required you to increase security. You want to reduce the chance of a virus spreading through email. What should you do?

○ A. Using the Security tab from the Options window in Outlook Express, select the option Warn Me When Other Applications Try to Send Mail as Me.

○ B. Using the Send tab from the Options window in Outlook Express, select the option Send Messages Immediately.

○ C. Using the Security tab from the Options window in Outlook Express, select the option Do Not Allow Attachments to Be Saved or Opened That Could Potentially Be a Virus.

○ D. Using the Security tab from the Options window in Outlook Express, change the Internet Explorer security zone to Restricted.

Answer Key for Practice Exam #2

. . . .

Answer Key

1. B	**16.** A	**31.** D
2. C	**17.** A	**32.** A, D
3. D	**18.** A, C	**33.** C
4. C	**19.** D	**34.** B
5. B	**20.** B	**35.** C
6. A	**21.** B	**36.** D
7. C	**22.** C	**37.** A
8. C	**23.** B, C	**38.** C
9. A	**24.** B	**39.** B
10. A, B	**25.** A	**40.** B
11. B	**26.** A, B	**41.** A
12. D	**27.** C	**42.** C
13. C	**28.** D	**43.** A
14. B, D	**29.** A	**44.** B
15. D	**30.** B	**45.** A

Question 1

Answer B is correct. To run the applications under both operating systems, the user must install Microsoft Office 2000 twice. To make applications available for both operating systems, they must be installed when booted in Windows XP and again in Windows 98. Answer A is incorrect. The permissions for the executables have not been changed so the user has permission to run all the applications. Answer C is incorrect because installing Microsoft Office 2000 on a different partition will not resolve the issue. Answer D is incorrect because changing the file system will not resolve the issue. Also, Windows 98 does not support NTFS.

Question 2

Answer C is correct. If pages that contain ActiveX and Java controls will not load correctly, the security level is more than likely too high. Answer A is incorrect because ICF would not cause the Web pages to load incorrectly. Answer B is incorrect because a permission problem would display an error message in the browser that access was denied. Answer D is also incorrect. If the Connection settings in Internet Explorer were misconfigured, the user would not be able to access any Web pages.

Question 3

Answer D is correct. To ensure that the problem doesn't occur again, you should reduce the amount of disk space available to the Temporary Internet Files folder. Answer A is incorrect because the Temporary Internet Files folder does improve performance. Answer B is incorrect because it is unreasonable to ask a user to reduce the number of Internet pages he views. Answer C is incorrect because the user has not indicated that the computer has a second hard drive.

Question 4

Answer C is correct. The source of the problem is likely caused by incorrect settings configured within Internet Explorer. If the settings on the Connection tab from the Internet Options window are not correctly configured, the user will not be able to access the Internet. Answers A and B are incorrect because you can successfully ping the computer. Answer D is incorrect because an access denied message would be displayed if the problem was related to permissions.

Question 5

Answer B is correct. If the user is unable to send email but can successfully receive email, verify that he typed in the correct name for the SMTP server. Answers A and C are incorrect. Because the user can successfully receive email, these two options can be eliminated as the source of the problem. Answer D is incorrect because this option would not affect a user's ability to send email.

Question 6

Answer A is correct. You can use the tracert command to quickly identify whether a router on the network is the source of the problem. Answers A and B are incorrect because each option would require more administrative effort. Answer D is incorrect because the ipconfig command is not used to test IP connectivity.

Question 7

Answer C is correct. You can use the ipconfig command to verify the IP address of the default gateway configured on a computer running Windows XP Professional. Answers A and B are incorrect because these commands will not display the required information. Answer D is incorrect because this command is used on computers running Windows ME and earlier.

Question 8

Answer C is correct. The first thing you should do when troubleshooting such a problem is to verify that the computer has network connectivity. You can do so by checking to see whether the link lights on the network adapter are on. Therefore, answers A, B, and D are incorrect.

Question 9

Answer A is correct. You can use POP3 to retrieve email messages from a mail server on the Internet. Answer B is incorrect because SMTP is used to send email. Answer C is incorrect because HTTP is used to view Web content. Answer D is incorrect because FTP is used to transfer files.

Question 10

Answers A and B are correct. To diagnose whether the problem is DNS related, try pinging the IP address and the DNS name of the Web site. If this approach fails, name resolution is more than likely failing. Answer C is incorrect because you can access other Web sites. Answer D is incorrect because pinging the IP address of a local computer will not test DNS name resolution.

Question 11

Answer B is correct. If you ping the loopback address (127.0.0.1) and receive a destination host unreachable error message, this would indicate that TCP/IP is not correctly installed on the computer. Answer A is incorrect because you have already verified that the network adapter is not causing the problem. Answer C is incorrect because the error message would not be received if TCP/IP was not correctly configured. Answer D is incorrect because the error message received from pinging indicates a problem with TCP/IP on the local computer.

Question 12

Answer D is correct. Aside from installing antivirus software, you need to update the signature files regularly; otherwise, the antivirus software will not protect your computers from any new viruses. Not updating the signature files defeats the purpose of installing the software. Answers A and B are incorrect. Although these two steps should be included in the overall plan to secure your network, it is the antivirus software that will detect and remove viruses. Answer C is incorrect because it is unreasonable to disable Internet access as a method of protecting against virus attacks.

Question 13

Answer C is correct. The next logical step would be to try printing from another program. This will determine whether the problem is application specific. Answers B and D are incorrect. Before performing either of these steps, you should gather some more information such as whether the problem is application specific or user specific. Answer A is incorrect because you have already determined that both the printer and computer have network connectivity.

Question 14

Answers B and D are correct. The cause of the problem could be an incorrect phone number being used or the remote access server not being online. Either one of these responses would explain why the user hears a ring when the modem dials but nothing happens. Answer A is incorrect because the user can successfully connect to her ISP. Answer C is incorrect because a permission problem would not cause this problem to occur.

Question 15

Answer D is correct. To improve the performance for loading previously viewed Web pages, you can increase the amount of disk space available for the Temporary Internet Files folder. Answers A, B, and C are incorrect because any of these options would decrease performance.

Question 16

Answer A is correct. Using the Folder Options applet within the Control Panel, you can change the program used to open files with different extensions. Answer B is incorrect because it does not solve the problem. Answer C is incorrect because WordPad does not need to be removed. Answer D is incorrect because the user has not indicated any error messages appearing in Microsoft Word. This approach would also not solve the problem.

Question 17

Answer A is correct. You can use the `nslookup` command to test name resolution. Answers B and C are incorrect because these two commands cannot be used to test hostname resolution. Answer D is incorrect because this command registers a computer's hostname with a DNS server.

Question 18

Answers A and C are correct. Antivirus software should be installed on all workstations and all servers on the network to protect against virus attack. Answers B and D are incorrect. Antivirus software does not need to be installed on routers (unless the routers are computers with routing enabled) or printers (unless the print device is attached to a computer).

Question 19

Answer A is correct. If all users are experiencing problems sending email, the likely cause of the problem is that the POP3 server is down. POP3 is used for sending email. Answer D is incorrect because SMTP is used for receiving email. Answer B is incorrect because all users can still browse the Internet. Answer C is incorrect because the problem did not occur the previous day.

Question 20

Answer B is correct. Because the Web server is accessible by IP address but not hostname, you can conclude that there is more than likely an incorrect DNS entry for the Web server. Answer A is incorrect because the Web server is accessible by IP address. Answer C is incorrect because other Web servers are accessible from the workstation. Answer D is incorrect because the Internet uses hostnames, not NetBIOS names.

Question 21

Answer B is correct. Share permissions only protect folders on the network. If a user has local access to a computer, share permissions do not apply. Therefore, a user accessed the files locally and changed the contents. Answer

A is incorrect because Read permission is the correct permission to use if you do not want others on the network changing the folder contents. Answer C is incorrect because Windows 98 does not support NTFS permissions. Answer D is incorrect because Read permission will allow users to view only the contents of a folder.

Question 22

Answer C is correct. To make the folder available to other users in the workgroup, you must share the folder and assign the Read-only share permission. Answer A is incorrect because this approach will create a hidden share. Answer B is incorrect because Windows 98 does not support NTFS. Answer D is incorrect because Share permissions cannot be set on a file, only folders.

Question 23

Answers B and C are correct. To begin troubleshooting the problem, have the user check that the modem is properly connected to the phone line and that the phone line is connected to the phone jack. Also, have the user check that the modem is properly seated. Answer A is incorrect because the modem is not dialing; therefore, checking the dial-up account properties will not solve the problem. Answer D is incorrect. This step may be performed if you have determined that the hardware and phone line are properly connected.

Question 24

Answer B is correct. By default, ICF will not allow any traffic to pass to the private network—that is, unless it matches a request that was initiated by a computer on the intranet. You can enable certain services such as FTP or HTTP using the Advanced tab from the properties window for the Internet connection. Doing so makes these services on the private network available to Internet users. Answers A and C are incorrect because ICF should be enabled to protect against Internet attacks. Answer D is incorrect because ICF should not be enabled on the LAN connection.

Question 25

Answer A is correct. If the characters appear garbled on the page, you should reinstall or update the printer driver. Answer B is incorrect because deleting the documents on the print queue will not solve the problem. Answer C is incorrect because the problem is not application specific. Answer D is incorrect. The problem can more than likely be solved by updating the printer driver instead of attaching it to another computer.

Question 26

Answers A and B are correct. If the user is unable to save to a CD using her CD burner, the problem is likely that it is not a rewritable CD or the rewritable CD does not have enough free space for the file. Answer C is incorrect because you can successfully save the file to another CD. Answer D is incorrect because the user has indicated that she has not encountered problems saving before.

Question 27

Answer C is correct. You can configure Outlook Express to remember the password by opening the properties window for the mail account. Select the Servers tab and check the Remember Password option. Therefore, answers A, B, and D are incorrect.

Question 28

Answer D is correct. If the user is not able to open some email attachments, open the Options window in Outlook Express. Select the Security tab and clear the check box beside the option Do Not Allow Attachments to Be Saved or Opened That Could Potentially Contain a Virus. Therefore, answers A, B, and C are incorrect.

Question 29

Answer A is correct. If the user is unable to open any Web pages, open the Internet Options window from within Internet Explorer. Verify that Internet Explorer is configured to use a proxy server and that the settings are correct. Therefore, answers B, C, and D are incorrect.

Question 30

Answer B is correct. You can use the Program Compatibility Wizard included with Windows XP to run legacy programs. Windows XP can emulate a specific environment in which the legacy program is designed to run. Therefore, answer D is incorrect. Answers A and C are also incorrect; these steps are not necessary because the Program Compatibility Wizard can be used.

Question 31

Answer D is correct. When Internet Explorer is configured to bypass the proxy server, it will not forward requests to the proxy server if the address is for a local host. Answer A is incorrect because this approach would result in a user not being able to access Internet resources. Answer B is incorrect because this approach would increase performance for loading recently viewed Web pages. Answer C is incorrect because this approach will only increase the length of time in which links to recently visited Web pages are kept in the History folder.

Question 32

Answers A and D are correct. Two possible causes for the problem are that the default Web page is currently unavailable. In such cases, a message would be displayed informing the user that the page is currently unavailable. Conversely, the problem may be due to the fact that the user has configured Internet Explorer to display a blank Web page when opened or when the Home button on the toolbar is selected. Answers B and C are incorrect because the user has indicated that she can successfully browse other Web pages.

Question 33

Answer C is correct. The user can move messages from Outlook Express into Microsoft Outlook using the Export function within Outlook Express. Therefore, answers A, B, and D are incorrect.

Question 34

Answer B is correct. The default port number used for POP3 is 110. Therefore, the port number should be changed back to the default. An incorrect port number would result in the user being unable to receive email. Answer A is incorrect because an SMTP server is not used to receive email; it is used for sending email. Answers C and D are incorrect because performing either of these tasks would not correct the problem.

Question 35

Answer C is correct. Using the Automatic Updates tab from the System Properties window, configure critical updates to be automatically downloaded and installed between the hours of 5 p.m. and 6 a.m. Answer A is incorrect. Although this option is feasible, it does not meet the requirements. Manually downloading critical updates would require administrative overhead. Answer B is incorrect because updates would be installed during business hours. Answer D is incorrect because Automatic Updates cannot be configured to perform both of these tasks.

Question 36

Answer D is correct. After installing antivirus software, you must update the signature files regularly to protect against new viruses. Therefore, answers A, B, and C are incorrect.

Question 37

Answer A is correct. To have messages available on multiple computers, you must configure Outlook to leave a copy of received messages on the server. Otherwise, they will be downloaded to the local computer only. Therefore, answers B, C, and D are incorrect.

Question 38

Answer C is correct. If a computer suddenly begins behaving erratically, you should consider scanning the computer with antivirus software. Make sure the signature files have been updated so recent viruses can be detected. Answers A and B are incorrect. Before performing either of these steps, you should attempt to troubleshoot and solve the problem. Answer D is incorrect because installing critical updates would more than likely not cause applications to suddenly begin behaving erratically.

Question 39

Answer B is correct. The Normal.dot template file stores several customized settings as well as the text. To ensure that no loss of configurations is experienced, you should edit the Normal.dot file to remove the text. Answers A and D are incorrect because the blank template is named Normal.dot. Answer C is incorrect because when the Normal.dot template is re-created, it loses all configuration settings the user has modified.

Question 40

Answer B is correct. Any Web pages on the private network can be added to the Local Intranet zone. Therefore, answers A, C, and D are incorrect.

Question 41

Answer A is correct. One of the most important things you can do to protect computers for virus attacks is install antivirus software and regularly update the signature files. Answers B and D are incorrect. Although performing these tasks can prevent virus attacks, the most important thing to do is to use antivirus software. Answer C is incorrect because computers are already using automatic updates.

Question 42

Answer C is correct. Using the Automatic Updates tab from the System Properties window, you can configure Windows XP to automatically download and install critical updates on a predefined schedule. The schedule should not be between the hours of 8 a.m. and 6 p.m. Answer A is incorrect because Windows XP supports the Automatic Updates feature for critical updates. Answer B is incorrect because the Microsoft Security Baseline Analyzer cannot be configured to download critical updates. Answer D is incorrect because this is not the default behavior for Windows XP.

Question 43

Answer A is correct. You can use the Microsoft Baseline Security Analyzer to scan a computer to identify configuration changes that should be made to increase security. Therefore, answers B, C, and D are incorrect.

Question 44

Answer B is correct. If messages are not being displayed correctly, Outlook Express may be configured to read all messages in plain text. Enabling this option prevents any HTML messages that may contain malicious code from harming a computer. Therefore, answers A, C, and D are incorrect.

Question 45

Answer A is correct. By configuring Outlook Express to notify users before an application can send email on their behalf, you can prevent viruses, such as worms, from spreading via email. Therefore, answers B, C, and D are incorrect.

Need to Know More?

Chapter 1

 Search the online version of TechNet using keywords such as *program compatibility* and *Windows XP*.

http://www.microsoft.com/windowsxp/pro/using/howto/
gettingstarted/multiboot.asp

 Microsoft Corporation. *Microsoft Windows XP Professional Resource Kit, Second Edition.* Seattle, Washington: Microsoft Press, 2003.

 Minasi, Mark. *Mastering Windows XP Professional, Second Edition.* Sybex, 2002.

 Siechert, Carl, and Ed Bott. *Microsoft Windows XP Inside and Out.* Seattle, Washington: Microsoft Press, 2001.

Chapter 2

 Search the online version of TechNet using keywords such as *Internet Explorer* and *Windows XP*.

 Microsoft Corporation. *Microsoft Internet Explorer 6.0 Resource Kit.* Seattle, Washington: Microsoft Press, 2001.

 Microsoft Corporation. *Microsoft Windows XP Professional Resource Kit, Second Edition.* Seattle, Washington: Microsoft Press, 2004.

Chapter 3

 Search the online version of TechNet using keywords such as *Internet Explorer*, *Outlook Express*, and *Windows XP*.

 Maran, Ruth. *Teach Yourself Visually More Windows XP.* Visual, 2002.

 Microsoft Corporation. *Microsoft Internet Explorer 6.0 Resource Kit.* Seattle, Washington: Microsoft Press, 2001.

 Microsoft Corporation. *Microsoft Windows XP Professional Resource Kit, Second Edition.* Seattle, Washington: Microsoft Press, 2004.

Chapter 4

 Search the online version of TechNet using keywords such as *Internet Explorer*, *Outlook Express*, and *Windows XP*.

 Microsoft Corporation. *Microsoft Office XP Resource Kit.* Seattle, Washington: Microsoft Press, 2001.

 Microsoft Corporation. *Microsoft Windows XP Professional Resource Kit, Second Edition.* Seattle, Washington: Microsoft Press, 2003.

Chapter 5

 Search the online version of TechNet using keywords such as *Outlook XP*, *Mail Account Configuration*, *Customization*, *Newsgroups*, *Office XP*, and *PST*.

 Microsoft Corporation. *Microsoft Office XP Resource Kit.* Seattle, Washington: Microsoft Press, 2001.

 Pearson Education. *Special Edition Using Microsoft Office 2003.* Indianapolis, Indiana: Que Publishing, 2004.

Chapter 6

 Search the online version of TechNet using keywords such as *Hardware, Printers, Device Manager*, and *Windows XP*.

 Microsoft Corporation. *Microsoft Office XP Resource Kit*. Seattle, Washington: Microsoft Press, 2001.

 Microsoft Corporation. *Microsoft Windows XP Professional Resource Kit, Second Edition*. Seattle, Washington: Microsoft Press, 2003.

Chapter 7

 Ogletree, Terry William. *Upgrading and Repairing Networks, Fourth Edition*. Indianapolis, Indiana: Que Publishing, 2003.

 Simmons, Curt, and James Causey. *Windows XP Networking Inside and Out*. Seattle, Washington: Microsoft Press, 2002.

 Thurrott, Paul. *Windows XP Home Networking*. John Wiley and Sons, 2002.

Chapter 8

 Search the online version of TechNet using keywords such as *NTFS permissions, Security, Auditing*, and *Office XP Security*.

 Microsoft Corporation. *Microsoft Office XP Resource Kit*. Seattle, Washington: Microsoft Press, 2001.

 Microsoft Corporation. *Microsoft Windows XP Professional Resource Kit, Second Edition*. Seattle, Washington: Microsoft Press, 2003.

Chapter 9

 Search the online version of TechNet using keywords such as *Virus*, *Automatic Updates*, and *Windows XP*.

 Glenn, Walter J., and Rowena White. *Windows XP Tips and Techniques*. McGraw Hill Osborne Media, 2002.

 Microsoft Corporation. *Microsoft Windows XP Professional Resource Kit, Second Edition*. Seattle, Washington: Microsoft Press, 2004.

 Thurrot, Paul. *Windows XP Home Networking*. John Wiley and Sons, 2002.

CD Contents and Installation Instructions

The CD features an innovative practice test engine powered by MeasureUp™, giving you yet another effective tool to assess your readiness for the exam.

Multiple Test Modes

MeasureUp practice tests are available in Study, Certification, Custom, Missed Question, and Non-Duplicate question modes.

Study Mode

Tests administered in Study Mode allow you to request the correct answer(s) and explanation to each question during the test. These tests are not timed. You can modify the testing environment *during* the test by selecting the Options button.

Certification Mode

Tests administered in Certification Mode closely simulate the actual testing environment you will encounter when taking a certification exam. These tests do not allow you to request the answer(s) and/or explanation to each question until after the exam.

Custom Mode

Custom Mode allows you to specify your preferred testing environment. Use this mode to specify the objectives you want to include in your test, the timer length, and other test properties. You can also modify the testing environment *during* the test by selecting the Options button.

Missed Question Mode

Missed Question Mode allows you to take a test containing only the questions you have missed previously.

Non-Duplicate Mode

Non-Duplicate Mode allows you to take a test containing only questions not displayed previously.

Random Questions and Order of Answers

This feature helps you learn the material without memorizing questions and answers. Each time you take a practice test, the questions and answers appear in a different randomized order.

Detailed Explanations of Correct and Incorrect Answers

You'll receive automatic feedback on all correct and incorrect answers. The detailed answer explanations are a superb learning tool in their own right.

Attention to Exam Objectives

MeasureUp practice tests are designed to appropriately balance the questions over each technical area covered by a specific exam.

Installing the CD

The minimum system requirements for the CD-ROM are

➤ Windows 95, 98, Me, NT4, 2000, or XP

➤ 7MB disk space for testing engine

➤ An average of 1MB disk space for each test

To install the CD-ROM, follow these instructions:

 NOTE If you need technical support, please contact MeasureUp at 678-356-5050 or email **support@measureup.com**. Additionally, you'll find Frequently Asked Questions (FAQ) at **www.measureup.com**.

1. Close all applications before beginning this installation.

2. Insert the CD into your CD-ROM drive. If the setup starts automatically, go to step 5. If the setup does not start automatically, continue with step 3.

3. From the Start menu, select Run.

4. In the Browse dialog box, double-click Setup.exe. In the Run dialog box, click OK to begin the installation.

5. On the Welcome Screen, click Next.

6. To agree to the Software License Agreement, click Yes.

7. On the Choose Destination Location screen, click Next to install the software to C:\Program Files\Certification Preparation.

8. On the Setup Type screen, select Typical Setup. Click Next to continue.

9. After the installation is complete, verify that Yes, I want to restart my computer now is selected. If you select No, I will restart my computer later, you will not be able to use the program until you restart your computer.

10. Click Finish.

11. After restarting your computer, choose Start, Programs, MeasureUp, MeasureUp Practice Tests.

12. Select the practice test and click Start Test.

Creating a Shortcut to the MeasureUp Practice Tests

To create a shortcut to the MeasureUp Practice Tests, follow these steps:

1. Right-click on your Desktop.

2. From the shortcut menu select New, Shortcut.

3. Browse to C:\Program Files\MeasureUp Practice Tests and select the MeasureUpCertification.exe or Localware.exe file.

4. Click OK.

5. Click Next.

6. Rename the shortcut MeasureUp.

7. Click Finish.

After you have completed step 7, use the MeasureUp shortcut on your Desktop to access the MeasureUp practice test.

Technical Support

If you encounter problems with the MeasureUp test engine on the CD-ROM, please contact MeasureUp at 678-356-5050 or email support@measureup.com. Technical support hours are from 8 a.m. to 5 p.m. EST Monday through Friday. Additionally, you'll find Frequently Asked Questions (FAQ) at www.measureup.com.

If you'd like to purchase additional MeasureUp products, telephone 678-356-5050 or 800-649-1MUP (1687) or visit www.measureup.com.

Glossary

. . . .

Access Control List (ACL)

A list Windows XP stores with every file and folder on the NTFS partition or volume. The ACL includes all the users and groups that have access to the file or folder. In addition, it indicates what access or specifically what permissions each user or group is allowed to that file or folder.

Address book

A feature similar to a traditional paper-based address book where you store the names, addresses, and phone numbers of your contacts. Most email programs allow you to configure and maintain an address book.

Administrative installation point

A shared network folder that contains all the Office files required to install Office on a user's computer.

Antivirus software

A program designed specifically to detect and remove viruses.

Auditing

This feature enables you to track security-related events that occur on a computer. It can be useful in detecting when attempts are being made to breach security. Security-related events can be viewed in the Security log within Event Viewer.

AutoArchive

A feature provided by some applications such as Microsoft Outlook that enables you to archive your data to a file called Archive.pst. When you do, your oldest data is placed into that file.

Automatic Update

A Windows feature that detects when you have an Internet connection and uses the connection to automatically connect to the Windows Update site. With Automatic Updates, you no longer need to search for critical updates pertinent to your computer.

Autoplay

The capability to determine how Windows will handle files stored on a removable device such as a CD-ROM.

CDR-ROM

A storage device that contains data you copy using a CD burner. It may contain company documents or applications written within the company. The maximum storage capacity is 700MB. The CDR-ROM disc can be written to only once.

CDRW-ROM

A storage device that allows you to copy data repeatedly using a CD burner. If you deem the information outdated or unnecessary, you can reformat the CD and delete the contents stored on the CD.

Critical update

An update considered critical to the normal operation of your computer. Most vendors, including Microsoft, release updates that can normally be downloaded from their Web sites. These updates are released to fix known issues and security vulnerabilities with an operating system or software program.

Device driver

Software that allows a computer to interact with and control a hardware device.

Device Manager

A feature that enables you to maintain, configure, and troubleshoot the devices physically connected to the computer system.

Digital ID (certificate)

An electronic attachment used to verify the authenticity of the sender.

Domain Name System (DNS)

Software used to map hostnames into IP addresses.

Drivers

Small programs, also referred to as *device drivers*, that allow a computer to communicate with and control hardware devices.

Effective permissions

The permissions that a user has been explicitly assigned or permissions that a user has inheritied because of permissions assigned to a group the user is a member of.

Email

An electronic mail message delivered via a virtual mailman in the form of an Exchange server. The message can be sent over a local area network or the Internet.

Export

A function available in many applications that allows you to export data from an application into a file. For example, you can export email messages from Outlook Express into a file.

Firewall

A barrier between a private network and the Internet. A firewall can be hardware or software based. It blocks any traffic initiated from the Internet unless otherwise permitted.

Hard drive

A drive that contains operating system files, as well as data. Some computers may have multiple hard drives to increase storage space. Hard drives can be internal or external.

Home page

The Web page that is automatically displayed when Internet Explorer is opened. It also determines which Web page is displayed when you click the Home button located on the toolbar within Internet Explorer.

Import

A function available in many applications that allows you to import data from one program into another. For example, you can import email from one program such as Outlook into Outlook Express.

Inbox Repair Tool

A utility you use to repair corrupt PST files in Microsoft Outlook. It works by repairing the PST file's header and then deleting anything in the file that it doesn't understand.

Internet Connection Firewall (ICF)

A software-based firewall component within Windows XP. It allows you to safely connect your computer or network to the Internet. Once enabled, ICF restricts the flow of packets between the Internet and your private network.

Internet Explorer

The default Web browser installed with Windows XP. With an Internet connection, Internet Explorer enables you to view information on the Web.

Internet

A worldwide network connecting millions of computers for the purpose of exchanging data.

IPCONFIG

A command used to view the IP parameters for a computer, such as the IP address, subnet mask, and default gateway. You can use the command to renew an IP address with a DHCP server, as well as empty the contents of the DNS resolver cache.

Local area network

A group of computers connected together for the purpose of sharing resources.

Macro

A mini-program that automates a procedure.

Microsoft Baseline Security Analyzer (MBSA)

A tool available from the Microsoft Web site. You can use the MBSA to scan a computer to identify any misconfigurations with the operating system or software such as Office 2000 to identify any misconfigurations.

Modem

A hardware device used to establish a connection with a remote access server or Internet service provider.

Multiboot

A single computer that has multiple operating systems installed. When you multiboot a computer, you are prompted to select which operating system to load during computer startup.

NetBIOS name

A name assigned to a computer on a network. A NetBIOS name is a 16-character name in which the first 15 characters identify a computer and the 16th character is a hexadecimal value used to identify a specific service on the computer. Prior to the introduction of Windows 2000, Network Basic Input/Output System (NetBIOS) names were used to identify computers, services, and other resources on Windows-based machines.

Network drive

A hard drive located on another computer on the network. Users can save and access data on network drives depending on permissions. In corporate environments, users are encouraged to store all data in their network drive to prevent the loss of data and maintain the ability to share information with multiple users.

Network interface card

The hardware that allows a computer to communicate on a network.

Newsgroup

An electronic means for people to exchange news, share information, and voice opinions. A newsgroup is normally dedicated to a specific topic and used by people with common interests. It serves as a type of message board where someone can post a comment or opinion (depending on the purpose of the newsgroup) that can be read by anyone else who accesses the newsgroup.

NTFS

The NT File System; one of the file systems supported by Windows XP, Windows NT4, Windows 2000, and Windows 2003. NTFS is the recommended file system because it offers many enhancements not available with the FAT and FAT32 file systems.

NTFS permissions

Permissions used to set resource security on files and folders within the NT File System (NTFS).

Outlook

A Microsoft Office application that allows you to send and receive email messages, manage contacts, schedule appointments, generate task lists, and leave personal notes.

Outlook Express

An email and newsgroup client that is installed along with Internet Explorer.

Personal Folder (.pst file)

A file that contains Outlook data, which may include email messages, contact information, and the like.

PING

A command-line utility used to verify connectivity with another TCP/IP host. Connectivity on the network is verified by sending Internet Control Message Protocol (ICMP) echo requests and replies. When the ping command is issued, the source computer sends four echo request messages to another TCP/IP host. The remote host, if reachable, then responds with echo replies.

Preview pane

The Outlook Express viewing pane that allows you to view the contents of an email message without having to open it in a separate window.

Printer

The software interface between the operating system and the print device.

Program Compatibility Wizard

A software feature that can be used to resolve compatibility problems that can arise when running legacy applications on Windows XP.

Proofing Tools

A Microsoft Office add-in that supplies a collection of tools, such as spelling and grammar checkers, thesauri, and AutoCorrect lists, for more than 45 languages. Microsoft Office comes with built-in proofing tools for commonly used languages.

Proxy server

A server that acts as a barrier between an intranet and the Internet. The proxy server receives requests for Internet resources (such as a Web page) from clients on the intranet. The proxy server acts on behalf of the client and retrieves the requested resource from the Internet. A proxy server can block Internet traffic from reaching the private network.

Share permissions

Permissions that determine what type of access a user has to a shared folder on the network. Share permissions include Full Control, Change, and Read.

Start menu

The menu used to access the most useful components installed on a computer. The Start menu consists of pinned items and the most frequently used items.

System Restore

A Windows XP feature that allows you to return the operating system to a prior state. For example, if a newly installed device driver causes computer problems, you can restore the computer to its state before the drive was installed.

Taskbar

A bar usually located along the bottom of the desktop that contains various buttons. The taskbar can be used to easily and quickly switch between open programs. Each program that is currently running has a button on the taskbar, making it easy for you to switch between programs.

TCP/IP

Transport Control Protocol/Internet Protocol; an industry standard suite of protocols that enables network communications between various hosts.

Template file

A framework of specifications for creating new documents. The template file specifies formats and may include some text and graphics.

Toolbar

A bar containing various buttons that can be used to easily perform different tasks. You can customize a window to display specific toolbars such as the Drawing toolbar in Microsoft Word.

TRACERT

A command used to determine the route taken to a specific destination. You may want to use the `tracert` command if you are not able to successfully ping the IP address of a remote host. The results of the `tracert` command indicate whether a problem exists with a router or gateway between the local computer and the remote destination.

Transform (.mst) file

A file used for automating and customizing the installation of Office XP on a user's computer.

Trojan horse

A virus designed to compromise security, such as stealing passwords. The purpose of a Trojan horse is to trick you into believing you are doing one thing when, in fact, you are doing something else.

Virus

A program or malicious code that secretly replicates itself by attaching to a medium such as another program, the boot sector, a partition sector, or a document that contains macros.

Windows Installer package

A file with an `.msi` extension used to automate the installation of an application such as Office XP.

Windows Update

A Windows feature that allows you to easily identify the updates available for your computer. Using the Windows Update Web site, you can have your computer scanned to determine the critical updates that are missing.

Worm

A form of malicious software that makes copies of itself. For example, after the worm is received, it can copy itself from one hard drive to another or spread by attaching itself to email. One of the most common ways of acquiring and spreading a worm is through email attachments.

Index

B - C

How can we make this index more useful? Email us at indexes@quepublishing.com

How can we make this index more useful? Email us at indexes@quepublishing.com